THE BOOK

OF TESTS

THE BOOK

OF TESTS

Allen D. Bragdon

PERENNIAL LIBRARY

Harper & Row, Publishers, New York
Grand Rapids, Philadelphia, St. Louis, San Francisco
London, Singapore, Sydney, Tokyo

FIRST EDITION

Library of Congress Cataloging-in-Publication Data

Bragdon, Allen D.
   The book of tests/Allen D. Bragdon—1st ed.
      p.   cm.
   ISBN 0-06-096358-1
   1. Questions and answers.   I. Title.
AG195.B67   1989   88-45924
031'.02—dc 19

89 90 91 92 93 RRD 10 9 8 7 6 5 4 3 2 1

Acknowledgments

As he did for our earlier book, *Can You Pass These Tests?*, David Gamon located, assembled and edited these examinations with his customary ingenuity, humanity and good judgment. For this book he wrote most of the introductions as well. Lisa Clark input, edited and formatted the text for page layout and typesetting using a Mac Plus, Quark Express and a high order of intelligence. Karen Ringnalda Altman proofread the laser-printed page proofs with the relentless skills that only true professionals command. Joe Piccione of Printastic set the type at a hassle-level of zero. Debbie Davies tidied up some artwork then, with flashing blade and a hot waxer, transformed repro to fast, clean mechanicals. John Miller, of For Art Sake Inc. design studio, executed the cover design with one shot. Daniel Bial, our editor at Harper & Row, helped to overcome the initial inertia of our idea and kept us happily motivated.

The editors would like to thank the following individuals who lent their goodwill and expertise to this project: Susan Boundy-Sanders of the Department of Geology and Geophysics at the University of California, Berkeley, who provided expert and conscientious help with the Geology section; Toshio Ohori of the Department of Linguistics at the University of California, Berkeley, who translated the *Kyotsu Ichiji;* Whitney Lowe of the Atlanta School of Massage, who gave unstintingly of his knowledge of massage therapy in formulating the questions and the informational introduction for that section; Pamela Blake of the Rutgers Office of TV and Radio, who was unwavering in her good humor despite the major and minor frustrations she was facing at the time; Ted Widmer, who graciously took time to explain the field of graphology to me; and Bill Green of the Boston Bartenders School, who displayed a rare and much-appreciated sense of humor.

Editor's note regarding any variations the reader might notice in the style and content of the introductions to the chapters of the book: The amount of humor and arresting information included in each introduction stands in inverse proportion to the number of legal department personnel who took the opportunity to veto passages from the manuscript.

Contents

Introduction

The relationship between test and testee is at its best when there is no penalty for failure. The number of questions you happen to answer correctly when you try your hand at one of the tests on the following pages probably will not effect your job security, professional credentials or academic tenure. In a relaxed state you may even be able to pick up succulent bits of trivia in a field about which you are expected to know nothing at all. To gain a temporary advantage over an auto mechanic, for example, it could be uselful to know that an electrical circuit is called an "open" when it contains a gap that does not allow it to be completed. Employ the word correctly early in your acquaintance and break off the conversation very soon after.

If you *are* expected to be profecient in the field in which you attempt one of these tests you, especially, already know that all experts have to look some things up. What differentiates experts from the rest of us is that they have learned about places (the location of which they don't feel compelled to blurt out) where they can find reliable information to reinforce their professional mystiques. Probably more than is permissible in most other dodges, professional writers appreciate the opportunity to look things up before taking credit for the way they put them down. Many of us would fail a fifth grade spelling test but that does not mean we are careless with the meaning of the words we callously misspell.

Even so, it is unwise not to keep an eye on self-professed experts caught being careless, especially with the trivia of their expertise. Imagine, for example, being greeted in these words by the grizzled Captain of an old-time sailing vessel as you step on board the first evening of a long-awaited cruise: "Red sky at night, sailors go light." Those of us who treat precise spelling as a tedious barrier to getting on with our meaning, also may be tempted to run red lights if we judge the coast is clear. In our more romanticized moments the 16th century's permissive enthusiasm about constructing English words seems appealing. To us it was an age rich in the stuff of greatness (never mind the plagues, despotic prelates, child labor, slavery and the like). It not only encouraged writers, it let them spell existing words as they thought fit, make up new words on the spot and capitalize the ones they knew their reader ought to pay extra attention to.

The trick, therefore, is to approach tests without anxiety and to apply their answers with as much guile as possible. Remarkably like life, what? (Did you spot the three spelling erors on this page, by the way?)

Allen Bragdon, South Yarmouth, March 1989

ASTROLOGY

Milo Kovar Astro-Psychology Institute

*Why hasn't anyone knowledgeable in this field ever
made a case for dating astrological calculations
from the moment of conception rather than the
moment of birth? That even seems more cosmically
significant to the individual, and delaying the calculation to the more easily moveable birth date may
even account for errors in astrological prediction.*

One of the best-known debates about the validity of astrology was conducted two and a half centuries ago by Edmund Halley (of Halley's Comet fame) and Sir Isaac Newton. Halley had nothing but scorn for the mere "pseudo-science"; Newton, on the other hand, was convinced of the validity of astrology. The argument was brought to a dramatic conclusion by Newton, who rose and rebuked Halley, "I have studied the subject, Mr. Halley; have you?"

In *Waite's Compendium of Natal Astrology*, long considered an essential reference book in the field, astrology is matter-of-factly defined as one of three arts (along with chronometry and navigation) derived from the science of astronomy. It has as its domain the influence of the heavenly bodies (as carefully measured using the techniques of astronomy) on the human experience of life on earth.

Skeptics among us may challenge the notion that the position of the planets could have any influence at all on our lives. Why should they, and how exactly would it work? Granted, the sun and moon do seem to influence our mood, but the stars? And why should the position of the planets, sun, and moon at the moment of our birth have an influence on us the rest of our lives? It just doesn't seem to fit in with the rest of the knowledge we've accumulated about the way the world works.

However, there is much in the world that happens regardless of whether we understand exactly how it happens. Also, considering the fact that accepted sources of knowledge and truth seem to be particularly arbitrary, changing with the times and from culture to culture, we might all do well to keep an open mind about things we were never taught about in elementary school. It's acceptable to discuss the finer points of black holes at cocktail parties, since scientists in white coats say they exist, and scientists in white coats are an accepted voice of authority in our culture. Yet how many of us know enough about physics to really judge the validity of arguments for the existence of black holes?

Actually, astrology is much easier to put to the test (or a test, at least) than are black holes. It doesn't take much time or money to have an accurate horoscope cast (a completely different matter from simply reading those general, simplified ones in the daily paper) or learn how to do so oneself, and from that to derive detailed horoscope readings for any day of one's life. If the readings seem to be silly, irrelevant hocum, then so much for astrology. However, if they seem to provide some kind of detailed insight into one's life, maybe there's something to it after all.

The questions that follow progress from the very general and introductory to the relatively technical and advanced, culminating in the casting of an accurate horoscope using information about the birth of a hypothetical individual. Even for those of us who know little about astrology, that final question is interesting for the light it sheds on the process an astrologer goes through in interpreting a person's character. The analysis and the other questions in this section were provided by Milo Kovar, director of the Milo Kovar Astro-Psychology Institute in San Francisco and author of numerous books on astrology, including *Astrology From A to Z*, a basic text for beginners. For information about classes at his school or his publications, contact him at 2640 Greenwich #403, San Francisco CA 94123, tel. (415) 921-1192.

Multiple Choice

1. Astrology would most accurately be characterized as
    (A) a science without qualification
    (B) an art without qualification
    (C) a science based on an art, since it involves accurate measurements and calculations using subjective experience as raw data
    (D) an art based on a science, since it rests on accurate measurements of the position of heavenly bodies but also involves the synthesis and interpretation of this information in a manner that varies according to the insight and ability of the astrologer

2. The word "zodiac," according to its Greek etymology, means
    (A) belt of animals
    (B) belt of stars
    (C) science of the stars
    (D) lore of the stars

3. Astrologers refer to our present time period as the age of
    (A) Sagittarius
    (B) Capricorn
    (C) Aquarius
    (D) Pisces

4. The 12 signs are collectively referred to as the
    (A) horoscope
    (B) zodiac
    (C) macrocosmos
    (D) system of houses

5. Of the following, which sign is most characteristically associated with homemaking skills?
    (A) Leo
    (B) Libra
    (C) Cancer
    (D) Gemini

6. Of the following, which sign would most characteristically be associated with musical ability?
    (A) Aries
    (B) Scorpio
    (C) Gemini
    (D) Cancer

7. Of the following, which sign would most characteristically be associated with ability as a salesperson?
    (A) Libra
    (B) Scorpio
    (C) Capricorn
    (D) Pisces

8. Of the following, which would most characteristically be associated with inclination toward a nursing profession?
    (A) Aries
    (B) Leo
    (C) Pisces
    (D) Libra

9. Each sign occupies how many degrees of a hypothetical circle or spherical ring around our planet?
    (A) 12
    (B) 15
    (C) 30
    (D) 45

10. The houses or departments of life
    (A) always occupy the same places in the horoscope
    (B) occupy different positions in the horoscope according to the birth hour of the individual
    (C) occupy different positions according to the positions of the signs

(D) occupy "default" positions in the horoscope which may be changed by unusual circumstances

11. The heavenly body that rules Aquarius is
    (A) Venus
    (B) Uranus
    (C) the Moon
    (D) Mercury

12. The term "aspect" refers to
    (A) the salient characteristic of a sign
    (B) the angle formed by two heavenly bodies (planets, Sun or Moon) relative to a fixed point on Earth
    (C) the angle formed by two heavenly bodies relative to some point on Earth corresponding to the physical position of an individual at a given point in time
    (D) the typical relative positions of two planets

13. When two planets are journeying within 10 degrees of each other they form the
    (A) conjunction aspect
    (B) semi-sextile
    (C) sextile
    (D) parallel aspect

14. The semi-square aspect is associated with the
    (A) planet Mercury
    (B) planet Venus
    (C) Sun
    (D) Moon

15. Two planets are in greatest conflict and tension when they are
    (A) closest to each other
    (B) 90 degrees apart
    (C) 150 degrees apart
    (D) parallel

16. The aspect when the planets exert their strongest influence is the
    (A) semi-sextile
    (B) parallel aspect
    (C) conjunction aspect
    (D) square

17. Another name for "star time" is
    (A) sidereal time
    (B) birth time
    (C) Greenwich Mean Time
    (D) astrological time

18. The characteristics commonly associated with your sign (i. e., your sun sign or the sign assigned to that part of the calendar year in which you were born) would, other things being equal, most strongly apply to your personality
    (A) if you were born during the middle of the period of the calendar year associated with that sign
    (B) if you were born at or near the beginning of the period of the calendar year associated with that sign
    (C) if you were born between 4 and 6 A.M.
    (D) if you were born between noon and 6 P.M.

19. If you were born at noon on May 10th, what would be your ascendant or rising sign?
    (A) Gemini
    (B) Cancer
    (C) Leo
    (D) Virgo

20. Which computation tells you how long each planet travels through one sign?
    (A) The revolution period of each planet's

travel around the earth divided by 12
(B) The revolution period of each planet's travel around the Sun divided by 12
(C) The revolution period of each planet's travel around the Sun divided by 12 plus the addition or subtraction of a number of hours determined by the sign involved
(D) There is no standard computation

21. Astrologically speaking, when a planet is "retrograde," that may mean that
(A) it is moving in an opposite direction from other planets
(B) it has a harmful influence due to its aspect
(C) some of the power of the planet is lost
(D) it appears to be slowing down

22. If an individual is born at 3 A.M on August 23rd in the northern hemisphere, and the sidereal time at noon for that day is 10 hours 04'-08", the corrected sidereal time at birth is
(A) 19 hours 05'-38"
(B) 10 hours 04'-38"
(C) 1 hour 04'-08"
(D) 1 hour 02'-38"

23. Sidereal time for places of birth in the southern hemisphere is calculated by
(A) adding 12 hours to the sidereal time we would normally calculate for the northern hemisphere
(B) subtracting 12 hours from the sidereal time we would normally calculate for the northern hemisphere
(C) adding 24 hours
(D) subtracting 24 hours

Matching

1. Match the following planets with their astrological symbols.
(A) Mercury   (1) ♀
(B) Venus   (2) ♃
(C) Sun   (3) ☉
(D) Moon   (4) ☿
(E) Mars   (5) ♆
(F) Jupiter   (6) ♇
(G) Saturn   (7) ♅
(H) Uranus   (8) ☽
(I) Neptune   (9) ♄
(J) Pluto   (10) ♂

2. Match the following sign names with their symbols.
(A) Aries   (1) ♉
(B) Leo   (2) ♋
(C) Gemini   (3) ♓
(D) Taurus   (4) ♊
(E) Pisces   (5) ♈
(F) Cancer   (6) ♌
(G) Libra   (7) ♏
(H) Virgo   (8) ♑
(I) Sagittarius (9) ♒
(J) Scorpio   (10) ♎
(K) Aquarius   (11) ♍
(L) Capricorn   (12) ♐

3. Match the following elements with their signs.
(A) Fire   (1) Aries, Leo, Sagittarius
(B) Water   (2) Gemini, Libra, Aquarius
(C) Earth   (3) Cancer, Scorpio, Pisces
(D) Air   (4) Taurus, Virgo, Capricorn

4. Match the following signs with the periods of the calendar year to which they correspond.

(A) Aries	(1) January 20-February 18
(B) Leo	(2) February 19-March 20
(C) Gemini	(3) March 21-April 20
(D) Taurus	(4) April 21-May 20
(E) Pisces	(5) May 21-June 20
(F) Cancer	(6) June 21-July 21
(G) Libra	(7) July 22-August 21
(H) Virgo	(8) August 22-September 21
(I) Sagittarius	(9) September 22-October 22
(J) Scorpio	(10) October 23-November 21
(K) Aquarius	(11) November 22-December 20
(L) Capricorn	(12) December 21-January 19

Casting a Simplified Horoscope

Cast a simplified horoscope for a client born at 3 P.M. on August 1. On Zodiac Clock Number 1 (below), mark the cusps with the zodiac signs and place the Sun in the appropriate house. The individual is interested in her horoscope reading on August 1, 1988, and in particular would like to anticipate the effect of the Moon on that day. A glance at the ephemeris tells you that the Moon occupies the sign Pisces on August 1, 1988. Place the Moon in the appropriate house on the zodiac clock. Provide a simplified horoscope reading for August 1, 1988, on the basis of the foregoing information.

Casting an Accurate Horoscope

A client asks you to cast an accurate horoscope. She tells you she was born on August 23, 1959, at 3 P.M. in San Francisco. Your ephemeris tells you that the Greenwich sidereal time at noon for that day is 10 hours 04'-08".

1. What is the corrected sidereal time at birth?

Your table of houses tells you that San Francisco has a latitude of 38 degrees north and a longitude of 122 degrees west. From the table of houses, you see that the closest sidereal time listed for that latitude gives the following: 18 degrees Libra tenth house, 15 degrees Scorpio eleventh house, 7 degrees Sagittarius twelfth house, 27 degrees-04' Sagittarius ascendant house, 3 degrees Aquarius second house, 13 degrees Pisces third house. On Zodiac Clock Number 2 (below), mark the cusps with the appropriate signs and degrees; include on the clock the "intercepted signs."

2. What is the GMT of birth?

The ephemeris tells you the Sun's position at 12 noon GMT 8/24/59 is 0 degrees 34'-22" Virgo and at 12 noon GMT 8/23/59 is 29 degrees 36'-32" Leo. Ascertain the position of the Sun at birth time in San Francisco and enter it in the clock. The ephemeris tells you the Moon's position at 12 noon GMT 8/24 is 10 degrees 32'-01" Taurus and 12 noon 8/23 is 28 degrees 30'-13" Aries. Calculate the position of the Moon in relation to the individual born in San Francisco and enter it in the clock. The ephemeris on the next page gives you needed information about the other planets.

Enter the appropriate details in the zodiac clock, including the Moon's nodes. Finally, figure out the Part of Fortune (Pars Fortuna) and enter into the clock. Now that you've completed the zodiac clock, provide an astrological portrait of the individual.

Venus—(8/23) =	13 degrees	03 minutes—(8/24) =	12 degrees	34 minutes in	Virgo
Mercury	11	13	12	13	Leo
Mars	21	22	22	02	Virgo
Saturn	0	35	0	34	Capricorn
Jupiter	23	51	23	56	Scorpio
Uranus	17	32	17	36	Leo
Neptune	04	35	04	36	Scorpio
Pluto	02	40	02	41	Virgo
No. Node	5	38	05	35	Libra

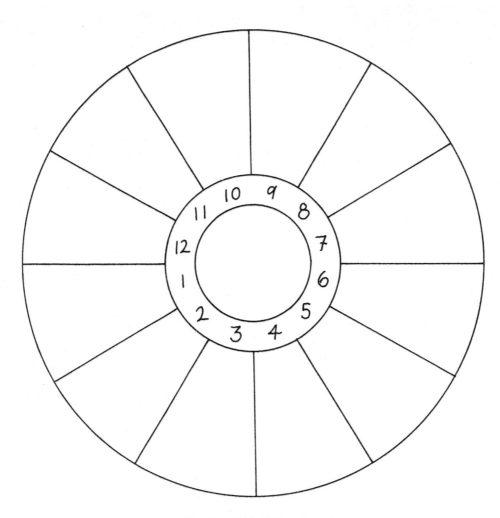

Zodiac Clock Number 1

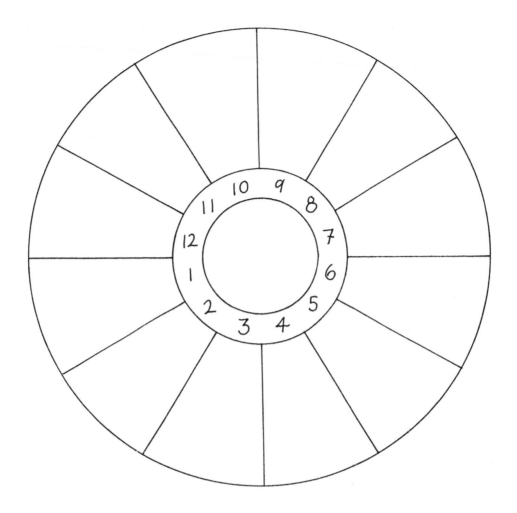

Zodiac Clock Number 2

ANSWERS!

Multiple Choice

1. D
2. A
3. C
4. B
5. C
6. C
7. A
8. C
9. C
10. A
11. B
12. C
13. A
14. A
15. B
16. A
17. A
18. C
19. C
20. B
21. C
22. D
23. A

Matching

1. A: 4
   B: 1
   C: 3
   D: 8
   E: 10
   F: 2
   G: 9
   H: 7
   I: 5
   J: 6
2. A: 5
   B: 6
   C: 4
   D: 1
   E: 3
   F: 2
   G: 10
   H: 11
   I: 12
   J: 7
   K: 9
   L: 8
3. A: 1
   B: 3
   C: 4
   D: 2
4. A: 3
   B: 7
   C: 5
   D: 4
   E: 2
   F: 6
   G: 9
   H: 8
   I: 11
   J: 10
   K: 1
   L: 12

Casting a Simplified Horoscope

The completed zodiac clock should look like this:

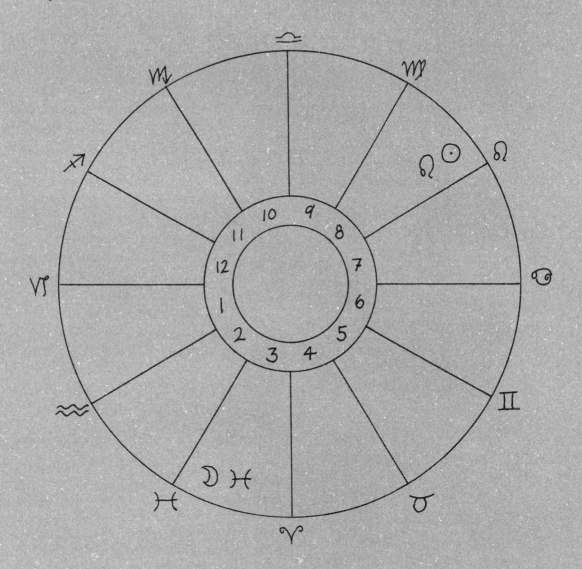

Zodiac Clock Number 1

The Moon stands for personality, people in general, changes of all kinds, travel, literary pursuits, brothers, sisters, when in the third house—it will activate the desire to travel, may urge you to write to relatives, brothers, sisters. It also activates our minds and intellects. Since the sign Pisces occupies the third house, the mind will be activated by matters relating to the twelfth house, meaning that of the basic Pisces sign and house activity. Some of the key words are: service, work in institutions, hospitals, confinement in them.

We conclude that the mind will be occupied by matters concerning sick friends or relatives. You may give a helping hand to someone in distress, travel to visit a sick friend, or be confined to a hospital yourself.

The Moon bestows sensitivity, particularly in a water sign such as Pisces. It will thus stimulate your imagination. You may think of a creative new approach to your ventures or contemplated activities. The Moon will also stimulate your relation with someone you love (eighth house—Leo). You may cherish loving thoughts about friends.

Since the Quincunx aspect of the Moon to the Sun represents an expansion aspect and the Sun is placed in the eighth house, which concerns psychic matters, death, and legacies, this aspect may cause you to think of some deceased member of the family. You might even travel to visit some relative's grave. You may also become involved with other matters connected with the eighth house: legacies, money matters, those of your associates, business partners, or marriage partner.

Casting an Accurate Horoscope

The completed zodiac clock is on the following page.

1. To account for each hour which elapsed from 12 noon, we allow 10 seconds for each hour that separates noon from native's birth hour:

S. T. 8/23	10 hours 04'-08"
Hour of birth	3 hours 00'-00"
Add correction	0 hours 00'-30"
Corrected S. T. at birth	13 hours 04'-38"

2. Our native was born in San Francisco, California, located 122 degrees west x 4'. We obtain 488 minutes (8 hours and 8 minutes), which represents the difference in time between Greenwich time and San Francisco local time. To convert the birth hour of our native, we add 8 minutes (122 degrees x 4 minutes) and obtain the relative Greenwich Mean Time for the birth of our native.

Local mean time	3 hours 00'-00"
Add: 4 minutes for each degree longitude	
(122 x 4)	8 hours 08'-00"
Greenwich Mean Time	11 hours 08'-00" P.M.

Sun's Position at Birth

We ascertain the position of the Sun in San Francisco relative to Greenwich in the following manner:

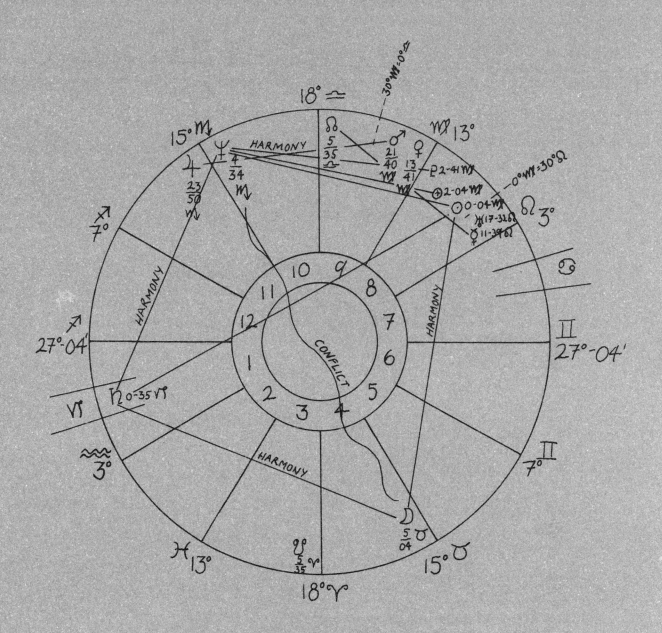

Zodiac Clock Number 2

Sun's position (12 noon) 8/24/59   00 degrees 34'-22" Virgo
Sun's position (12 noon) 8/23/59   29 degrees 36'-32" Leo

We cannot subtract 00 degrees from 29 degrees, and we rearrange the calculation in the following manner:

       30 degrees 34'-22"
less 29 degrees 36'-32"
       00 degrees 57'-50"

If the sun moves 58' in 24 hours, it will move 2½' in 1 hour. Thus, Sun at 11:08 P.M. GMT would have traveled 11 x 2½'—about 28'. The position of the Sun will then be: 29 degrees 36'-32" Leo plus 28' = 00 degrees 04'-32" Virgo.

Moon's Position at Birth

	(30 degrees)
Moon at 12 noon GMT 8/24	10 degrees 32'-01" Taurus
Moon at 12 noon GMT 8/23	28 degrees 30'-13" Aries
Moon traveled in 24 hours	12 degrees 01'-48"
Moon at 12 noon 8/23	28 degrees 30'-13" Aries
11:08 GMT interval	06 degrees 34'-00"
	35 degrees 04'-13"
(borrowed above)	-30 degrees
Moon at 11:08 GMT	5 degrees 04'-13" Taurus

For the other planets, recall the information from the ephemeris.

Apply equation: Planets' daily travel time—24 hours x GMT 10 hours 04 minutes, add result to each planet at noon 8/23. Since planets marked * are in retrograde motion, result of the above equation must be subtracted rather than added to the position of the given planet for 8/23.

Part of Fortune

The formula that applies: ASCENDANT + Moon − Sun

The chart of our native shows ASC = Sagittarius = Ninth sign from the first (Aries).

ASC-Sagittarius Ninth	27 degrees 04'
Add Moon (Taurus) Second	05 degrees 04'
Eleventh	32 degrees 08'
Subtract Sun (Virgo) Sixth	00 degrees 04'
Fifth	32 degrees 04'
Part of Fortune is found in the Sixth	02 degrees 04' Virgo

To verify the correctness of our computation, we compare the distance of the Ascendant and the Part of Fortune. This should equal the distance between the Moon and the Sun—115 degrees.

Astrological Portrait

The Sun, the "focus of life," in Virgo, a practical mind sign, in the eighth house, a department of secrets, hidden things, and death, points to professions relating to matters and activities connected with secrets and the dead, e.g., undertakers, title companies, and criminal investigators. The purpose of life is enlarged by an extra energy channeled through Pluto, Venus, Mars, and the Part of Fortune in Virgo—the latter, in particular, signifying the fortunate outcome of things pertaining to the sign and house the Part of Fortune is placed in. Venus and Mars in the ninth house speak of the capacity to excel in academic studies, suggesting a teacher or professor in a field relating to one of the above areas, also in the field of health (Virgo!).

The zenith of the chart, the Midheaven ruled by Libra, points to a creative mind, artistic inclinations, showmanship, public relations, which characteristics are confirmed by Mercury, Uranus in Leo; both planets form a sextile (= harmony aspect) to Dragon's Head or North Node in Libra.

Virgo inclinations mentioned above are enhanced by another sextile-harmony aspect of Jupiter and Neptune in Scorpio, the former providing energy that expands in professional pursuits (tenth house) such as indicated under Virgo in the eighth house, the latter (Neptune) describing a source of psychic energy and its preferred area or scope.

The rising sign Sagittarius speaks of a husky body and tall build. The Capricorn interception enlarges and diversifies the role of the two signs' (Capricorn's and Sagittarius's) influence upon the personality. The presence of the two signs speaks of considerable struggle, an inner rift between the conservatism of Capricorn traits and expansionist, go-getter, show-off Sagittarius. Capricorn traits predominate in the second half of life as Saturn gains ground and forces the Capricorn image upon the native, who might at that time respond more readily to those features of her makeup and accept them more readily than the Sagittarius ones. South Node or Dragon's Tail in Aries (third house) is the opposite pole of North Node/Dragon's Head in Libra. Whatever one labors for, putting out one's best (denoted by the Dragon's Head), one can take the Dragon's Tail for granted. Thus it would be an easy chore for the Virgo native to capitalize on the talents of the intellect (= Aries). By sheer coincidence, the Dragon's Tail is placed in the third house, which by its own nature and content relates to the pursuits of the intellect and mind.

Last but not least, the Moon in Taurus in the department of the home and family speaks of an affinity of "trine" (= harmony aspect) to native's Virgo Sun sign's traits. An Earth sign by its zodiacal category, the Moon responds readily and passes all its emotional energy to the Sun to utilize and operate within its worldly surroundings and environment.

AUTO MECHANICS

Denver Automotive and Diesel College

Time was, a mechanic could cock his ear to an idling engine, sniff the fluid leaks, finger the residue inside the exhaust pipe, and tell you what was wrong. Then he'd take out the faulty part, rebuild it, and put it back in. Now it's dial-reading and "R&R" (remove and replace). Before yearning for the old days though, bear in mind that in the 16th century, Johann Hautach produced a vehicle propelled only by coil springs and nobody had yet invented full-color wall calendars.

Auto mechanics, according to the Automotive Information Council's definition, repair, service, and adjust mechanical and electrical parts of automobiles, trucks, recreational vehicles, buses, tractors, and other gasoline-powered equipment. They perform preventive maintenance, diagnose trouble, make adjustments, estimate costs, repair or replace defective parts, rebuild assemblies, and test all repairs to ensure proper operation. Some mechanics perform all kinds of repair work; others specialize in one or two types of repair, such as engine repair (gasoline or diesel), turbo-charging, fuel injection, front-wheel drive, transaxles, automatic transmission, drive-train and rear axle, front end, brakes, electrical systems, heating and air conditioning, engine tune-ups, electronics, and auto body.

Auto mechanics are employed in independent auto repair shops, new and used car dealers' service departments, gas stations, trucking and utility companies, taxicab companies, service departments of companies maintaining fleets of trucks or cars, and government agencies such as the postal service and law enforcement agencies.

Currently, the ratio of vehicles to mechanics is over 235 to 1. According to the AIC, that ratio should ideally be cut in half in order to achieve the kinds of maintenance needed. Their studies indicate that the job market could absorb 160,000 properly-trained mechanics in the next few years.

Probably the best way to get training in the field is from a trade, technical, or vocational school offering courses in automotive repair. It used to be that apprenticeship programs and informal on-the-job training were readily available, but with ever-higher levels of technological complexity manufactured into vehicles, such opportunities are rare these days. In the section that follows, you'll find questions from the Denver Automotive and Diesel College, one of the country's leading training centers in the automotive and diesel mechanics, collision repair, and paint fields. For information about their programs, call them at 1-800-525-8956, or write to 460 South Lipan, Denver CO 80223.

We've also included some sample test questions from ASE, or the National Institute for Automotive Service Excellence. ASE was established in 1972 to provide a standard of competence in the automotive service industry. Through a voluntary competency testing and certification program, ASE measures and recognizes the diagnostic and repair skills and knowledge of automobile and heavy-duty truck technicians, body repairers, and painters. It also encourages and assists in the development of effective training programs.

A minimum of two years' work experience as a technician is required to be eligible for certification by ASE. One year's credit is given in some cases for established courses in accredited trade and vocational schools. Tests are offered in the following areas of automobile technician certification: Engine Repair; Automatic Transmission/Transaxle; Manual Drive Train and Axles; Suspension and Steering; Brakes; Electrical Systems; Heating and Air Conditioning; and Engine Performance. Also, six tests are administered for heavy-duty truck technicians and one test each for auto body painters and repairers.

Although ASE testing is voluntary and not a form of licensing, certification through the ASE exams is very highly regarded in the industry. For information about their certification process, contact ASE at 1920 Association Drive, Reston VA 22091-1502.

Multiple Choice

1. The venturi in a carburetor is
   (A) a calibrated restriction within a carburetor bore
   (B) a restriction within the intake manifold
   (C) a part of the idle circuit

2. In the carburetor, fuel flows from the idle circuit because of
   (A) the low pressure created by air moving through the venturi
   (B) atmospheric pressure applied to the air bleeds
   (C) the difference in pressure between atmospheric pressure in the float bowl and the low pressure below the throttle plates
   (D) the flow of air around the throttle plates

3. The carburetor main metering circuit is a circuit generally used in what mode of operation?
   (A) Idle
   (B) Cruise
   (C) Accelerating
   (D) Decelerating

4. The carburetor circuit that allows the engine to operate at very high speeds or heavy load conditions is the
   (A) off idle circuit
   (B) choke circuit
   (C) power enrichment circuit
   (D) accelerator pump circuit

5. Supercharging is defined as the use of an air pump to increase pressure to the cylinders, greater than atmospheric.
   (A) True
   (B) False

6. Which of the following pollutants would be primarily found in unburned fuel?
   (A) Carbon monoxide
   (B) Hydrocarbons
   (C) Oxides of nitrogen
   (D) Oxides of sulfur

7. What type of electricity is used in automobiles?
   (A) Direct current
   (B) Alternating current

8. An ampere is a measure of
   (A) a charge
   (B) resistance
   (C) current flow
   (D) difference in potential

9. Another term for voltage is electrical pressure.
   (A) True
   (B) False

10. A series circuit has more than one path for current flow.
    (A) True
    (B) False

11. A parallel circuit has more than one path for current flow.
    (A) True
    (B) False

12. Battery electrolyte is a mixture of water and
    (A) lead peroxide
    (B) sulfuric acid
    (C) lead sulfate

13. When a technician is checking for "voltage drop" in a circuit,
    (A) current must be flowing in the circuit
    (B) only the insulated portion needs to be tested

(C) the load component should be disconnected from the circuit

(D) both A and C

14. An "open" is an incomplete path for current flow.
    (A) True
    (B) False

15. The process of converting AC current to DC current in the alternator is called
    (A) induction
    (B) rectification
    (C) calibration
    (D) condensation

16. Which of the following is in the low voltage circuit of the ignition system?
    (A) Condenser
    (B) Rotor
    (C) Distributor cap
    (D) Spark plugs

17. Which of the following is in the high voltage circuit of the ignition system?
    (A) Battery
    (B) Spark plugs
    (C) Ignition switch
    (D) Ballast resistor

18. The distributor rotates at _____ the speed of the engine's crankshaft.
    (A) one-half
    (B) the same speed as
    (C) twice
    (D) none of the above

19. The oil pressure light stays on whenever the engine is running. The oil pressure has been checked and it meets specs. Technician A says that a ground in the circuit between the indicator light and the pressure switch could be the cause. Technician B says that an open in the pressure switch could be the cause. Who is right?
    (A) A only
    (B) B only
    (C) Both A and B
    (D) Neither A nor B

20. The starter will not 'crank,' and the solenoid does not 'click' on a vehicle with an automatic transmission. All of these could be the cause *except*
    (A) a misadjusted neutral safety switch
    (B) an open solenoid hold-in winding
    (C) an open circuit between the solenoid and the ignition switch
    (D) an open in the solenoid ground circuit

21. Low heater output can be caused by all of these except
    (A) a low engine coolant level
    (B) a stuck open cooling system thermostat
    (C) a restricted heater control valve
    (D) a disengaged clutch-type radiator fan

22. There is blue smoke coming from the exhaust pipe of a vehicle. Technician A says that blocked cylinder head oil return passages could be the cause. Technician B says that a stuck open thermostat could be the cause. Who is right?
    (A) A only
    (B) B only
    (C) Both A and B
    (D) Neither A nor B

23. A warm fuel-injected engine has a high idle speed. Technician A says that an open cold start injector could be the cause. Technician B says that an open auxiliary-air regulator (valve) could be the cause. Who is right?

(A) A only
(B) B only
(C) Both A and B
(D) Neither A nor B

24. A vehicle with rear-wheel drive was in a rear-end collision. It now has a vibration that happens only during hard acceleration. Repairman A says that a bad universal joint could be the cause. Repairman B says that a misaligned drive shaft could be the cause. Who is right?
(A) A only
(B) B only
(C) Both A and B
(D) Neither A nor B

25. An original acrylic enamel finish is to be spot repaired with an acrylic lacquer. Which of these should the painter do to get good adhesion?
(A) Sand with 220 grit paper
(B) Use an enamel sealer
(C) Use an enamel primer
(D) Sand with 400 grit paper

26. After a high-metallic acrylic lacquer is sprayed on a door panel, the color is lighter than the original finish. Which of these could be the cause?
(A) The paint was not mixed enough
(B) The paint was sprayed too wet
(C) The air pressure was too high
(D) The thinner was too slow

27. A compression test shows that one cylinder is too low. A leakage test on that cylinder shows that there is too much leakage. During the test, air could be heard coming out of the tail pipe. Which of these could be the cause?
(A) Broken piston rings
(B) A bad head gasket

(C) A bad exhaust valve
(D) An exhaust valve not seating

28. Technician A says that in a liquid cooling system, a thermostat that is installed backwards will cause the engine to run at a lower-than-normal temperature. Technician B says that a radiator pressure cap that is not fully seated will cause the coolant to boil over at a higher-than-normal temperature. Who is right?
(A) A only
(B) B only
(C) Both A and B
(D) Neither A nor B

29. A vehicle with an automatic transmission and a properly tuned engine accelerates poorly from a stop. Acceleration is normal above 35 mph. Which could be the cause?
(A) A bad torque converter
(B) A worn front pump
(C) A bad governor valve
(D) A low fluid level

30. An automatic transmission does not work right. What should the technician do first?
(A) Take a pressure test
(B) Adjust the bands
(C) Check the fluid level
(D) Check the engine vacuum

31. All of these could cause the clutch to chatter or grab when engaging *except*
(A) oil or grease on the clutch disc linings
(B) clutch disc binding on the transmission input (clutch) shaft
(C) pilot bearing out of lubricant
(D) binding in the clutch pedal linkage

32. The steering wheel of a vehicle is not centered when traveling straight down the road. Technician A says that the steering

wheel can be removed from the steering column and its position changed. Technician B says that the steering wheel can be turned to the center position and the toe-in readjusted. Who is right?
(A) A only
(B) B only
(C) Both A and B
(D) Neither A nor B

33. All of these could cause tire wear if not within manufacturer's specs *except*
(A) caster
(B) wheel balance
(C) toe-in
(D) camber

34. The brake pedal on a vehicle with power-assisted disc/drum brakes moves slowly to the floor during braking. Which of these could be the cause?
(A) A leaking master cylinder primary cup
(B) A leaking power brake booster
(C) A leaking master cylinder residual check valve
(D) An internal leak in the combination valve

Matching
Match the following terms to the list of definitions.

_____1. Pattern the abrasive cuts into the metal when grinding
_____2. Grinding motion is from side to side using the top of the disc only
_____3. Finish grinding with a fine disc to obtain a smooth surface after metal finishing is complete
_____4. File used to file convex and reverse curves
_____5. Paper, cloth or fiber that the abrasive is bonded to
_____6. Using the pick hammer to raise metal during grinding and filing of metal finishing
_____7. Filing in one direction only
_____8. Grinding motion where grinder is moved up and down using the top portion of the grinding disc
_____9. Disc used for grinding paint off the surface and any other coating which might plug up and ruin a closed coat disc
_____10. Filing in one direction followed by filing a second time across the first at a 45-degree angle; method of check filing
_____11. Disc cut special to clean damaged areas and welds
_____12. Filing in one direction followed by filing a second time across the first at a 90-degree angle the other direction; method of check filing
_____13. Disc used for grinding metal after paint has been removed

Definitions
A. Buffing
B. Crosscutting (discing)
C. Metal polishing
D. Crosscut
E. Closed coat disc
F. Open coat disc
G. Backing
H. Hexagon or square-cut disc
I. Picking
J. Cross filing
K. X filing
L. Line filing
M. Half-round or shell file

ANSWERS! ☞

Multiple Choice

1.	A	19.	A
2.	C	20.	B
3.	B	21.	D
4.	C	22.	A
5.	A	23.	B
6.	B	24.	C
7.	A	25.	D
8.	C	26.	C
9.	A	27.	D
10.	B	28.	D
11.	A	29.	A
12.	B	30.	C
13.	A	31.	C
14.	A	32.	B
15.	B	33.	A
16.	A	34.	A
17.	B		
18.	A		

Matching

1. D
2. B
3. C
4. M
5. G
6. I
7. L
8. A
9. F
10. K
11. H
12. J
13. E

BARBER

Moler Barber College, Inc.

The era of the old-fashioned straight razor with the barber tugging your skin taut with his thumb is now over; not because barbers don't learn how to shave a customer that way anymore, but because the age of AIDS requires the use of single-use blades and disposable rubber gloves.

Most states have Boards of Barber Examiners which oversee the granting of licenses to barber establishments and individuals working in those establishments. If you work with customers in a barber establishment, you must own a license. To get a license, you must pass a State Board Examination, the format of which varies from state to state. In some states, the exam consists of two parts, one practical and one written. In others, there is only a written exam. In Oregon, for example, the entire exam consists of 100 multiple-choice questions including ones pertaining to a range of professional knowledge, safety, and laws and regulations.

In California, one of the states with a two-part exam, the practical section requires you to bring a model. Models must have two days' beard growth on all parts of the face and neck (from which we may infer that models must be male and postpubescent), and hair at least ½" long. Applicants are required to demonstrate knowledge of shaving, scientific rest facial, scientific scalp massage, haircutting, and shampooing, the last using both the incline and the recline method. Applicants should take care to restrain themselves during the haircutting demonstration, as the next part of the exam requires the creation of a hairstyle enhancing the appearance of the model, and demonstration of the proper use of a heated curling iron. Finally, the applicant must perform three demonstrations of chemicals used in barbering: hair coloring chemicals, hair straightener (sodium hydroxide), and hair waver (sodium thiogylcolate). After all this, models are unchained and ungagged and permitted to leave.

The questions that follow are provided by Moler Barber College in Portland, OR, and are used in their curriculum to prepare students for the state exam. The shortage of qualified barbers and the demand for their graduates are so great that Moler currently has a 100 percent placement rate. (The editor can vouch for the quality of the curriculum there, as he found them to give the best and and most reasonably priced haircuts in town while he was a student in Portland.) We have omitted any questions about laws and regulations, as those tend to vary considerably from state to state. Questions about dermatology are included, since a barber must be able to recognize infectious skin diseases as well as symptoms of health problems that would make certain barbering techniques dangerous for the customer. For information about Moler's classes, contact Moler Barber College at 517 SW 4th Street, Portland OR 97204, tel. (503) 223-9818.

1. A person with a prominent nose should have a
   (A) pyramid moustache
   (B) large moustache
   (C) narrow moustache
   (D) small moustache

2. A person with a round face and regular features should have a
   (A) triangular-shaped moustache
   (B) small moustache
   (C) semi-square moustache
   (D) pyramid-shaped moustache

3. What is the purpose of steaming the face?
   (A) Soothes and relaxes patron
   (B) Softens cuticle layer of hair
   (C) Lubrication stimulates action of oil glands
   (D) All of the above

4. Lather is rubbed into the beard with the
   (A) knuckles
   (B) palms
   (C) nail tips
   (D) cushion tips of fingers

5. Shaving the face too closely may cause
   (A) acne
   (B) alopecia
   (C) ingrown hairs
   (D) all of the above

6. A patron may find fault with a shave because of
   (A) offensive body odor
   (B) foul breath or tobacco odor
   (C) unclean hands, towels, or shaving cloths
   (D) all of the above

7. Lathering the face for shaving serves to
   (A) keep the hair in an erect position
   (B) soften the follicles in the hair
   (C) relax the hair of the face
   (D) keep the hair flat on the face

8. When should a hot towel not be applied to the face?
   (A) When the face is chapped or blistered
   (B) When the person has extremely oily skin
   (C) When the moustache is large
   (D) When the person has ingrown hairs

9. Which of these points is it most important for the barber-stylist to know about the patron's skin and hair before shaving?
   (A) Condition and sensitivity of skin
   (B) Texture of hair
   (C) Slope and grain of beard
   (D) All of the above

When a barber shaves a customer, the razor is held in one of three different positions to shave each of the 14 numbered zones in the illustration.

10. These three razor positions are called "freehand," "backhand," and "reverse backhand." Which position is used for shaving which group of zones?
    1, 3, 4, 8, 11, 12 _____
    2, 6, 7, 9 _____
    10, 13, 5, 14 _____

11. The grain of the beard changes direction from zone to zone. Draw an arrow in each zone to indicate the direction in which the razor is drawn.

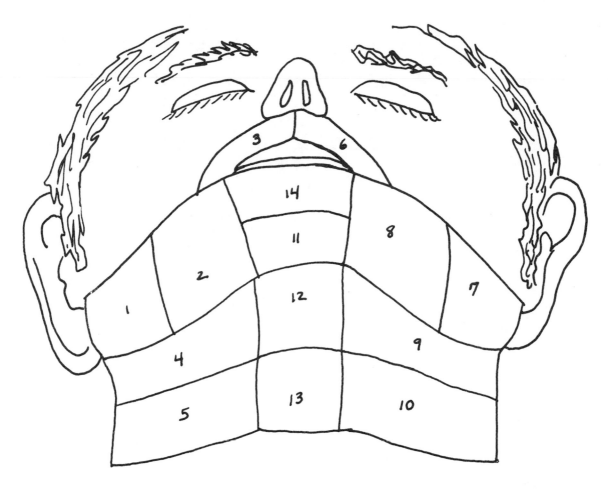

12. In shaving the face once over, the strokes are made
    (A) against the grain of the hair
    (B) with the grain of the hair
    (C) across the grain of the hair
    (D) opposite the grain of the hair

13. In order to stretch the skin tightly while shaving, the left hand is kept
    (A) in back of the razor
    (B) in front of the razor
    (C) alongside the razor
    (D) on top of the razor

14. What are the nine requirements of a good shave?
    (1)_____
    (2)_____
    (3)_____
    (4)_____
    (5)_____
    (6)_____
    (7)_____
    (8)_____
    (9)_____

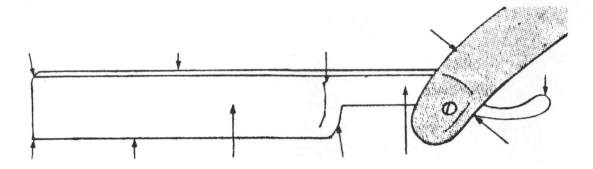

15. Of the 11 parts of a straight razor, 5 are named for parts of the human body. Write them next to the appropriate arrow in the illustration.

16. The art of temporarily reshaping the patron's hair with the aid of a styling dryer, comb, and brush is
    (A) finger waving
    (B) thermal waving
    (C) iron waving
    (D) air waving

17. Some barber-stylists prefer to use metal combs when air waving because these combs
    (A) transmit and retain heat longer
    (B) protect the patron's scalp
    (C) lose heat rapidly
    (D) are cooler to the touch

18. Barber-stylists find it easier to brush hair into desired styles with
    (A) broad brushes
    (B) square brushes
    (C) narrow brushes
    (D) wide brushes

19. To achieve hair lifts or fullness in various parts of the head, the hair must be
    (A) perfectly dry
    (B) slightly damp
    (C) cut very short
    (D) saturated

20. In air waving, a higher temperature is required for
    (A) fine hair
    (B) coarse hair
    (C) thin hair
    (D) damaged hair

21. A shadow wave differs from a regular wave in that it has
    (A) deep ridges
    (B) reverse ridges
    (C) no ridges
    (D) low ridges

22. An example of a general infection is
    (A) a boil
    (B) blood poisoning
    (C) a nose discharge
    (D) a skin lesion

23. The chemical reaction that takes place when peroxide and a tinting solution are combined is called
    (A) decoloration
    (B) oxidation
    (C) neutralization
    (D) certification

24. A hydrometer measures the strength of
    (A) peroxide
    (B) quaternary ammonium
    (C) shampoo concentrate
    (D) bleach

25. Oil lighteners are usually mixtures of hydrogen peroxide and
    (A) glycerine oil
    (B) sulfonated oil
    (C) gential oil
    (D) olive oil

26. To speed the liberation of oxygen gas from hydrogen peroxide, add a small quantity of
    (A) sodium hydroxide
    (B) 20 vol. oxygen
    (C) 28% ammonia
    (D) paraphenylene

27. When removing pigment from the hair shaft, one of the ingredients is
    (A) analine derivatives
    (B) hydrogen peroxide
    (C) sodium hydroxide
    (D) softening agent

28. Color rinses contain
    (A) sodium hydroxide
    (B) certified colors
    (C) analine derivatives
    (D) thioglycolate colors

29. To overcome the prolonged processing time of the acid-balanced permanent wave solution, the barber-stylist must apply
    (A) alkaline
    (B) protein fillers
    (C) heat
    (D) additional solution

30. The length of time required for the hair strands to absorb the waving solution and complete the total rearrangement of the chemical bonds around the rods is called
    (A) processing time
    (B) testing time
    (C) oxidation time
    (D) neutralizing time

31. The ability of hair to expand and contract is called
    (A) elasticity
    (B) texture
    (C) porosity
    (D) condition

32. The cross-bonds of the hair are found in the
    (A) medulla layer
    (B) cortical layer
    (C) cuticle layer
    (D) all of the above

33. Permanent wave solution is required in order to break the
    (A) peptide links
    (B) hydrogen bonds
    (C) sulfur bonds
    (D) polypeptides

34. Another name for dandruff is
    (A) alopecia
    (B) steatoma
    (C) pityriasis
    (D) dermatitis

35. The function of the neutralizer is to
    (A) reform the cross-bonds
    (B) break the polypeptides
    (C) soften the hair
    (D) condition the hair

36. The sanitized end of a comedone extractor is used to remove
(A) blackheads
(B) moles
(C) scales
(D) whiteheads

37. Dermatology deals with the structure, functions, and diseases of the
(A) nails
(B) hair
(C) heart
(D) skin

38. Which implement is used to protect the patron from scalp burns when iron curling?
(A) Scissors
(B) Comb
(C) Swivel
(C) Clamp

39. When combing chemically processed hair, use a
(A) styling comb
(B) barber comb
(C) steel comb
(D) wide-tooth comb

40. Canities is the technical term for
(A) black hair
(B) brown hair
(C) blonde hair
(D) gray hair

41. In air waving, a higher temperature is required for
(A) fine hair
(B) resistant hair
(C) thin hair
(D) damaged hair

42. Superfluous hair or abnormal development of hair on the body is called
(A) alopecia
(B) hypertrichosis
(C) canities
(D) monilithix

43. Bromidrosis means
(A) lack of perspiration
(B) excessive perspiration
(C) foul-smelling perspiration
(D) prickly heat

44. A severe disease of short duration is described as being
(A) acute
(B) chronic
(C) congenital
(D) occupational

45. Liver spots on the skin is known as
(A) naevi
(B) leucoderma
(C) chloasma
(D) albinism

46. The direction used in razor stripping is
(A) the same as that used in honing
(B) the reverse of that used in honing
(C) of no particular consequence
(D) clockwise

47. An aniline derivative tint should not be used if the allergy test results are
(A) positive
(B) negative
(C) neutral
(D) clean

48. The two general classifications of hair processors are the ammonium thioglycolate and the
(A) thio products
(B) petrolatum
(C) hydrogen peroxide
(D) sodium hydroxide

49. Baldness in spots is known as alopecia
    (A) adnata
    (B) senilis
    (C) areata
    (D) prematura

50. Effleurage is used in massage for its
    (A) stimulating effects
    (B) soothing and relaxing effects
    (C) heating effects
    (D) magnetic effects

51. The main divisions of the skin are the epi-
    dermis and the
    (A) subcutaneous tissue
    (B) dermis
    (C) cuticle
    (D) scarf skin

52. Acne is a disorder of the
    (A) sweat glands
    (B) oil glands
    (C) bloodstream
    (D) scalp

53. Herpes simplex or fever blisters usually
    occur around the
    (A) scalp
    (B) ears
    (C) eyes
    (D) lips

54. Hair that protrudes from moles should
    (A) be cut
    (B) be pulled out
    (C) be cut with clipper only
    (D) not be treated

55. Abnormal white patches present on the
    skin are called
    (A) chloasma
    (B) albinism
    (C) leucoderma
    (D) naevi

56. The common term for keratoma is
    (A) callous
    (B) wart
    (C) tumor
    (D) birthmark

57. Trichology deals with the study and dis-
    eases of the
    (A) skin
    (B) hair
    (C) nails
    (D) bones

ANSWERS! ☛

1. B
2. C
3. D
4. D
5. C
6. D
7. A
8. A
9. D
10. 1, 3, 4, 8, 11, 12   Freehand
    2, 6, 7, 9   Backhand
    5, 10, 13, 14   Reverse freehand
11. See illustration

12. B
13. A
14. (1) Hand, razor, and towel properly
       sanitized
  (2) Razor properly honed and stropped
  (3) Beard well lathered
  (4) Towels properly heated and applied
  (5) Beard cut smoothly
  (6) Lather completely removed
  (7) Astringent or face lotion properly
       applied
  (8) Face dried thoroughly
  (9) Powder evenly applied

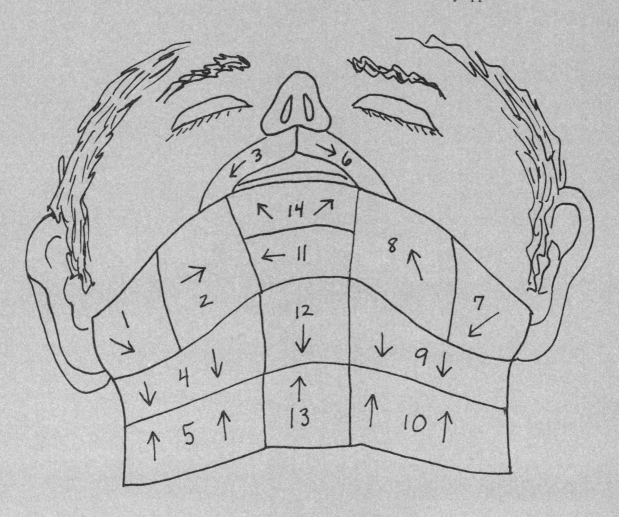

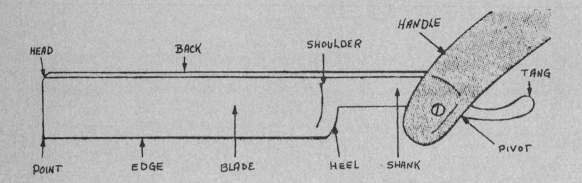

15. See illustration above
16. D
17. A
18. C
19. B
20. B
21. D
22. B
23. B
24. A
25. B
26. C
27. B
28. B
29. C
30. A
31. A
32. B
33. C
34. C
35. A
36. A

37. D
38. B
39. D
40. D
41. B
42. B
43 C
44. A
45. C
46. B
47. A
48. D
49. C
50. B
51. B
52. B
53. D
54. D
55. C
56. A
57. B

BARTENDING

Boston Bartenders School of America

Who said this first?

*"I pray thee let me and my fellow have
a haire of the dog that bit us last night."*

*"And he that will to bed go sober
Falls with the leaf still in October."*

The skills involved in being a good bartender run the gamut from knowing how to make and serve drinks to knowing when to stop serving them. Of the two skills just mentioned, the first can be learned in a fairly steady and systematic manner out of a bartender's recipe guide or in a mixology course at a bartending school. The second requires not only book learning but live experience with human beings. You can't learn from a book how to slow someone's drinking rhythm without making them angry, or how to tell whether someone is becoming belligerent from drinking too much or just has a blunt (but harmless) personality—you have to have, or cultivate through experience, a certain way with people. If you don't have a way with people, if, perhaps most importantly, you don't *like* people, maybe bartending isn't the field for you—which, if you have nothing more than an interest in mixing up strangely colored concoctions with odd-sounding names, is probably just as well, since you can make your mother happier by working in a chemistry lab.

The final exam from the Boston Bartenders School will test your knowledge of mixology, wet bar operation, bar management, spotting excessive drunkenness and preventing drunk driving, common sense, and a little trivia. BBS offers a comprehensive 40-hour course featuring hands-on training in a cocktail lounge atmosphere, and 100 hours supervised practice at no extra charge for those who choose it. For information about their program, contact Boston Bartenders School at 719 Boylston Street, Boston MA 02116, tel. (617) 536-7272.

Or, if setting up Sazeracs in the Big Easy is more your style, you might be interested in the questions about New Orleans specialty drinks. If nothing else, those questions will provide you with great material for stumping your local barkeep (I'll bet he doesn't know how to make a Sazerac *or* a Hurricane, and I'll bet he wouldn't dare try to make a pousse-café).

John Heywood (1497–1580)
Note: Eighty-three years is an unusual life span for that period.

John Fletcher (1579–1625)
The Bloody Brother, *Act II, Sc. 2*

Short Answer

1. How is the percentage of alcohol in any bottle of liquor determined?

2. What is a garnish "flag"?

3. What is the origin of the name of the cocktail "Manhattan"?

4. What is the difference between champagne and white wine?

5. What does the year (vintage date) on a bottle of wine indicate: date of bottling or year the grapes were picked?

6. What is the difference between white tequila and gold tequila?

7. Champagne was discovered by whom?

8. The frosty looking substance found on the skin of grapes is what?

9. Which wine is often referred to as the "Wine of Celebration"?

10. Found on a bottle of cognac, what does V.S.O.P. stand for?

11. Which alcohol was originally used in religious ceremonies?

12. Scotch whiskey's flavor is from what?

13. What liquor is used frequently in tropical drinks? What is it made from?

14. What was Prohibition? How long did it last?

15. Define the Dram Shop Acts?

16. What is Midori?

17. Gin's flavor is from what?

18. What place does tequila come from? What is tequila made from?

19. What is the difference between brandy and cognac?

20. Name the four essential ingredients for making beer.

21. Name the four steps in making beer.

22. How is draft beer different from other types of beer, such as ales, pilsners, and stouts?

23. What is the brand name of the unpasteurized canned or bottled beer?

24. What is the name and location of the bar that sells more alcohol than any other bar in the world?

25. What tropical drink (created in New Orleans) held a patent for 10 years after it was invented?

26. Define "Pousse Café."

27. What New Orleans drink has rye whiskey as a primary ingredient?

28. Galliano is a product of what country?

29. What is Drambuie?

30. Metaxa is a product of what country?

31. What is Grand Marnier?

32. Grenadine is nonalcoholic and made from what?

33. What type of ice is used in a mist?

34. What kind of liqueur is Kahlua?

35. What kind of liqueur is Amaretto?

36. What do the seven coded buttons on a soda gun, C, X, S, Q, G, W, and L, stand for?

37. What is an apertif?

38. What is a liqueur?

39. List three important things to check when accepting a major credit card.

40. List three popular cognacs.

41. Name two sherries.

42. List four procedures to follow in opening a bar.

43. List the three categories of wine you handle.

44. Briefly tell how you would please a customer who says his screwdriver is not strong enough.

45. How is a "pre-mix" soda system different from a "post-mix" soda system?

46. Why is rotating bottled beer important?

47. Name four behavior cues you should be aware of when deciding whether to continue serving a patron drinks.

48. Name three strategies a bartender could use to slow a patron's drinking rhythm.

49. What steps should "the house" take to prevent an intoxicated person from driving?

50. Some people seem to be affected by alcohol more quickly than others because of absorption rate factors. Name at least seven factors that could increase absorption rate.

51. What type of setting stimulates people to drink?

Multiple Choice

1. Ingredients for a J. B. Spritzer include
   (A) a Collins glass, ⅔ J. B., fill with club soda
   (B) a rocks glass, 1 ounce J. B., fill with club soda
   (C) a highball glass, 1 ounce J. B., fill with club soda
   (D) a wine glass, 1 ounce J. B., fill with club soda

2. Which is *not* a procedure for opening a bar?
   (A) Preparing garnishes
   (B) Stocking wine and liquor
   (C) Getting ice
   (D) Removing rubbish

3. Which one of the following drinks is *always* shaken?
   (A) California Root Beer
   (B) Screwdriver
   (C) Gibson
   (D) Sombrero

4. Which one of the following does not take an orange and cherry garnish?
(A) Collins
(B) Manhattan
(C) Sour
(D) Old-fashioned

5. Ingredients for a whiskey sour on the rocks include
(A) Brandy snifter, 1 ounce blended whiskey, 2 ounces sour mix
(B) rocks glass, 1 ounce blended whiskey, fill with sour mix
(C) highball glass, 1 ounce blended whiskey, 2 ounces sour mix, orange and cherry garnish
(D) highball glass, 1 ounce blended whiskey, 2 ounces sour mix, lemon twist

6. When is the *best* time for a bartender to ask to serve the next round?
(A) When the customer requests one
(B) When the customer has finished his or her drink
(C) When the drink is ⅔ gone
(D) When the bar is not busy

7. The three ingredients in sour mix are lemon juice and
(A) club soda and sugar
(B) egg whites and sugar
(C) egg whites and club soda
(D) simple syrup and club soda

8. An apertif is always served
(A) straight up in a pony glass
(B) on the rocks with a lemon twist
(C) in a sherry glass
(D) in a highball glass with a lemon wheel

9. How many ounces are there in a drink served "on the rocks"?

(A) 2 ounces
(B) 1½ ounces
(C) 1 ounce
(D) ¾ ounce

10. "PAR" refers to
(A) money each bartender starts with in his or her register
(B) number of customers served on a daily basis
(C) back-up schedule of employees available for fill-in work
(D) reserve storage of liquor and supplies for one day's operation

11. Most American wine is produced in the state of
(A) Massachusetts
(B) California
(C) New York
(D) Oregon

12. Cognac is a product of
(A) France
(B) Germany
(C) England
(D) United States

13. Call gin is a product of
(A) France
(B) Germany
(C) England
(D) United States

14. Other than water, what is the main ingredient in all spirits?
(A) Corn
(B) Alcohol
(C) Sugar
(D) Yeast

15. What is the most popular brew in the United States?

(A) Lager
(B) Porter
(C) Stout
(D) Light

Labeling

Label each drink either (A) Call or (B) No Call

1. _____Screwdriver
2. _____Bacardi cocktail
3. _____Presbyterian
4. _____Dry Southern Comfort Manhattan
5. _____Cutty on-the-rocks with a slash of soda

True or False

1. _____60 percent alcohol is equal to 30 proof.
2. _____You should under all circumstances acknowledge your regular customers by name.
3. _____Galliano is considered both a proprietary brand name and a generic spirit.
4. _____Wine is identified by its alcohol content and liqueur by its proof.
5. _____Imported liquors will always demand top shelf price.
6. _____Gin and sloe gin may be used interchangeably.
7. _____As a bar manager, handle waiter and waitress problems in public, so others can learn from the mistake.
8. _____A bartender should check a customer's ID if he/she is in doubt of the customer's age.
9. _____Fortified wines are always over 15 percent alcohol.
10. _____There is no difference between draft beer and bottled beer.

ANSWERS! ☞

Short Answer

1. Divide the proof by two.
2. An orange slice and a maraschino cherry
3. From a bar in Manhattan, New York, by Winston Churchill's mother.
4. Champagne is double fermented.
5. Year the grapes were picked
6. White tequila is not aged.Gold tequila is aged 2½ years in a charred white oak barrel.
7. Dom Perignon
8. Yeast
9. Champagne
10. Very Superior Old Pale
11. Wine; it is still used for this purpose today.
12. Peat smoke
13. Rum, which is made from sugar cane (originally grown in the tropics).
14. Prohibition was a movement, then a law that lasted 13½ years, prohibiting the sale, manufacture, importation, and exportation of alcoholic beverages.
15. Dram Shop Acts are federal laws that prohibit the sale of alcoholic beverages to intoxicated persons and minors
16. Japanese melon liqueur
17. Juniper berries
18. Tequila comes from Tequila, Mexico and is made from the root of the blue agave cactus. It is a special type of mezcal (the primary Mexican spirit).
19. Cognac is distilled from the Grand Champagne grape, which is grown only in the Cognac region of France. Brandy is distilled from wine or other fermented fruit juices.
20. (A) Malt
    (B) Water
    (C) Hops
    (D) Yeast
21. (A) Mashing
    (B) Brewing
    (C) Fermenting
    (D) Lagering
22. Draft beer is not pasteurized; others are.
23. Coors; it's passed through ultrafine filters to remove impurities.
24. Pat O'Brian's, in New Orleans, LA
25. The Hurricane; the patent covered the ingredients, name, and glasses, which were individually hand-blown.
26. A specialty drink made by layering cordials, syrups, and brandies according to their specific gravities, resulting in a rainbow appearance.
27. The Sazarac
28. Italy
29. Scotch liqueur
30. Greece
31. Orange-based cognac
32. Pomegranate
33. Crushed
34. Coffee
35. Almond
36. C: Cola
    X: Diet
    S: Soda
    Q: Quinine
    G: Ginger ale
    W: Water
    L: Seven-up
37. A before-dinner drink of fortified wine with higher than 15 percent alcohol
38. An after-dinner drink that is 21.5 percent sugar
39. (A) Expiration date
    (B) Check delinquent list
    (C) Authorization
40. Hennessey, Martell, Remy Martin, Courvoisier (sample answers)
41. Harvey's, Dry Sack (sample answers)
42. (A) Check ice quantity
    (B) Fill three sinks
    (C) Do bank
    (D) Check glasses, garnishes, and mixes; bleed guns

43. (A) House
    (B) Fortified
    (C) Champagne-Sparkling
44. Remove stirrer and add lace
45. Pre-mix system: ⅛ syrup to ⅞ soda; post-mix system: all syrup, add club soda
46. Shelf life is six months
47. Impaired or reduced
    (A) coordination
    (B) judgment
    (C) reaction time
    (D) inhibition
48. (A) Give food
    (B) Give ice water
    (C) Give bad service
49. Try to get one of the intoxicated customer's friends to drive. If that doesn't work, take away his/her car keys.
50. The following all increase alcohol absorption rate: carbonation, an empty stomach, drinking in gulps rather than sips, drinking straight liquor, drinking stronger alcohol, stress or exhaustion, and some drugs. All other things being equal, lighter people will be affected faster than heavier people. A man and a woman who weigh the same will not be equally affected—women's bodies have a higher ratio of body fat to muscle, which increases absorption rate.
51. Music and dim lights

Multiple Choice

1. C
2. D
3. D
4. B
5. C
6. A or C
7. B
8. B
9. B
10. D
11. B
12. A
13. C
14. C
15. A

Labeling

1. B
2. A
3. B
4. A
5. A

True or False

1. F
2. F
3. T
4. T
5. F
6. F
7. F
8. T
9. T
10. F

BROADCASTING

Columbia School of Broadcasting

Let's imagine that you're applying for an education or a job (or both) in that segment of the entertainment industry that calls itself Broadcasting. You are short, speak with a lateral lisp, and you have a mild facial tic. You make your pitch. You hear, in response, "The field is terribly crowded at the moment. Thanks for coming in. Don't call us. Goodbye." At that you do your best gravelly voiced imitation: "Whatever you sshay, Baby. If you need me, just whishtle." Then watch 'em bogey the whole. Be warned though, broadcasting has little patience for slow-fuse humor and, reasonably enough, can't cope with bad puns whose meager justification derives from the written word.

If you project your personality well, and you fall within the normal range in reading and writing ability, and your speech is free of stuttering, stammering, and lisping, you might be able to work in what many consider to be a dream field—being paid for playing records, talking about sports, and the like. You don't need to have a voice that can light a gasoline-soaked rag at fifty paces. It would probably help, though, to have something more than your native charm to rely on when trying to get into the broadcasting business. You have to learn about FCC regulations, broadcast signal frequencies, and V.U. meters, not to mention spots, tags, music beds, jingles, doughnuts, segues, and voiceovers. Various schools offer courses that will teach you the requisite skills (assuming, in the case of the responsible one, that you meet the above prerequisites—you'll have to take the reading and writing test and submit a voice recording before enrolling); probably the best known is the Columbia School of Broadcasting, the "official broadcast training school for the National Football League Players Association." CSB offers courses not only in radio announcing but also, for those of us with stammers, stutters, lisps, or other inclinations, radio/television advertising sales and commercial copywriting. They also have a course in Spanish language radio announcing.

The Radio Announcing course consists of six sections or "phases." The first phase involves instruction in breathing techniques, pronunciation, and articulation. Phase two covers commercial delivery technique and instruction in types of commercials, timing, marking, jingles, inserts, and tags. Phase three involves news gathering, interviewing, and news writing and delivery. The fourth phase deals with music: station formats and music policies, programming, and DJ show content and delivery. Phase five covers specialty reports, including sports reports, farm reports, business and financial reports, weather reports, and traffic reports. The final phase culminates in the production of an audition tape, for which you'll need to polish your intros and outros, avoid straight segues, and generally keep your board tight and free of dead air. After passing the final review and the final written exam, you can start sending out your resume and audition tape, and hopefully, before too long, land that dream major-market broadcasting job.

Realistically, according to responsible industry educators like CSB, you can expect to work a midnight-to-six A.M. shift in Salt Lick, Utah, maybe performing double duty as the night janitor, before you work your way up to that job in a larger market—and we're still not talking morning DJ with NBC radio in New York City. However, given ambition, perseverance, and unwavering belief in the American Dream, who knows? Maybe you could become the next generation's Larry King or Casey Casem.

The questions that follow are from CSB's Radio Announcer final exam; 70 percent correct is considered passing. For more information about CSB's programs, check your phone book to see if there's a school in your area, or contact them at: Columbia School of Broadcasting, P.O. Box 1970, Hollywood CA 90078-9990, tel. (213) 469-8321.

Multiple Choice

1. A "remote" is a broadcast that
    (A) is broadcast too faintly to be easily received far away
    (B) originates from a location other than the studio
    (C) is announced early and taped in order to broadcast at a later time

2. Amplitude Modulation Stations transmit their signals by
    (A) varying the frequency of the broadcast signal
    (B) varying the strength of the broadcast signal
    (C) neither of the above methods

3. A "V.U." meter shows the operator
    (A) the line voltage at the control board
    (B) the volume of the sound being produced by the equipment
    (C) the wattage of the transmitter

4. Which of the following is NOT a good practice to follow in planning a popular music show?
    (A) Every other selection should be a current hit tune
    (B) For every slow tune played, two bright, cheery tunes should be played
    (C) Mix classical and rock-and-roll music

5. A "Copy Book" primarily contains
    (A) news broadcasts
    (B) the weather reports
    (C) commercials

6. When you are planning a question for a Man-on-the-Street Program, you should phrase it so that it will
    (A) express your own opinion on the subject
    (B) excite varied response from many people
    (C) do neither of these things

7. A "promo" is
    (A) a political announcement
    (B) an announcement about a new feature or about a station's program
    (C) a prerecorded program

8. Which of the following sentences offers you, as the broadcaster, the most protection from a libel suit?
    (A) John Smith, the bank robber, was caught by police as he fled from the scene of the crime
    (B) John Smith, the suspect, was caught by police as he fled from the scene of his crime
    (C) John Smith, the suspect, was caught by police as he fled from the scene of his alleged crime

9. When you place your hand on your chest to see if you can feel it vibrate, you are testing
    (A) the resonance of your delivery
    (B) the pitch of your voice
    (C) the loudness of your voice

10. "Availability" is a broadcasting term which means
    (A) that an announcer is available for work at a certain time
    (B) radio time that can be sponsored by a prospective advertiser
    (C) time that a station has available for a national network broadcast

11. On a telephone call-in program you should NOT
    (A) clarify a topic for a listener
    (B) place a time limit on the calls, as this

inhibits those persons who wish to express their opinions
(C) express your own opinions on the topics

12. Which of the following is NOT an advantage of Frequency Modulation stations?
(A) They are not affected by interference noise
(B) They can broadcast good high-fidelity sound
(C) They are limited to line-of-sight transmission, just as television stations are

13. A "daytimer" is
(A) a listener who listens only during the day, usually a housewife
(B) an announcer who refuses to work the night shift
(C) a station that is allowed to broadcast only from local sunrise to local sunset

14. "Cold Copy" is a broadcasting term used to indicate
(A) copy which is unpracticed by an announcer and is read for the first time
(B) copy which hasn't been used by a station in a long time
(C) the station's log

15. It is always best, when ad-libbing,
(A) to stick to one subject
(B) to speak at your normal announcing speed
(C) to do both of these things

16. Every three years the FCC requires all radio stations to renew their licenses and to
(A) submit a complete analysis of all programs and commercials

(B) promise to do a better job of broadcasting in the next three years
(C) submit a complete program guide for the next three years

17. The log's most important function is to
(A) list the announcers who are on duty for the day
(B) list the commercials that are to be announced during each program
(C) give the station manager an idea of what an announcer plans to do on his program

18. In order to handle a remote program interruption well, you should
(A) always have a brief announcement explaining that there is a technical difficulty
(B) be prepared with a substitute program that will fill what would otherwise be dead air
(C) do both of these things

19. A "tag" is
(A) a label on a record that tells how long each song is
(B) a live announcement that follows a commercial
(C) the closing three lines of a DJ show

20. Radio stations make money by
(A) belonging to a national network
(B) broadcasting local commercials
(C) either or both of these methods

21. Which of the following types of musical programs is the rarest in the United States?
(A) Country and western
(B) Jazz
(C) Rock and roll

True or False

1. _____Always announce the manufacturer of a record you play.
2. _____Beginning announcers should try to be as humorous as possible; it relaxes them.
3. _____All radio stations east of the Rockies have call letters beginning with W.
4. _____All radio stations broadcast with at least 10,000 watts of power.

ANSWERS!☞

Multiple Choice

1. B
2. B
3. B
4. C
5. C
6. B
7. B
8. C
9. A
10. B
11. C
12. C
13. C
14. A
15. C
16. A
17. B
18. C
19. B
20. C
21. B

True or False

1. F
2. F
3. F
4. F

BUILDING CONTRACTOR

American Schools

Who hasn't observed, often critically, the apparent confusion and waste that surrounds a building site while one is watching, often with apprehension, the fascinating process by which all the pieces come together at each stage of construction? If it happens to be your own house going up, those feelings are hardly trivial.

Most states have contractor licensing boards, which administer examinations requiring a demonstration of an adequate understanding of state laws, codes, and regulations and of practical knowledge in about twenty "knowledge areas" (in the case of General Contractor) or in one of more than three dozen special fields (in the case of the specific-classification contractors licenses). These special fields range from the mundane (concrete, plumbing, painting) to the relatively arcane (mill work, acoustical, ornamental metal).

From the contractor's point of view, the advantage to having the license is that it allows one to charge more than a given amount for a given job—typically, around $300, including materials. In other words, if you don't have a license and you advertise your services as a painter, say, you wouldn't be legally permitted to charge more than $300, in the typical case, for any painting job. Obviously, that makes it hard to make a serious living. If you're a consumer, the main advantage to hiring a licensed contractor is that you're protected from the consequences of bad work by a bond the contractor has to deposit with the Contractors State License Board, so that if a General Contractor you've hired to remodel your bathroom turns your living room into a swimming pool, the cost of damages is covered. You can also arrange to have a licensed contractor obtain a payment and completion bond so that, if the contractor is unable to complete the work or the job goes sour, bonding company funds will be available to finish the work and pay the bills. Also, of course, the license is intended to be a confirmation of the builder's skill and knowledge, so the chances of bad workmanship are reduced.

The questions that follow are from the American Schools home study courses, which prepare people to pass the General Building Contractor License and about twenty other classification exams in the state of California. You can get more information about their courses by calling American Schools at 1-(800)-63-STUDY.

Steel Reinforcing

1. What is the smallest size of rebar used in a single-story residence?
   (A) No. 1
   (B) No. 2
   (C) No. 3
   (D) No. 4

2. What are reinforcing bars primarily used for?
   (A) Absorbing tensile strength
   (B) Absorbing compressive strength
   (C) Supporting underground utility conduits
   (D) None of the above

3. At what depth should anchor bolts be placed in residential concrete footing?
   (A) 3 inches
   (B) 6 inches
   (C) 9 inches
   (D) 12 inches

Concrete

1. The best method of placing concrete under water is
   (A) sacked concrete
   (B) gunite
   (C) tremie pouring
   (D) none of the above

2. The most suitable condition for pouring concrete under water is
   (A) when water temperature is under 45 degrees F
   (B) when water is flowing with a velocity greater than 10 feet per minute
   (C) when water is flowing with a velocity less than 10 feet per minute
   (D) onto a sloped underwater surface

3. A cleat is a
   (A) device for spacing the sides of a form when pouring a concrete footing
   (B) a device used between units of a structure
   (C) a post or column extending into and above the ground and supporting a structural member of a building
   (D) none of the above

4. Honeycombing can occur when
   (A) the forms are not tight
   (B) the concrete separates
   (C) the concrete has not been consolidated
   (D) all of the above

Drywall Construction

1. The vertical and horizontal angles in a steel soffit assembly should be
   (A) horizontal, straight, and level
   (B) level, parallel, and plumb
   (C) straight, level, and plumb
   (D) parallel, vertical, and level

2. The metal screw-on stud wall system has only three major components; studs, track, and
   (A) partition
   (B) soffit
   (C) framing
   (D) gypsum

Electrical

1. What type of thermostat is normally used for controlling the air-conditioning unit in a residence?
   (A) Zero stage
   (B) One stage
   (C) Two stage
   (D) Three stage

2. Proper color codes for identifying conductors in a 220-v circuit are
   (A) white or gray and any other color combination
   (B) black or green and any other color combination
   (C) blue or red and any other color combination
   (D) yellow or red and any other color combination

3. Romex cable that is approved for underground work is classified as
   (A) UF
   (B) HSE
   (C) MTW
   (D) SD

Earthwork and Paving

1. Concrete paving costs are usually expressed in
   (A) square feet
   (B) square yards
   (C) linear feet
   (D) linear yards

2. A sack of cement
   (A) weighs 94 pounds
   (B) weights 376 pounds
   (C) contains 1 cubic foot
   (D) A and C

3. Two-thirds cubic yard of fine aggregate, mixed with 2 cubic yards of coarse aggregate with 33⅓% voids, yields _____ of mixed aggregate.
   (A) 1⅓ cubic yards
   (B) 2 cubic yards
   (C) 2⅓ cubic yards
   (D) 2⅔ cubic yards

4. A _____ is one part cement, two parts sand, and three parts coarse aggregate.
   (A) lean mix
   (B) medium mix
   (C) rich mix
   (D) none of these

5. When the water-cement ratio is high, the strength of the concrete is
   (A) high
   (B) low
   (C) unaffected
   (D) none of the above

Carpet

1. Pile made of wool or synthetic fibers that is machine-stitched into a backing made beforehand is
   (A) tufted
   (B) woven
   (C) punched
   (D) none of the above

2. Which factors must be taken into account when planning the layout of a carpet in a room?
   (A) Pile direction
   (B) Run the longest seam in the room toward the major light source
   (C) Keep seams away from high traffic areas
   (D) All of the above

3. Which of the following should be done prior to beginning a carpet re-installation?
   (A) Remove grilles from heating vents
   (B) Nail uneven boards
   (C) Sweep the floor
   (D) All of the above

Windows and Doors

1. Why should putty be applied with adequate pressure to complete the facing operation on the first pass of the putty knife?
    (A) To prevent the putty from falling from the rabbet
    (B) To conserve on putty
    (C) To ensure a cleaner job
    (D) Because the putty will become increasingly difficult to handle with each subsequent pass

2. If the rubber channel is stretched too far while installing a sliding sash,
    (A) runs may develop in the glass
    (B) the glass may shift in the frame
    (C) water can enter through the rubber channel
    (D) the frame may bow

3. Which of the following is the most important factor to remember regarding glazing sliding windows?
    (A) You must allow for expansion of the glass
    (B) Your measurements must accommodate the pull hardware
    (C) All measurements must be accurate
    (D) The light should be free of distortions

4. Under which conditions will putty not stick to a sash?
    (A) If the sash is too warm
    (B) If the sash is bowed or warped
    (C) If the sash is greasy or dirty
    (D) None of the above

5. Which stop does the glazier apply first when installing glass into a wood sash with stops?
    (A) Top
    (B) Right
    (C) Bottom
    (D) Left

Heating, Ventilating, and Air Conditioning

1. How many fans are required to provide proper airflow through a 240,000-cubic-foot building if building requirements state that the air must be replenished four times an hour? Each fan moves 2,000 cubic feet per minute.
    (A) 6
    (B) 8
    (C) 10
    (D) 12

2. Internal heat can be best maintained during the winter by installing the smallest number of regular single glass windows on which side(s) of a residence?
    (A) North
    (B) South
    (C) East or west
    (D) Northeast or northwest

3. If a metal heating duct is exposed, it should be insulated
    (A) when it is in the attic
    (B) when it is exposed to the exterior
    (C) when it leads into a plenum
    (D) at all times

Landscape Contracting

1. The settling factor when backfilling with loam soil approximates
    (A) 5%
    (B) 12%
    (C) 25%
    (D) 35%

2. Grass-seed labels show all the following information except
   (A) purity
   (B) weed seed
   (C) number of seeds per pound
   (D) lot number

3. A benefit of spring-retracted heads is
   (A) a reduction in the amount of damage done to sprinklers by mowing equipment
   (B) greater water coverage per sprinkler head
   (C) lower initial cost
   (D) none of the above

Masonry

1. What is a dwarf wall?
   (A) That part of a wall from which an arch is suspended
   (B) The lowest part of a wall, pier, monument or column
   (C) A wall or partition which does not extend to the ceiling
   (D) A projection from the face of a wall used to support an ornamental feature

2. What is the minimum thickness of a stone masonry wall?
   (A) 6 inches
   (B) 8 inches
   (C) 16 inches
   (D) 20 inches

3. Construction of natural or cast stone laid in mortar with all joints thoroughly filled is called _____ masonry.
   (A) random rubble stone
   (B) coursed rubble stone
   (C) stone
   (D) all of the above

4. What is a frog and what is another term used for it?
   (A) A section of a wall built up and racked back on successive courses at the corners of a wall, also called a lead
   (B) A fragment or chip of stone or brick, especially bad or broken brick, also called a gallet
   (C) A depression in the bed surface of a brick, also called a panel
   (D) None of the above

Painting and Decorating

1. What should be painted first when painting a room?
   (A) Walls
   (B) Windowsills
   (C) Trim and mouldings
   (D) Ceilings

2. The best paint for kitchen walls is
   (A) semi-gloss
   (B) flat latex
   (C) oil-base flat
   (D) polyurethane

3. When cleaning a latex brush, it is best to use
   (A) alcohol
   (B) gasoline
   (C) water
   (D) turpentine

4. Prior to papering new plaster walls, they must be
   (A) coated with wallpaper paste
   (B) sandpapered
   (C) coated with wall sizing
   (D) washed with water and detergent

Plastering

1. Which of the following materials cannot have portland cement plaster applied directly over it?
(A) Gypsum masonry
(B) Gypsum plaster
(C) Gypsum lath
(D) All of the above

2. What is the minimum number of inches above the grade with which one can place weep screeds?
(A) 1 inch
(B) 3 inches
(C) 6 inches
(D) 12 inches

Structural Steel

1. Which of the following is a method for binding metal together with heat?
(A) Fission
(B) Compression
(C) Combustion
(D) None of the above

2. What is the name of a material that will dissolve oxides on a surface, leaving it clean?
(A) Flux
(B) Rubbing compound
(C) Pantothenic acid
(D) None of the above

3. Which of the following is a type of rivet used in steel framing?
(A) Buttonheads
(B) Knuckleheads
(C) Countersunk
(D) Both A and C

Solar

1. A solar heating system that depends on mechanical devices to move and distribute the sun's heat from the collector is called a(n)
(A) active solar system
(B) passive solar system
(C) direct solar system
(D) closed-loop solar system

2. A(n) _____ system utilizes both active and passive solar technology.
(A) direct
(B) indirect
(C) hybrid
(D) hydronic

3. A differential thermostat regulates the operation of a solar system by responding to differences in
(A) pressure
(B) circulation
(C) temperature
(D) all of the above

Electrical Signs

1. Which of the following formulas will measure the current flow in a circuit?
(A) E times R
(B) R times I
(C) E divided by R
(D) I divided by R

2. Which of the following terms is used to designate the positive pole of an electric terminal?
(A) Cathode
(B) Geode
(C) Anode
(D) None of the above

3. Which of the following terms is used to designate the negative pole of an electric terminal?
(A) Cathode
(B) Geode
(C) Anode
(D) None of the above

4. How is wattage found?
(A) Voltage times resistance
(B) Voltage times amperes
(C) Resistance times amperes
(D) Ohms times volts

Roofing

1. A good wood shingle roof is never less than _____ layer(s) thick.
(A) one
(B) two
(C) three
(D) four

2. Which type of new roof does not require a felt underlay?
(A) Wood shingle
(B) Asphalt strip shingle
(C) Gravel
(D) Fiberglass shingle

3. When the shingles are woven or laced back and forth, forming the valley, it is a
(A) closed valley
(B) full-lace valley
(C) half-lace valley
(D) smooth valley

Plumbing

1. A DWV piping system is a
(A) drain, water, and vent system which empties into a sewer, septic tank, cesspool, or lagoon
(B) dynamic water, vent system which empties into a septic tank or cesspool
(C) drain, waste, vent piping system which empties into a sewer, septic tank, cesspool, or lagoon
(D) water supply piping which is fed by a municipally owned water main

2. Who is responsible for trenching between street connections and a building's foundation?
(A) The city or town
(B) The contractor or plumber
(C) Both A and B
(D) The owner of the building

3. Who will tap the water main, install the corporation stop, the curb stop, and the "B" box?
(A) The building owner
(B) City workers
(C) The plumber or contractor
(D) Both B and C

4. Who is responsible for opening up the sewer main and for installing the sleeve connector and the lateral line to the building?
(A) The sewer department
(B) The building owner
(C) The city workers
(D) The plumber

Safety

1. Which of the following is not a recommended practice for someone who is handling epoxies and mastics?
(A) Do not use in a room with an open flame
(B) Use water to wash off any spills on the hands

(C) Use only in rooms that are tightly
    closed
(D) Read the label before using

2. Which one of the following is not a recom-
    mended safety measure to be followed
    when electrical equipment is being used?
    (A) Ground all electrical tools
    (B) While they are in use, keep extension
        cords looped over nails
    (C) Use only heavy-duty extension cords
    (D) If the supporting surface is wet, wear
        rubber-soled shoes

3. If someone working nearby should come
    into contact with a live power wire, the
    very first thing that should be done is
    (A) try to shake the person
    (B) turn off the power
    (C) administer first aid
    (D) pull the person off the wire without
        contacting either the person or the
        energized object

4. What must an employer do prior to starting
    work on a job that involves substantial risk
    to employees?
    (A) Rope off the danger area
    (B) Install scaffolding
    (C) Obtain a project permit from the Divi-
        sion of Occupational Safety and
        Health
    (D) Place warning signs around the project

ANSWERS!☞

Steel Reinforcing

1. D
2. A
3. B

Concrete

1. C
2. C
3. A
4. D

Drywall Construction

1. C
2. D

Electrical

1. C
2. A
3. A

Earthwork and Paving

1. A
2. D
3. B
4. C
5. B

Carpet

1. A
2. D
3. D

Glazing

1. A
2. C
3. C
4. C
5. A

Heating, Ventilating and Air Conditioning

1. B
2. A
3. D

Landscape Contractor

1. B
2. C
3. A

Masonry

1. C
2. C
3. D
4. C

Painting and Decorating

1. D
2. A
3. C
4. C

Plastering

1. C
2. C

Structural Steel

1. B
2. A
3. D

Solar

1. A
2. C
3. C

Electrical Signs

1. C
2. C
3. A
4. B

Roofing

1. C
2. A
3. B

Plumbing

1. C
2. B
3. B
4. D

Safety

1. C
2. B
3. D
4. C

COSMETOLOGY

Professional Licensing Examination

As far as we know, none of the formal training curricula in this field contain courses in keeping secrets or writing popular fiction.

Most states require those employed in beauty salons to pass the state cosmetology license exam, administered by the Board of Cosmetology Examiners in each state. As with the barber exams, the cosmetology exams vary from state to state.

Typically, the exam covers all branches of cosmetology (about which more in a minute), and consists of two parts, one practical and one written. In the case of the California exam, the total possible examination score consists of 400 points: 300 for the practical and 100 for the written section. To pass the exam, the applicant must achieve at least 300 points overall or 75 percent, including a score of at least 225 points in the practical part. Typically, an average of 75 percent of applicants pass the exam at each sitting for all state cosmetology exams nationwide.

For the practical section, the applicant must bring a female model at least fifteen years of age, and perform scalp treatments, hair cutting, hair tinting, permanent waving, finger-waving, and basic hairstyling. It is advisable to bring someone with whom you are on good terms and to inform her beforehand that you will be performing these techniques, so as to avoid any unnecessary stress during the examination.

Subjects covered on the written part include makeup, facial massage, manicuring, bacteriology and sanitizing, trichology, histology, superfluous hair, cosmetic dermatology, wigs, and hair shampooing, styling, cutting, shaping, waving, straightening, and coloring. The reader may have noticed that much of the knowledge required on this exam overlaps with the barber license exam; which one you want to get should be determined partly by what kind of establishment you want to work in, one with a barber license or one with a cosmetology license. Also, the standard cosmetology curriculum lacks instruction in tapering hair with clippers and shaving and trimming beards and mustaches.

Of the many institutions that prepare applicants for the cosmetology exam, probably the best known is the Wilfred Beauty Academy, which has about 40 schools around the country. The questions that follow are from the State Board Review Examinations text Wilfred uses in its curriculum, and cover all subject areas. For more information about Wilfred's programs, check your phone book for a school in your area or contact: Wilfred American Educational Corp., 1657 Broadway, New York NY 10019-6707, tel. (212) 582-6690.

Shampooing

1. A shampoo is required before
   (A) a permanent wave
   (B) a hot oil treatment
   (C) bleaching hair
   (D) caustic hair straightening

2. The hair will become more lustrous and dirt will be eliminated with
   (A) haircutting
   (B) proper pin curls
   (C) hair brushing
   (D) air waving

3. Bleached hair is best shampooed with
   (A) powdered dry shampoo
   (B) a mild shampoo
   (C) benzine
   (D) a soapless product

4. Of the following types of shampoo, the one that is least effective with hard water is
   (A) egg
   (B) soap
   (C) cream
   (D) synthetics

5. It is advisable to brush hair before shampooing because
   (A) it helps remove foreign matter from the hair
   (B) it will require the use of less shampoo
   (C) it avoids irritating the scalp
   (D) it makes the setting last longer

6. The standard shampoo procedure requires
   (A) one soaping
   (B) three soapings
   (C) four soapings
   (D) two soapings

7. Soft water does which of the following?
   (A) Rinse shampoo out easily
   (B) Clean hair without shampoo
   (C) Not work well with shampoo
   (D) Not help to lather up

8. It's best not to rub or brush the scalp when using a
   (A) soapless shampoo
   (B) coco castile shampoo
   (C) liquid dry shampoo
   (D) lanolin shampoo

9. Following the shampoo, begin to comb the patron's hair
   (A) in the front
   (B) at the nape
   (C) over the ears
   (D) from the roots

Hairstyling

1. A center-back parting gives the illusion to the head of
   (A) length
   (B) height
   (C) depth
   (D) breadth

2. To locate a natural tendency to wave in the hair
   (A) comb the hair toward the face
   (B) comb the hair away from the face and push forward
   (C) brush the hair up from the scalp
   (D) locate the crown and work down

3. A long thin neck looks best with the neck-line cut
   (A) in a V-shape
   (B) close at the sides
   (C) longer than its natural shape
   (D) at an angle

4. For a patron with a long, thin face, the hairstyle should be
   (A) full at the sides
   (B) high at the top
   (C) snug and tight at the sides
   (D) parted in the middle

5. The arrangement of hair at the back of the head in a smooth vertical molded line is called a
   (A) French twist
   (B) page boy fluff
   (C) beehive
   (D) chignon

6. For the patron with a narrow face, a parting should be
   (A) at the middle of the forehead
   (B) slanted outward from inner end of eyebrow
   (C) straight back from middle of the eyebrow
   (D) diagonally from outer end of eyebrow toward crown

7. The purpose of fingerwaving is to
   (A) center the hairstyle
   (B) mold the hair into even ridges
   (C) add height to the style
   (D) flatten the hair

8. The blow dryer usually has two to four heat settings. Medium heat is used for
   (A) drying the hair
   (B) controlled styling
   (C) final touches
   (D) tight curling

9. When blow drying the hair, use the cool temperature for
   (A) short hair
   (B) faster drying
   (C) final touches
   (D) coarse hair

Men's Haircutting, Hairstyling, and Hair Care

1. The movement for men to go to the cosmetologist instead of the barber for haircuts and hair services in the early 1970s was triggered by
   (A) women
   (B) longer hairstyles
   (C) short haircuts
   (D) the economy

2. Which of the following is more aging for a man?
   (A) Gray hair
   (B) Tinted hair
   (C) A gray moustache and/or beard
   (D) Gray sideburns

3. The final styling details of a man's hairstyle are placed with a
   (A) comb
   (B) curling iron
   (C) round styling hair brush
   (D) 1500-watt hair blower

4. Over-curly hair has long been plaguing men because
   (A) it needs frequent haircutting
   (B) it must be shampooed daily
   (C) it needs frequent brushing
   (D) it limits the way the hair may be combed

Hairpieces

1. First-quality human hairpieces are made of
   (A) European Caucasian hair
   (B) Indian hair
   (C) Asiatic hair
   (D) American hair

2. It is advisable to clean human hairpieces with
   (A) soap and water
   (B) a detergent
   (C) a nonflammable wig cleaner
   (D) cream rinse

3. Before coloring a wig, it is advisable to
   (A) use henna as a base
   (B) always make a strand test
   (C) use an aniline dye
   (D) lighten before tinting

4. Compared to hand-tied wigs, wefted wigs are
   (A) heavier
   (B) lighter
   (C) thinner
   (D) shorter

Hair Shaping

1. A light growth of hair down the sides of the neck is best removed with the
   (A) clipper
   (B) thinning shears
   (C) razor
   (D) tips of the scissors

2. Split hair ends are best eliminated by
   (A) blunt cutting
   (B) ruffing
   (C) thinning
   (D) epilating

3. Cutting hair straight across, while it is held between the fingers, is known as
   (A) blunt cutting
   (B) club cutting
   (C) slithering
   (D) tapering

4. It may be necessary to thin closer to the ends with
   (A) gray hair
   (B) hennaed hair
   (C) coarse hair
   (D) fine hair

Permanent Waving

1. The greatest risk in permanent waving may be expected with hair that is
   (A) over-bleached
   (B) bleached
   (C) dyed with amino dye
   (D) white

2. If the ends of the hair are frizzy after a permanent wave, it is usually due to
   (A) highly tapered ends
   (B) hair not being clean
   (C) too much neutralizer
   (D) blunt cut ends

3. When cold waving tinted hair causes hair breakage, it may be the result of
   (A) temporary color applications
   (B) continuous overlapping
   (C) a vegetable tint application
   (D) continued use of hair color creams

4. A permanent curl should last
   (A) six months
   (B) the life of the hair
   (C) a year
   (D) a lifetime

5. If cold wave lotion is dripped onto the skin near the face area, it is best to
   (A) apply a lemon pack
   (B) cover with cotton
   (C) apply neutralizer to skin
   (D) apply cholesterol

6. The softness of the completed curl in cold waving is determined partially by the
   (A) processing time
   (B) texture of the hair
   (C) conditioning treatment
   (D) density of the hair

Super Curly Hair

1. Super curly hair should always be brushed in line with its growth pattern
   (A) downward and toward the scalp
   (B) backward away from the face
   (C) up and close to the scalp
   (D) up and away from the scalp

2. Super curly hair usually grows
   (A) faster than the usual ½ inch per month
   (B) long, without losing its shape or style
   (C) slower than the usual ½ inch per month
   (D) at the nape area only

3. Super curly hair should always be cut
   (A) wet—after the shampoo
   (B) dry—before or after the shampoo
   (C) wet—before the shampoo
   (D) before combing the hair

4. When super curly hair becomes exposed to moisture or dampness, it will
   (A) revert
   (B) straighten
   (C) develop soft large waves
   (D) grow stronger

5. Most super curly hair has poor elasticity and
   (A) extra strong qualities
   (B) no cuticle protective cells
   (C) poor porosity
   (D) is very porous

6. When super curly hair is to be combed while in a dry state, the technique is to
   (A) "lift" the comb through the hair
   (B) pull the comb through the hair
   (C) pull the comb back and over the hair
   (D) comb the hair as flat as possible

7. Super curly hair stands out from the head because of its
   (A) density and texture
   (B) texture, density, and elasticity
   (C) spiral form and lack of weight
   (D) elasticity and texture

Hair Straightening

1. Chemical hair straightener will cause hair to
   (A) swell and soften
   (B) curl
   (C) bleach
   (D) kink

2. In straightening kinky hair, a soft press means
   (A) no oil and lukewarm pressing comb
   (B) wax and marcel iron, passed quickly
   (C) oil and one treatment with pressing comb
   (D) croquignole marcel on cool iron

3. Hair pressing treatments between shampoos are called
   (A) patch tests
   (B) hair treatments
   (C) curl reversion
   (D) touch ups

4. The pressing treatment that is least
   injurious to the hair is a
   (A) hard press
   (B) soft press
   (C) double iron press
   (D) double comb press

5. The most difficult type of hair to press is
   (A) medium, curly hair
   (B) coarse, curly hair
   (C) coarse, kinky hair
   (D) fine, kinky hair

6. Difficult to straighten hair requires a
   (A) soft press
   (B) regular press
   (C) comb press
   (D) hard press

7. To avoid breakage in pressing fine hair,
   use
   (A) no pressing cream
   (B) more heat and pressure
   (C) less heat and pressure
   (D) more heat and less pressure

Hair Coloring

1. Bleached or tinted hair is easier to comb
   when wet, after applying a little
   (A) cold wave lotion
   (B) cream hair dressing
   (C) boric acid
   (D) phenol

2. To correct damaged hair to absorb color
   evenly, use a
   (A) color neutralizer
   (B) basic color
   (C) shampoo tint
   (D) color filler

3. According to the federal Food, Drug, and
   Cosmetic Law, an allergy (predisposition)
   test must be made
   (A) before the first application of oxidation
       dyes
   (B) before any application of vegetable
       coloring
   (C) before every application of oxidation
       dyes
   (D) when the scalp shows open lesions

4. If the hair feels like rubber after bleaching,
   it usually means
   (A) too much ammonia in peroxide
   (B) hair is badly over-bleached
   (C) hair was too oily
   (D) peroxide was not strong enough

5. For best effects, all bleaching agents and
   dyes must be
   (A) kept wet on the hair for full time
   (B) allowed to remain on the hair for
       exactly 15 minutes
   (C) allowed to dry quickly
   (D) dried under infra-red lamp

6. When changing the color of hair to a much
   lighter shade, the hair should always be
   (A) developed
   (B) pre-lightened
   (C) over-processed
   (D) drabbed

7. Hair color is absorbed fastest at the
   (A) crown area
   (B) hair ends
   (C) nape area
   (D) scalp area

8. Hair that is devoid of red or gold
   highlights is known as
   (A) drab hair
   (B) bleached hair

(C) hennaed hair
(D) frosted hair

9. Application of hair bleach may cause breakage to hair previously colored with
(A) white henna
(B) peroxide shampoo
(C) a gray rinse
(D) a metallic hair dye

10. Bleached hair must be treated with care because it may become
(A) unruly
(B) overactive
(C) very oily
(D) dry and fragile

11. Bleaching a strand of hair in the front area is known as
(A) parting
(B) streaking
(C) tipping
(D) frosting

12. Dermatitis venenata (hair dye poisoning) is the same condition as
(A) sunburn
(B) psoriasis
(C) hives
(D) ivy poisoning

Cosmetic Dermatology

1. Which of the following conditions should not be treated in the beauty shop without medical approval?
(A) Canities
(B) Eczema
(C) Seborrhea
(D) Lentigo

2. White hair at birth is usually a sign of
(A) hypertrichosis
(B) melanism
(C) albinism
(D) early baldness

3. One of the following conditions of the nails should not be treated in the beauty shop:
(A) Eggshell nails
(B) Bluish nail
(C) Tinea
(D) Hangnails

Facial Massage

1. The heaviest movements in facial massage are recommended for
(A) circles under the eyes
(B) a scrawny neck
(C) heavy jowls and chin
(D) a florid complexion

2. A facial treatment should not be given to skin that shows a condition of
(A) freckles
(B) extreme oiliness
(C) eczema
(D) extreme dryness

3. A clay pack is used as a treatment for
(A) dandruff
(B) hand massage
(C) dry skin
(D) blackheads

Makeup

1. For a more effective application of pressed powder eye shadow, use
(A) a wet brush
(B) absorbent cotton
(C) a sponge
(D) your fingertips

2. Mascara skin stains are easily removed with the use of
   (A) acetone
   (B) a sponge
   (C) a cotton swab
   (D) a tissue

3. When applying makeup, the cream base is known as
   (A) massage cream
   (B) acne cream
   (C) foundation cream
   (D) lemon cream

4. As a healthy, sanitary measure, lip rouge should be applied with a
   (A) cotton swab
   (B) powder puff
   (C) sanitized brush
   (D) orangewood stick

Scalp Treatments

1. Hair that is weak, dry, and lifeless may be the result of
   (A) good food
   (B) oily treatments
   (C) poor blood circulation
   (D) scalp massage

2. When the condition of the scalp is dry and the hair is limp and lifeless, the cosmetologist should advise
   (A) a cream shampoo
   (B) a vapor shampoo
   (C) a coloring treatment
   (D) corrective treatments

3. The most effective movement in the usual routine for scalp massage is
   (A) linear stroking
   (B) palmar rotation
   (C) slapping
   (D) rolling

Superfluous Hair

1. Permanent removal of hair (no regrowth) requires
   (A) that the papilla be dissolved
   (B) that the hair be cut
   (C) bleach before treating
   (D) a wax treatment

2. The depth of insertion of an electrolysis needle will vary according to the
   (A) color of the skin
   (B) sensitivity of the skin
   (C) size of the needle
   (D) coarseness of the hair

3. After applying the current through the needle, remove the hair
   (A) by cutting
   (B) with a tweezer
   (C) with the needle
   (D) with the fingers

Manicuring

1. A proficient manicurist has the necessary skills to give a long manicure within
   (A) 30 minutes
   (B) 60 minutes
   (C) 5 minutes
   (D) 10 minutes

2. Pumice stone is used
   (A) to shorten nails
   (B) to remove nail enamel
   (C) to remove light stains from skin around the nails
   (D) to smooth nails

3. When shaping nails, the file should be directed

(A) from the corners toward the middle
(B) in a straight line
(C) from the middle toward the corners
(D) in a continuous curve

4. A substance used to contract the skin to stop bleeding from minor cuts is called
(A) an astringent
(B) an antiseptic
(C) a styptic
(D) a spatula

Bacteriology & Sanitizing

1. The best metal for instruments that must withstand regular sanitizing is
(A) brass
(B) stainless steel
(C) tin-plated copper
(D) aluminum

2. The growth of bacteria will be prevented by
(A) washing
(B) intense heat
(C) cold water
(D) moles

3. When not in use, the comb should always be kept
(A) in the hairdresser's pocket
(B) tucked into the patron's hair
(C) on the table
(D) behind the hairdresser's ear

Anatomy in Beauty Culture

1. Which of the nine systems do not come within the province of the cosmetologist?
(A) endocrine and reproductive
(B) digestive
(C) vascular
(D) excretory and nervous

2. The skeletal system consists of
(A) 80 bones
(B) 62 bones
(C) 64 bones
(D) 206 bones

3. The function of nervous tissue is to
(A) carry food to the cells
(B) bind structures together
(C) convey impulses
(D) form a protective covering

Chemistry for Cosmetologists

1. The cause of trouble with soap and hard water is the dissolution of
(A) acids
(B) organic matter
(C) bacteria
(D) metallic salts

2. The hydrogen peroxide used for bleaching and dyeing hair should be of the following quality:
(A) 3%, 10 volume
(B) 15%, 47 volume
(C) 5-6%, 17-20 volume
(D) 4%, 12 volume

3. In a cream shampoo, the essential cleansing ingredient is
(A) casein from milk
(B) white of egg
(C) synthetic detergent
(D) neutral soap

4. The symbol for aluminum is
(A) Km
(B) Al
(C) Am
(D) Ag

5. A compound that contains hydrogen

atoms that are positively charged is
(A) iron
(B) acid
(C) alkali
(D) gas

6. A homogeneous mixture of one or more substances dissolved into another is called a(n)
(A) mixture
(B) emulsion
(C) solution
(D) salt

7. A pigment that can produce black, brown, yellow, or red color is
(A) melanin
(B) cortex
(C) natural
(D) cuticle layer

Trichology

1. The first cycle of hair growth is known as
(A) catagen
(B) telagen
(C) the cuticle
(D) anagen

2. The chemical symbol for the chemical bonds in the hair, prior to the application of permanent wave lotion, is
(A) H-O-N
(B) S-H-O-H-S
(C) S-H-H-S
(D) S-S

3. The first stage in the development of hair covering usually lasts from one to three years. The third stage is the permanent hair covering. The secondary stage lasts until about the age of
(A) 12

(B) 6
(C) 18
(D) 21

4. Because hair will react to either acid or alkaline substances, it is referred to as
(A) logarithmic
(B) cysteine
(C) amphoteric
(D) neutral

5. The number of hair follicles per square inch on the average scalp is approximately
(A) 1000
(B) 500
(C) 2000
(D) 2500

6. The approximate area of the average scalp is
(A) 220 square inches
(B) 120 square inches
(C) 60 square inches
(D) 200 square inches

7. The number of hairs on the average scalp is
(A) 200,000
(B) 1,000
(C) 120,000
(D) 50,000

Histology

1. The normal rate of hair growth on the head is about
(A) $\frac{1}{16}$ inch per month
(B) $\frac{1}{2}$ inch per month
(C) $\frac{3}{4}$ inch per week
(D) 1 inch per year

2. The thickest part of the skin is found on the

(A) palms
(B) fingers
(C) chin
(D) eyelids

3. The thinnest area of the skin is found on the
   (A) chin
   (B) eyelids
   (C) nape of the neck
   (D) crown

4. The normal life of hair on the head is
   (A) 2-4 months
   (B) 6-8 months
   (C) 2-4 years
   (D) more than 10 years

5. If coloring matter is not present, the hair will become
   (A) blue
   (B) black
   (C) red
   (D) gray

6. Wet natural hair can be stretched about
   (A) 60%
   (B) 25%
   (C) 10%
   (D) 40%

Beauty Salon Management

1. A cosmetologist's best source of income is from
   (A) haircutting
   (B) appointments
   (C) merchandising
   (D) working late hours

2. The highest percentage of expense from income is
   (A) wages and salaries

(B) supplies
(C) electric, heat, and water
(D) fees, taxes, and legal services

3. It is recommended that employers send their cosmetologists to school for a short course in advanced training
   (A) every month
   (B) once every five years
   (C) once a year
   (D) every 10 years

4. Straight salaries
   (A) increase incentive
   (B) lower incentive
   (C) eliminate withholding taxes
   (D) are paid on a weekly basis only

ANSWERS! ☞

Shampooing

1. A
2. C
3. B
4. B
5. A
6. D
7. A
8. C
9. B

Hairstyling

1. D
2. B
3. C
4. A
5. A
6. D
7. B
8. B
9. C

Men's Haircutting, Hairstyling, and Hair Care

1. B
2. C
3. A
4. D

Hairpieces

1. A
2. C
3. B
4. A

Hair Shaping

1. D
2. A
3. A
4. C

Permanent Waving

1. A
2. A
3. B
4. B
5. C
6. A

Super Curly Hair

1. D
2. C
3. B
4. A
5. D
6. A
7. C

Hair Straightening

1. A
2. C
3. D
4. B
5. C
6. D
7. C

Hair Coloring

1. B
2. D
3. C
4. B
5. A
6. B
7. B
8. A
9. D
10. D
11. B
12. D

Cosmetic Dermatology
1. B
2. C
3. C

Facial Massage
1. C
2. C
3. D

Makeup
1. A
2. C
3. C
4. C

Scalp Treatments
1. C
2. D
3. B

Superfluous Hair
1. A
2. D
3. B

Manicuring
1. A
2. C
3. A
4. C

Bacteriology & Sanitizing
1. B
2. B
3. C

Anatomy in Beauty Culture
1. A
2. D
3. C

Chemistry for Cosmetologists
1. D
2. C
3. C
4. B
5. B
6. C
7. A

Trichology
1. D
2. B
3. A
4. C
5. A
6. B
7. C

Histology
1. B
2. A
3. B
4. C
5. D
6. D

Beauty Salon Management
1. C
2. A
3. C
4. B

CPA

American Institute of Certified Public Accountants

If you aren't born with the understanding of how a Balance Sheet behaves and why it makes practical sense for it to do so, no amount of training will ever liberate you from accepting that esoterica as an act of faith.

The Uniform CPA Examination prepared by the Board of Examiners of the American Institute of Certified Public Accountants is the most widely used exam in the licensing process of the various state boards of accountancy to ensure the technical and professional competence of CPA candidates. (If you managed to work your way through that introductory sentence, maybe you won't find the questions so terribly difficult.)

The exam consists of four sections: Accounting Practice, Auditing, Business Law, and Accounting Theory. Each section tests candidates' knowledge by the use of multiple-choice (60 percent of each section), essay, or problem-type questions. Scoring 75 percent correct is considered passing for each section. Multiple-choice questions are graded by an optical scanning machine, and essay and problem-type questions are graded by a professional staff specifically engaged for this purpose, with the roles reversed on leap years to provide a mutual check and to make sure everyone is awake and free of malfunctions.

Accounting Practice

1. On January 1, 1986, Carr Company purchased Fay Corporation 9% bonds with a face amount of $400,000 for $375,600, to yield 10%. The bonds are dated January 1, 1986, mature on December 31, 1995, and pay interest annually on December 31. Carr uses the interest method of amortizing bond discount. In its income statement for the year ended December 31, 1986, what total amount should Carr report as interest revenue from the long-term bond investment?
   (A) $40,000
   (B) $37,560
   (C) $36,000
   (D) $34,440

2. On July 1, 1986, Hart signed an agreement to operate as a franchisee of Ace Printers for an initial franchise fee of $120,000. The same date, Hart paid $40,000 and agreed to pay the balance in four equal annual payments of $20,000 beginning July 1, 1987. The down payment is not refundable and no future services are required of the franchisor. Hart can borrow at 14% for a loan of this type. Present and future value factors are as follows:

   Present value of 1 at 14% for 4 periods: 0.59
   Future amount of 1 at 14% for 4 periods: 1.69
   Present value of an ordinary annuity of 1 at 14% for 4 periods: 2.91

   Hart should record the acquisition cost of the franchise on July 1, 1986, at
   (A) $135,200
   (B) $120,000

(C) $98,200
(D) $87,200

3. Kew Company leased equipment for its entire nine-year useful life, agreeing to pay $100,000 at the start of the lease term on December 31, 1985, and $100,000 annually on December 31 of the next eight years. The present value on December 31, 1985, of the nine lease payments over the lease term, discounted at the lessor's implicit rate known by Dew to be 10%, was $633,000. The December 31, 1985 present value of the lease payments discounted at Kew's incremental borrowing rate of 12% was $597,000. Kew made a timely second lease payment. The total lease liability at December 31, 1986, was
   (A) $0
   (B) $100,000
   (C) $694,000
   (D) $750,000

4. On January 17, 1987, an explosion occurred at a Cord Company plant causing extensive property damage to area buildings. Although no claims had yet been asserted against Cord by March 10, 1987, Cord's management and counsel concluded that it is reasonably possible Cord will be responsible for damages, and that $2,500,000 would be a reasonable estimate of its liability. Cord's $10,000,000 comprehensive public liability policy has a $500,000 deductible clause. In Cord's December 31, 1986 financial statements, which were issued on March 25, 1987, how should this item be reported?
   (A) No footnote disclosure or accrual is necessary
   (B) As a footnote disclosure indicating the possible loss of $500,000
   (C) As an accrued liability of $500,000

(D) As a footnote disclosure indicating the possible loss of $2,500,000

5. The Tone Company is the defendant in a lawsuit filed by Witt in 1985 disputing the validity of a copyright held by Tone. On December 31, 1985, Tone determined that Witt would probably be successful against Tone for an estimated amount of $400,000. Appropriately, a $400,000 loss was accrued by a charge to income for the year ended December 31, 1985. On December 15, 1986, Tone and Witt agreed to a settlement providing for cash payment of $250,000 by Tone to Witt, and transfer of Tone's copyright to Witt. The carrying amount of the copyright on Tone's accounting records was $60,000 at December 15, 1986. What would be the effect of the settlement on Tone's income before income tax in 1986?
(A) No effect
(B) $60,000 decrease
(C) $90,000 increase
(D) $150,000 increase

6. On January 1, 1984, Bray Company purchased for $240,000 a machine with a useful life of ten years and no salvage value. The machine was depreciated by the double declining balance method and the carrying amount of the machine was $153,600 on December 31, 1985. Bray changed retroactively to the straight-line method on January 1, 1986. Bray can justify the change. What should be the depreciation expense on this machine for the year ended December 31, 1986?
(A) $15,360
(B) $19,200
(C) $24,000
(D) $30,720

7. Joe Neil, CPA, has among his clientele a charitable organization that has a legal permit to conduct games of chance for fund-raising purposes. Neil's client derives its profit from admission fees and the sale of refreshments, and therefore wants to "break even" on the games of chance. In one of these games, the player draws one card from a standard deck of 52 cards. A player drawing any one of four "queens" wins $5, and a player drawing any one of 13 "hearts" wins $2. Neil is asked to compute the price that should be charged per draw, so that the total amount paid out for winning draws can be expected to equal the total amount received from all draws. Which one of the following equations should Neil use to compute the price (P)?

(A) $5 - 2 = \dfrac{35\,P}{52}$

(B) $\dfrac{4}{52}(5) + \dfrac{13}{52}(2) = \dfrac{35\,P}{52}$

(C) $\dfrac{4}{52}(5 - P) + \dfrac{13}{52}(2 - P) = P$

(D) $\dfrac{4}{52}(5) + \dfrac{13}{52}(2) = P$

Auditing

1. Which of the following statements best describes the auditor's responsibility regarding the detection of material errors and irregularities?
(A) The auditor is responsible for the failure to detect material errors and irregularities only when such failure results from the nonapplication of generally accepted accounting principles
(B) Extended auditing procedures are required to detect material errors and

irregularities if the auditor's examination indicates that they may exist

(C) The auditor is responsible for the failure to detect material errors and irregularities only when the auditor fails to confirm receivables or observe inventories

(D) Extended auditing procedures are required to detect unrecorded transactions even if there is no evidence that material errors and irregularities may exist

2. When unable to obtain sufficient competent evidential matter to determine whether certain client acts are illegal, the auditor would most likely issue

(A) an unqualified opinion with a separate explanatory paragraph

(B) either a qualified opinion or an adverse opinion

(C) either a disclaimer of opinion or a qualified opinion

(D) either an adverse opinion or a disclaimer of opinion

3. When there are few property and equipment transactions during the year, the continuing auditor usually makes a

(A) complete review of the related internal accounting controls and performs compliance tests of those controls being relied upon

(B) complete review of the related internal accounting controls and performs analytical review tests to verify current year additions to property and equipment

(C) preliminary review of the related internal accounting controls and performs a thorough examination of the balances at the beginning of the year

(D) preliminary review of the related internal accounting controls and performs

extensive tests of current year property and equipment transactions

4. Without the consent of the client, a CPA should *not* disclose confidential client information contained in working papers to a

(A) voluntary quality control review board

(B) CPA firm that has purchased the CPA's accounting practice

(C) federal court that has issued a valid subpoena

(D) disciplinary body created under state statute

5. Prior to commencing the compilation of financial statements of a nonpublic entity, the accountant should

(A) perform analytical review procedures sufficient to determine whether fluctuations among account balances appear reasonable

(B) complete the preliminary phase of the study and evaluation of the entity's internal accounting control

(C) verify that the financial information supplied by the entity agrees with the books of original entry

(D) acquire a knowledge of any specialized accounting principles and practices used in the entity's industry

6. When an independent accountant's report based on a review of interim financial information is incorporated by reference in a registration statement, the Securities and Exchange Commission requires that the prospectus clarify that the accountant's report is not

(A) a part of the registration statement within the meaning of the Securities Act of 1933

(B) subject to the Statements on Standards for Accounting and Review Services

(C) to be relied upon due to the limited nature of the procedures applied

(D) included in the company's quarterly report on Form 10-Q

7. Which of the following best describes the auditor's reporting responsibility concerning information accompanying the basic financial statements in an auditor-submitted document?
    (A) The auditor should report on all the information included in the document
    (B) The auditor should report on the basic financial statements but may not issue a report covering the accompanying information
    (C) The auditor should report on the information accompanying the basic financial statements only if the auditor participated in the preparation of the accompanying information
    (D) The auditor should report on the information accompanying the basic financial statements only if the document is to be distributed to public shareholders

8. Parker is the in-charge auditor with administrative responsibilities for the upcoming annual audit of FGH Company, a continuing audit client. Parker will supervise two assistants on the engagement and will visit the client before the field work begins.

    Parker has started the planning process by preparing a list of procedures to be performed prior to the beginning of field work. The list includes:
    (1) Review correspondence and permanent files
    (2) Review prior year's audit working papers, financial statements, and auditor's reports

(3) Discuss with CPA firm personnel responsible for audit and nonaudit services to the client, matters that may affect the examination
(4) Discuss with management current business developments affecting the client

Required: Complete Parker's list of procedures to be performed prior to the beginning of field work.

Business Law

Questions 1–3 are based on the following information:

White, Grey, and Fox formed a limited partnership. White is the general partner and Grey and Fox are the limited partners. Each agreed to contribute $200,000. Grey and Fox each contributed $200,000 in cash while White contributed $150,000 in cash and $50,000 worth of services already rendered. After two years, the partnership is insolvent. The fair market value of the assets of the partnership is $150,000 and the liabilities total $275,000. The partners have made no withdrawals.

1. If Fox is insolvent and White and Grey each have a net worth in excess of $300,000, what is White's maximum potential liability in the event of a dissolution of the partnership?
    (A) $62,500
    (B) $112,500
    (C) $125,000
    (D) $175,000

2. Unless otherwise provided in the certificate of limited partnership, which of the following is correct if Fox assigns her

interest in the partnership to Barr and only White consents to Barr's admission as a limited partner?

(A) Barr will not become a substituted limited partner unless Grey also consents
(B) Barr will have the right to inspect the partnership's books
(C) The partnership will be dissolved
(D) Barr will become a substituted limited partner because White, as general partner, consented

3. Unless otherwise provided in the certificate of limited partnership, which of the following is correct if Grey dies?

(A) Grey's executor will automatically become a substituted limited partner
(B) Grey's executor will have all the rights of a limited partner for the purpose of settling the estate
(C) The partnership will automatically be dissolved
(D) Grey's estate will be free from any liabilities which may have been incurred by Grey as a limited partner

Questions 4 and 5 are based on the following information:

On March 1, Mirk Corp. wrote to Carr offering to sell Carr its office building for $280,000. The offer stated that it would remain open until July 1. It further stated that acceptance must be by telegram and would be effective only upon receipt.

4. For this question only, assume that Carr telegrammed its acceptance on June 28 and that it was received by Mirk on July 2. Which of the following statements is correct?

(A) A contract was formed when Carr telegrammed its acceptance
(B) A contract was formed when Mirk received Carr's acceptance

(C) No contract was formed because three months had elapsed since the offer was made
(D) No contract was formed since the acceptance was received after July 1

5. For this question only, assume that on May 10, Mirk mailed a letter to Carr revoking its offer of March 1. Carr did not learn of Mirk's revocation until Carr received the letter on May 17. Carr had already sent a telegram of acceptance to Mirk on May 14, which was received by Mirk on May 16. Which of the following statements is correct?

(A) Carr's telegram of acceptance was effective on May 16
(B) Mirk's offer of March 1 was irrevocable and therefore could not be withdrawn prior to July 1
(C) Mirk's letter of revocation effectively terminated its offer of March 1 when mailed
(D) Carr's telegram of acceptance was effective on May 14

6. Baker fraudulently induced Able to sell Baker a painting for $200. Subsequently, Baker sold the painting for $10,000 to Gold, a good faith purchaser. Able is entitled to

(A) Rescind the contract with Baker
(B) Recover the painting from Gold
(C) Recover damages from Baker
(D) Rescind Baker's contract with Gold

Questions 7 and 8 are based on the following information:

On April 5, 1987, Anker, Inc. furnished Bold Corp. with Anker's financial statements dated March 31, 1987. The financial statements contained misrepresentations which indicated that Anker was solvent when in fact it was insolvent. Based on Anker's financial statements, Bold agreed to sell Anker 90 computers, "F.O.B.—Bold's loading dock." On April 14, Anker received 60 of the computers. The remaining 30 computers are in the possession of the common carrier and in transit to Anker.

7. If, on April 28, Bold discovered that Anker was insolvent, then with respect to the computers delivered to Anker on April 14, Bold may
   (A) reclaim the computers upon making a demand
   (B) reclaim the computers irrespective of the rights of any subsequent third party
   (C) not reclaim the computers since ten days have elapsed from its delivery
   (D) not reclaim the computers since it is entitled to recover the price of the computers

8. With respect to the remaining 30 computers in transit, which of the following statements is correct if Anker refuses to pay Bold in cash and Anker is not in possession of a negotiable document of title covering the computers?
   (A) Bold may stop delivery of the computers to Anker since their contract is void due to Anker's furnishing of the false financial statements
   (B) Bold may stop delivery of the computers to Anker despite the fact that title had passed to Anker
   (C) Bold must deliver the computers to Anker on credit since Anker has not breached the contract
   (D) Bold must deliver the computers to Anker since the risk of loss had passed to Anker

9. On March 1, Dun purchased $50,000 of equipment from Lux Corp. for use in Dun's manufacturing process. Dun paid for the equipment with funds borrowed from Best Bank that same day. Dun executed a security agreement and financing statement covering Dun's existing and after-acquired equipment. On March 7, Dun was involuntarily petitioned into bankruptcy under the liquidation provisions of the Bankruptcy Code and a trustee in bankruptcy was appointed. On March 9, Best properly filed the financing statement. Which of the parties will have a superior security interest in the equipment?
   (A) Best, because it perfected its security interest within the permissible time limits
   (B) Best, because it had a perfected purchase money security interest without having to file a financing statement
   (C) The trustee in bankruptcy because the trustee became a lien creditor prior to the time Best perfected its security interest
   (D) The trustee in bankruptcy because the filing of the financing statement after the commencement of the bankruptcy case would be deemed a preferential transfer

10. John Reed, a wealthy businessman, established an inter vivos trust on January 1, 1986 to provide for the financial needs of his son and wife. The written trust agreement signed by Reed provided for income to his wife, Myrna, for her life with the remainder to his son, Rodney. Reed named Mini Bank as the sole trustee and transferred stocks, bonds, and two commercial buildings to the trust. The accounting period selected for the trust was the calendar year.

During the first year of the trust's existence, Mini made the following allocations to principal and income arising out of transactions involving the trust property:
• With regard to the sale of $25,000 of stock, $20,000 to income representing the gain on the sale of stock and $5,000 to principal representing the cost basis of the stock
• $95,000 to income from rental receipts earned and received after the trust was created
• $60,000 to income and $2,000 to principal as a result of a stock dividend of 400m shares of $5 par value common stock at a time when the stock was selling for $20 per share
• $10,000 to income for bond interest received and which is payable semiannually on April 1 and October 1
• $35,000 to principal as a result of mortgage payments made by the trust on the commercial buildings

The instrument creating the trust is silent as to the allocation of the trust receipts and disbursements to principal and income.

Required: Answer the following, setting forth reasons for any conclusions stated.
(A) Have the requirements been met for the creation of a valid inter vivos trust?
(B) Indicate the proper allocation to principal and income of the trust receipts and disbursements described above under the majority rules, ignoring the tax effect of each transaction.

Accounting Theory

1. A company borrowed cash from a bank and issued to the bank a short-term noninterest-bearing note payable. The bank discounted the note at 10% and remitted the proceeds to the company. The effective interest rate paid by the company in this transaction would be
   (A) equal to the stated discount rate of 10%
   (B) More than the stated discount rate of 10%
   (C) Less than the stated discount rate of 10%
   (D) Independent of the stated discount rate of 10%

2. A December 15, 1986, purchase of goods was denominated in a currency other than the entity's functional currency. The transaction resulted in a payable that was fixed in terms of the amount of foreign currency and was paid on the settlement date, January 20, 1987. The exchange rates between the functional currency and the currency in which the transaction was denominated changed at December 31, 1986, resulting in a loss that should
   (A) not be reported until January 20, 1987, the settlement date
   (B) be included as a separate component of stockholders' equity at December 31, 1986
   (C) be included as a deferred charge at December 31, 1986
   (D) be included as a component of income from continuing operations for 1986

3. Five thousand (5,000) shares of common stock with a par value of $10 per share were issued initially at $12 per share. Subsequently, one thousand (1,000) of these shares were acquired as treasury stock at $15 per share. Assuming that the par value method of accounting for treasury stock transactions is used, what is the effect of

the acquisition of the treasury stock on each of the following?

	Additional Paid-in Capital	Retained Earnings
(A)	Increase	No effect
(B)	Increase	Decrease
(C)	Decrease	Increase
(D)	Decrease	Decrease

4. An inventory loss from a market price decline occurred in the first quarter. The loss was not expected to be restored in the fiscal year. However, in the third quarter the inventory had a market price recovery that exceeded the market decline that occurred in the first quarter. For interim financial reporting, the dollar amount of net inventory should
   (A) decrease in the first quarter by the amount of the market price decline and increase in the third quarter by the amount of the market price recovery
   (B) decrease in the first quarter by the amount of the market price decline and increase in the third quarter by the amount of decrease in the first quarter
   (C) not be affected in the first quarter and increase in the third quarter by the amount of the market price recovery that exceeded the amount of the market price decline
   (D) not be affected in either the first quarter or the third quarter

5. An investment in marketable securities was accounted for by the cost method. These securities were distributed to stockholders as a property dividend in a nonreciprocal transfer. The dividend should be reported at the
   (A) fair value of the asset transferred
   (B) fair value of the asset transferred or the recorded amount of the asset transferred, whichever is higher
   (C) fair value of the asset transferred or the recorded amount of the asset transferred, whichever is lower
   (D) Recorded amount of the asset transferred

6. A proposed project has an expected economic life of eight years. In the calculation of the net present value of the proposed project, salvage value would be
   (A) excluded from the calculation of the net present value
   (B) included as a cash inflow at the estimated salvage value
   (C) included as a cash inflow at the future amount of the estimated salvage value
   (D) included as a cash inflow at the present value of the estimated salvage value

ANSWERS! ☞

Accounting Practice

1. B
2. C
3. C
4. B
5. C
6. C
7. D

Auditing

1. B
2. C
3. D
4. B
5. D
6. A
7. A
8. Additional procedures to be performed prior to the beginning of field work are:
    (5) Read the current year's interim financial statements
    (6) Discuss the scope of the examination with management of the client
    (7) Establish the timing of the audit work
    (8) Arrange with the client for adequate working space
    (9) Coordinate the assistance of client personnel in data preparation
    (10) Establish and coordinate staffing requirements including time budget
    (11) Hold a planning conference with assistants assigned to the engagement
    (12) Determine the extent of involvement, if any, of consultants, specialists, and internal auditors
    (13) Consider the effects of applicable accounting and auditing pronouncements, particularly recent ones
    (14) Consider the need for an appropriate engagement letter
    (15) Prepare documentation setting forth the preliminary audit plan
    (16) Make preliminary judgment about materiality levels
    (17) Make preliminary judgment about reliance to be placed on internal accounting controls
    (18) Update the prior year's written audit program

Business Law

1. C
2. A
3. B
4. D
5. A
6. C
7. A
8. B
9. A
10. (A) Yes. The elements necessary to set up a valid inter vivos trust have been met. John Reed as the creator (grantor or settlor) transferred stocks, bonds, and buildings which constituted the trust res (corpus or principal) to the trust with a present intent to create a trust. The trust instrument which designated Mini as trustee was set up for a lawful purpose and named Myrna as the income beneficiary and Rodney as the remainderman.

(B) Where the trust instrument is silent as to the allocation of the trust receipts and disbursements to principal and income, the following rules apply:

With respect to the $25,000 proceeds on the sale of the stock, most states require that the entire $25,000 be allocated to principal. Therefore, the allocation of $20,000 to income and $5,000 to principal is incorrect.

The allocation of $95,000 in rental receipts to income is correct since the entire amount was earned and received after the creation of the trust.

The allocation of stock dividend to principal and income is incorrect in the vast majority of states. Even under the minority rule, an allocation of a stock dividend to principal based on the par value of the shares distributed is incorrect, i.e., 400 shares x $5 par value = $2,000. Under the majority rule, the entire stock dividend is allocated to principal.

The allocation of the full $10,000 bond interest to income is incorrect since one-half ($2,500) of the semiannual payment received on April 1, 1986, had already accrued when the trust was created on January 1, 1986. Therefore, the proper allocation should be $2,500 to principal and $7,500 to income.

The $35,000 of mortgage payments allocated to principal is correct to the extent such payments represent a repayment of the mortgage debt. Any portion of such payments which are deemed to be interest on the mortgage should be allocated to income.

Accounting Theory

1. B
2. D
3. D
4. B
5. A
6. D

EXECUTIVE SECRETARY

Katharine Gibbs School

"Take a letter, George."
"Yes, Ma'am."

Your secretary may well know more than you do about Hotel and Restaurant Management, Travel Planning, and Microcomputing/Accounting if she acquired her skills at the Katharine Gibbs School. And in case you think that Gibbs is attended mostly by young ladies from good Boston families, it may be news to you that there are now eight Katharine Gibbs campuses (five of which are outside of New England), that those campuses are attended by men as well as women, and that financial aid is available.

Most of the Katharine Gibbs programs feature vocational courses in such areas as business math, shorthand, and accounting. Gibbs straddles the line between academics and vocational training with its Associate in Applied Science in Secretarial Arts program, a two-year degree program that not only involves courses in such skills as shorthand, keyboarding, and information processing, but also requires students to take more traditional academic courses in the humanities and social sciences, such as literature, macro- and microeconomics, and psychology. The "international" version of that program, leading to the same degree, features a "junior year abroad"-type option to study in a foreign country and courses in international relations and foreign languages.

The questions that follow are from the Executive Secretarial program, an eight-and-a-half month program designed to prepare students to enter the job market with a comprehensive array of secretarial skills.

For more information about all the programs that Gibbs offers, contact the campus nearest you; check the Credits section for the addresses of all the campuses.

Business Communications

1. Which of the following cannot be modified by an adverb?
   (A) Adjective
   (B) Adverb
   (C) Verb
   (D) Noun

2. Which sentence is expressed correctly?
   (A) It is she whom we believe will be promoted.
   (B) It is she who we believe will be promoted.
   (C) It is her whom we believe will be promoted.
   (D) It is her who we believe will be promoted.

3. Which of the following is acceptable in modern business writing?
   (A) As per your instructions
   (B) In accordance with your instructions
   (C) Following your instructions
   (D) Pursuant to your instructions

4. Indicate which sentence is expressed correctly.
   (A) All the secretarys received a three week's vacation.
   (B) All the secretaries received a three week's vacation.
   (C) All the secretarys received a three weeks' vacation.
   (D) All the secretaries received a three weeks' vacation.

5. Which of the following words is spelled correctly?
   (A) Accommodate
   (B) Subpeona
   (C) Procede
   (D) Questionaire

Speedwriting Shorthand

1. The primary rule in any shorthand system is
   (A) write what you hear
   (B) write all vowels
   (C) write the first three letters of each word
   (D) write out all numerals

2. In Speedwriting shorthand the capital letter "N" stands for
   (A) in, not
   (B) "ence"—"end"—"ent"
   (C) number
   (D) "ing" or necessary

3. The shorthand symbol / represents
   (A) per month
   (B) it is, its, it's
   (C) it, at
   (D) to, too

4. In Speedwriting the capital, printed, and disjoined T represents
   (A) subway
   (B) transportation
   (C) travel/trip
   (D) "trans"

5. In Speedwriting shorthand the symbol for the period (.) is
   (A))
   (B) @
   (C) x
   (D) \

Business Math

1. Pat Alves bought a new refrigerator for $695.75. Pat gave the salesperson seven $100 bills. What change did Pat receive?
   (A) $433.05
   (B) $217.90
   (C) $27.05
   (D) $4.25

2. Harry Morton traveled 9,880 miles. His car averaged 19 miles per gallon. Assuming a gallon of gas costs $1.45, what was Harry's gasoline cost for the trip?
   (A) $547
   (B) $754
   (C) $574
   (D) $457

3. A note dated July 15 and due on September 18 runs for exactly
   (A) 71 days
   (B) 54 days
   (C) 65 days
   (D) 15 days

4. What number increased by 2,000 equals 4,768?
   (A) 1,768
   (B) 4,012
   (C) 2,768
   (D) 768

5. To convert a percent to a decimal,
   (A) move the decimal point two places to the left
   (B) add a second % symbol
   (C) move the decimal point four places to the right
   (D) multiply by 90 and delete the % symbol

Accounting

1. The record used to record the original transactions in their entirety is called a
   (A) journal
   (B) ledger
   (C) capital statement
   (D) personal withdrawal

2. The process of transferring the amounts from the journal to the ledger is called
   (A) journalizing
   (B) recording
   (C) ledgerizing
   (D) posting

3. The general journal has two amount columns; the *left* column is the
   (A) debit column
   (B) credit column
   (C) total column
   (D) items column

4. The form used for detailed listing of items being deposited in the bank is the
   (A) signature card
   (B) check record
   (C) deposit slip
   (D) bank statement

5. The entry to record the sale of merchandise on account requires a debit to
   (A) accounts payable
   (B) accounts receivable
   (C) sales
   (D) cash

Keyboarding

1. Page numbering of all pages after page 1 of unbound and leftbound reports appears
   (A) on line 7 at the top right margin
   (B) on line 4 at the top right margin
   (C) centered on line 4

2. The most common method of citing references within a report is by
   (A) using a reference list at the end of the report
   (B) using internal referencing within the report (author, date, page number)
   (C) typing footnotes at the bottom of the page on which they are cited

3. How many horizontal spaces are available on paper that is 8½ by 11 inches, using elite pitch?
   (A) 102
   (B) 85
   (C) 66

4. The most commonly used letter style in offices today is
   (A) block style
   (B) Administrative Management Society style
   (C) modified block style

5. When an attention line is used in a letter it appears as
   (A) a double space above the salutation
   (B) the second line in the address
   (C) a double space below the salutation

Machine Transcription

1. The best way to transcribe machine dictation is to
   (A) type as you listen
   (B) listen to the whole tape before you type from it
   (C) listen to as much as you can memorize, then type it

2. The most important transcription skill is
   (A) fast typing
   (B) good listening skills
   (C) formatting documents
   (D) English skills

3. One advantage of machine transcription as compared with shorthand is
   (A) the secretary is with the executive who is dictating
   (B) the transcriptionist works from the actual voice of the dictating person, so work can often be more accurate
   (C) machine transcription requires that the executive be in his or her office

4. When you receive a tape to be transcribed, you should preview the work before you begin typing. One of the things you do in this preview is
   (A) listen to any correction messages or special instructions
   (B) set your margins
   (C) enter the date at the top of the stationery

5. After a letter is typed, it should be
   (A) sent immediately to the originator
   (B) signed and mailed by the transcriptionist
   (C) inspected and proofread for quality
   (D) checked and mailed by the proofreader without being returned to the originator

Office Procedures

1. The professional organization for secretaries is known as
   (A) American Secretaries Association
   (B) Professional Secretaries International
   (C) Administrative Secretaries International
   (D) Society of Professional Secretaries

2. Which of the following is NOT an acceptable time management principle?
   (A) Assign priorities to work
   (B) Set deadlines for work
   (C) Follow a daily work plan
   (D) Do routine items during the most productive time of day

3. The following class of mail may be insured:
   (A) first class
   (B) second class
   (C) third and fourth classes
   (D) all of the above

4. A letter containing valuable legal papers should be sent
   (A) certified
   (B) insured
   (C) registered
   (D) special handling

5. Which of the following travel duties may be performed for the employer by the secretary?
   (A) Preparing an itinerary
   (B) Obtaining a passport
   (C) Purchasing traveler's checks
   (D) All of the above

6. If an error is found in the minutes at subsequent meetings of an organization, the secretary should
   (A) recopy the minutes to incorporate the changes
   (B) attach a separate sheet at the end of the original minutes to show the changes
   (C) have the chairperson make the corrections on the original copy
   (D) make the corrections and additions on the original copy

ANSWERS! ☞

Business Communications

1. D
2. B
3. C
4. D
5. A

Speedwriting Shorthand

1. A
2. B
3. C
4. D
5. D

Business Math

1. D
2. B
3. C
4. C
5. A

Accounting

1. A
2. D
3. A
4. C
5. B

Keyboarding

1. B
2. B
3. A
4. C
5. B

Machine Transcription

1. C
2. D
3. B
4. A
5. C

Office Procedures

1. B
2. D
3. D
4. C
5. A
6. D

FASHION DESIGN

Progressive Fashion School

If the diameter of Queen Victoria's midsection measured 18 inches on the morning of her wedding, how long was the waistband of her wedding dress?

(d = C/pi), (pi = 3.1416)

The glamorous careers in fashion design—the kind of career the term "fashion design" commonly evokes—actually represent only a tiny fraction of the more than six million fashion-related jobs in the U.S. A few designers have become household names, but most in the fashion design field lead more anonymous existences as technical artists, pattern makers, dressmakers, illustrators, and fashion coordinators. Designers who work for large clothes manufacturing firms are typically more preoccupied with selecting styles, fabric, and trimmings that allow the manufacturer to churn out the product at a low enough price than they are with the finer points of *haute couture*. Some designers work in the entertainment field, but strictly behind the scenes, designing and making costumes for theatrical productions, television shows, and the like.

To work in the field, the most important prerequisite is a solid knowledge of tailoring techniques and pattern making. There are post-secondary schools that offer programs that prepare you for careers in fashion design; some have one-year programs, others have more involved four-year bachelors-type programs. The questions that follow are from Progressive Fashion School in Cleveland, Ohio, and test knowledge of technical details of sewing and dressmaking techniques as well as sewing trivia. Actually, we've gone a little heavy on the trivia. Did you know that the notion that women are particularly susceptible to fainting fits comes from the time when corsets were used to squeeze a woman's waist size down to socially acceptable dimensions? That the inventor of the sewing machine was tarred and feathered and driven out of town by a bevy of seamstresses? That Queen Victoria not only owned an industrial-strength corset, but had mice in her hair? Should this section of the book whet your appetite for such sartorial lore, or for the more sober technicalities of fashion design, drop Jean Salata a line at Progressive Fashion School, 2012 West 25th Street, Cleveland OH 44113, tel. (216) 781-4595.

1. A thimble is used for hand sewing
   (A) sometimes
   (B) always
   (C) when needed
   (D) when thought about

2. What size needle is used for hand sewing in tailoring?
   (A) #6 sharps
   (B) #5-7 betweens
   (C) #9 betweens
   (D) #1 sharps

3. What is a sloper block?
   (A) Piece of wood
   (B) Tool
   (C) Basic pattern
   (D) Completed pattern

4. Another term for power sewing machine is
   (A) domestic sewing machine
   (B) home sewer
   (C) industrial sewing machine
   (D) top of the line sewing machine

5. When in the fabric store and you see fabric that you like, not sure of the design, how much fabric would you buy?
   (A) Approximately 4 yards
   (B) Ask salesperson
   (C) Look in a pattern book for closely related garment
   (D) Know your length from shoulder to hem for the front and back plus 1 yard for sleeves, plus ½ yard

6. Size ¾-inch button is the commercial size
   (A) #30
   (B) #25
   (C) #16
   (D) #18

7. What did Queen Victoria's waist measure?
   (A) 20"
   (B) 18"
   (C) 25"
   (D) 23"

8. The standard length of a lady's sleeve placket is
   (A) 3"
   (B) 4"
   (C) 6"
   (D) 8 "

9. The first sewing machine patented was
   (A) straight stitch
   (B) chain stitch
   (C) overcast stitch
   (D) running stitch

10. What year was the first sewing machine invented?
    (A) 1818
    (B) 1830
    (C) 1825
    (D) 1755

11. Who designed the buttons on the sleeve, at the wrist, of a tailored suit?
    (A) Napoleon
    (B) Queen Victoria
    (C) Tailors Union
    (D) Button manufacturers

12. What was the first method of patternmaking?
    (A) Flat system
    (B) Draping
    (C) Trial & error
    (D) Cut & trim

13. 100% Silk was first made in
    (A) China
    (B) Italy
    (C) Korea
    (D) Japan

14. In designing a garment that would slip
    over the head, with no opening, how large
    should the neckline at least measure?
    (A) 22½ to 23 inches
    (B) 14½ to 15 inches
    (C) 16½ to 17 inches
    (D) 21 to 22½ inches

15. What type of interfacing is used for tai-
    lored garments?
    (A) Woven
    (B) Canvas
    (C) Hymo-canvas
    (D) Fusible

16. Three-dimensional patternmaking is used
    for
    (A) ladies' garments
    (B) toys
    (C) hats
    (D) shoes

17. The flat patternmaking system is used for
    (A) custom designing
    (B) mass production
    (C) dressmaking
    (D) samplemaking

18. Banrol is found in
    (A) collars
    (B) cuffs
    (C) waistbands
    (D) lapels

ANSWERS! ☛

1.	B	10.	D
2.	B	11.	A
3.	C	12.	B
4.	C	13.	D
5.	D	14.	A
6.	A	15.	C
7.	B	16.	B
8.	A	17.	B
9.	B	18.	C

FIREFIGHTING

Mental and Physical Ability Requirements

*Q: Which nationally known fire-fighting institution
is best known to the general public?*

A: Smokenders.

Pretty much every kid (male kid, at least) has dreamed about rescuing fair maidens from burning buildings and riding lickety-split down Main Street in a gleaming red fire engine, sirens blaring. See if the following description squares with your childhood image.

A firefighter must fight fires while wearing work apparel and equipment weighing 45 to 55 pounds. While in full gear the firefighter may be required to carry 50 pounds of hose or rescue a citizen inside a burning building. (So far, squares pretty well, doesn't it?) A firefighter's duties may include fire prevention, emergency calls, and postfire salvage and cleanup. (Hmm, don't know about this part, sounds too much like cleaning your room.) A firefighter must be a team player and must be able to get along with a variety of people. A firefighter must have good judgment, good communication skills, mechanical aptitude, the ability to perform arithmetic computations, and the ability to comprehend and learn firefighting material. (Hmm, sounds too much like school.)

A firefighter must be able to work in a paramilitary organization; that is, a firefighter must be able to follow orders. In addition, a firefighter must be able to live at close quarters and work nontraditional hours. A firefighter usually works a 24-hour shift, with 48 or 72 hours off between shifts, depending on the department.

In case the forgoing has revived your childhood dreams, you might want to know about salary and qualifications. Starting salaries for firefighters these days run from about $24,000 to $30,000. In most departments, a firefighter must be at least 18, have a valid driver's license, be a high-school graduate, pass a medical exam, have normal night vision, color vision, depth perception, and hearing, and have a good driving record and a background free of felony convictions.

If you're still interested, you might want to know that you have to pass an examination to be eligible for hiring. Most departments have a three-stage examination: a written test, a physical agility test (see the sidebar following this section), and an oral interview. The written test is sometimes the only component of the exam that determines your rank on an eligibility list. Usually, though, the written test has a weight equal to 35-60 percent of the final grade. Most physical ability tests are simply pass/fail, but some are given a small weighting. The oral interview is usually given a weight of 40-60 percent of the final grade.

The written test usually measures verbal reasoning, table interpretation, reading comprehension, mechanical aptitude, map reading, and mathematics. Occasionally, the ability to comprehend and learn firefighting material, fire chemistry, and building construction is measured by the written test, in which case the selecting agency usually provides a study guide containing material the candidate is expected to learn before the test.

The oral interview usually measures interpersonal relations, oral communication, judgment, and motivation to become a firefighter. Open-ended questions are usually asked during the interview. For example, in order to evaluate the candidate's motivation to be a firefighter, the candidate may be asked, "Why do you want to be a firefighter?" (To which a favorable response might involve a discussion of what you would like to contribute to the community, reference to the respect you have for someone who is a firefighter, or the like).

The exam that follows is typical of those administered by city fire departments. It was provided by Deborah P. Ashton, Ph.D., Office of Personnel Resource Management, City of Oakland, CA.

Multiple Choice

Before answering the multiple choice questions make sure you have a watch. It is important to bring a watch to the written test as written tests are normally timed.

Verbal Reasoning

1. If A is bigger than B but smaller than C; and D is smaller than A but bigger than B then
   (A) A is the biggest
   (B) B is the smallest
   (C) C is smaller than B
   (D) D is bigger than C

2. If a person falls through thin ice while walking across the ice, the best way for you to try to rescue the person is to:

   (A) run across the ice to the person and pull the person out of the icy water as quickly as possible

   (B) tie one end of a rope to your car and the other end to your waist and walk across the ice

   (C) tie one end of a rope to your car and the other end to your waist and crawl across the ice on your stomach

   (D) walk across the ice very carefully on the tip of your toes then pull the person to safety

3. Energy in a gaseous state is fuel for a fire. Energy in a solid or liquid state is a fuel source. If the previous statements are true, which of the following statements is the best answer?
   (A) If oil gas is energy in a liquid state; oil gas is fuel for a fire
   (B) If dichlorosilane is energy in a gaseous state; dichlorosilane is fuel for a fire
   (C) If hay is energy in a solid state; hay is a fuel source
   (D) Both statements A and B are correct
   (E) Both statements B and C are correct

4. All oxidizers are inflammable gases. All inflammable gases are combustible. Some inflammable gases are poisonous. Therefore:
   (A) all oxidizers are poisonous
   (B) all poisonous gases are oxidizers
   (C) all combustible gases are oxidizers
   (D) all oxidizers are combustible

5. 37.94 X .65
   (A) 2.4661
   (B) 24.161
   (C) 24.661
   (D) 241.61

6. 243 is 27% of
   (A) 9.0
   (B) 65.61
   (C) 656.1
   (D) 900.0

7. 5 feet, 8 inches
   −2 feet, 10 inches

   (A) 2 feet, 8 inches
   (B) 2 feet, 10 inches
   (C) 3 feet, 2 inches
   (D) none of the above

8. If fire helmets were 10 for $80.00 and are now 12 for $111.00, what is the percent of increase?
   (A) 1.25%
   (B) 15.625%
   (C) 27.93%
   (D) 72.072%

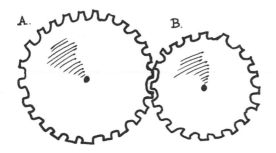

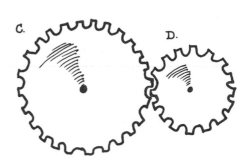

9. Which gear has the most rotations per minute (rpm's)?
   (A) Gear A
   (B) Gear B
   (C) Gear C
   (D) Gear D
   (E) Both Gears A and C

10. Which drawing is the best way to move the boulder?
    (A) Drawing A
    (B) Drawing B
    (C) Drawing C
    (D) Drawing D
    (E) Drawing E

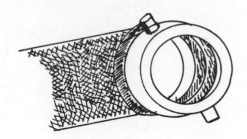
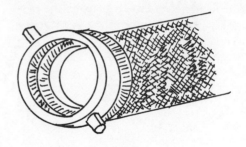

11. Above are the ends of two hoses. Which device below would you use to connect these two ends?
(A) Device A
(B) Device B
(C) Device C
(D) Device D

A.

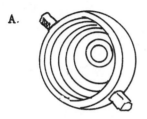

B.

C.

D.

Reading Comprehension

The City of Lobos hires approximately 30 firefighter trainees every two years. The individuals selected must pass the written test, the physical agility, and the oral interview. The candidates selected usually are within the top 10% of the list established from the firefighter test. Once hired as trainees, they attend the City's Fire Academy for 12 weeks. Trainees must pass the academy in order to become firefighters. Of the 30 candidates selected as trainees, only 25 complete the training at the academy.

The academy focuses on the home fire safety program, fire behavior, and fire fighting. The academy emphasizes that the most important aspect of the home fire safety program is the proper installation of smoke detectors. The second most important aspect is a family escape plan. The third most important aspect is minimizing fire hazards by not smoking in bed or when intoxicated, by not leaving children alone at home, and by not cleaning with inflammable liquid, like kerosene.

The academy instructors teach the basic facts about the behavior of fire. The most important element to fire is heat. Even if fuel for a fire exists, it cannot ignite without heat and oxygen. Heat travels in three ways:

1. Conduction, which is from solids to solids which are in contact with each other;
2. Convection, which is through the circulation of heated liquids and gases; and
3. Radiation, which is when a hot body transmits heat to a cold body, for example, light transmitted through a magnifying glass

Fire is most likely to spread if heat is traveling through convection. Air has enough oxygen to keep a fire burning. That is why it is important to either eliminate the heat or to reduce the amount of oxygen (smother the fire).

According to the academy lectures, fire can be fought by one or a combination of the following:

1. By removing fuel from the fire area
2. By removing oxygen from the fire area
3. By cooling the involved or exposed combustible materials to a temperature lower than their ignition temperature

Please answer questions 12–14 using the previous text.

12. How many firefighter trainees are successful in completing the training at the academy?
    (A) 10
    (B) 12
    (C) 25
    (D) 30

13. According to the Fire Academy for the City of Lobos, the second most important aspect to the home fire safety program is
    (A) not smoking in bed or when intoxicated
    (B) the proper installation of smoke detectors
    (C) not leaving children alone
    (D) a family escape plan

14. According to the text, fire is most likely to travel if heat is traveling through
    (A) conduction.
    (B) convection.
    (C) radiation.
    (D) air.

Table Interpretation

15. According to Table 1 (on the following page), which shift is on duty at 2:00 A.M. on November 17th?
    (A) Shift A
    (B) Shift B
    (C) Shift C

Answer Questions 16 and 17 using Table 2 on the following page.

16. How much pump pressure is needed to pump 600 gpm through two 200-foot leads of 2¾-inch hose at 80 NP?
    (A) 90
    (B) 95
    (C) 100
    (D) 105

Table 1: Fire Department Work Schedule for November*

*Each shift is 24 hours. Each shift begins at 0800/8:00 A.M. of the date listed.

△ "A" Shift Working

○ "B" Shift Working

▽ "C" Shift Working

NOVEMBER calendar

SUN	MON	TUE	WED	THU	FRI	SAT
OCTOBER	OCTOBER	1 △	2 ○	3 ▽	4 △	5 ○
6 ▽	7 △	8 ○	9 ▽	10 △	11 ○	12 ▽
13 △	14 ○	15 ▽	16 △	17 ○	18 ▽	19 △
20 ○	21 ▽	22 △	23 ○	24 ▽	25 △	26 ○
27 ▽	28 △	29 ○	30 ▽			

Table 2: Hydraulics Chart

GPM	NO LEADS	HOSE SIZE	NP PSI	FL/100'	PUMP PRESSURE NEEDED FOR 200'	300'	400'
250	1	2 3/4"	80	10 PSI	100	110	120
600	2	2 3/4"	80	12 PSI	105	115	130
700	2	2 3/4"	100	16 PSI	130	150	165
800	2	2 3/4"	80	20 PSI	120	140	160
600	3	2 3/4"	80	6 PSI	90	100	105
700	3	2 3/4"	100	8 PSI	115	125	130
800	3	2 3/4"	80	10 PSI	100	110	120
250	1	3"	80	5 PSI	90	95	100
600	2	3"	80	8 PSI	95	105	110
700	2	3"	100	12 PSI	125	135	150
800	2	3"	80	16 PSI	110	130	145
600	3	3"	80	4 PSI	85	90	95
700	3	3"	100	6 PSI	110	120	125
800	3	3"	80	8 PSI	95	105	110

GPM = gallons per minute; waterflow

No. Leads = number of hoses

NP = nozzle pressure = amount of pressure created by water being discharged from a nozzle

PSI = pressure in pounds per square inch

FL/100' = friction loss per 100 feet of hose

200', 300', and 400' = length of hose

17. How much FL/100 feet is there for 800 gpm being pumped through three leads of 3-inch hose at 80 NP?
    (A) 8 PSI
    (B) 10 PSI
    (C) 16 PSI
    (D) 20 PSI

Answer Questions 18-20 using the map given on the following page.

18. If there is a fire located in section C7, the most likely location of the fire dwelling is
    (A) the Community Shopping Center on the corner of D Street and Machado Court
    (B) the library on Stevens Street
    (C) the corner of Hardeman Street and Maude Avenue
    (D) the corner of D Street and Stratton Court

19. If there is a fire located in section B3, the most likely location of the fire dwelling is
    (A) the corner of East Castro Valley Blvd. and Old Dublin Road
    (B) the Palomares School on Palomares Road
    (C) the corner of Crow Canyon Road and Beacon Hill Drive
    (D) Fairview Elementary School on Maude Avenue

20. If you are located at the fire station on Cull Canyon Road in section B3 and there is a fire at the corner of Elm Street and Pine Street in section A4, the best route to take to the fire scene is to go south on Cull Canyon Road to Crow Canyon Road:
    (A) take a left on Crow Canyon Road and proceed north to Cold Water Drive; take a right on Cold Water Drive and proceed northeast to Jensen Road; take a right on Jensen Road and pro-

ceed southeast to East Castro Valley Blvd.; take a right on East Castro Valley Blvd. and proceed southwest to Grove Way; continue southwest on Grove Way to Redwood Road; take a right on Redwood Road and proceed north to Pine Street; take a right on Pine and proceed east to the corner of Elm Street and Pine Street
    (B) continue south on Crow Canyon Road to Castro Valley Blvd.; take a right on Castro Valley Blvd. and proceed west to Aspen Avenue; take a left on Aspen and proceed south to Pine Street; take a right on Pine Street and proceed west to the corner of Elm Street and Pine Street
    (C) continue south on Crow Canyon Road to East Castro Valley Blvd.; take a left onto East Castro Valley Blvd. and proceed east to the 580 Freeway; take I-580 West to the Greenview Drive exit. At Greenview Drive, make a right onto Elm Street; proceed north to the corner of Elm Street and Pine Street
    (D) continue south on Crow Canyon Road to the 580 Freeway; take the I-580 West to Grove Way and proceed southwest to Redwood Road; take a right on Redwood and proceed north to Pine Street; take a right on Pine Street and proceed to the corner of Elm Street and Pine Street

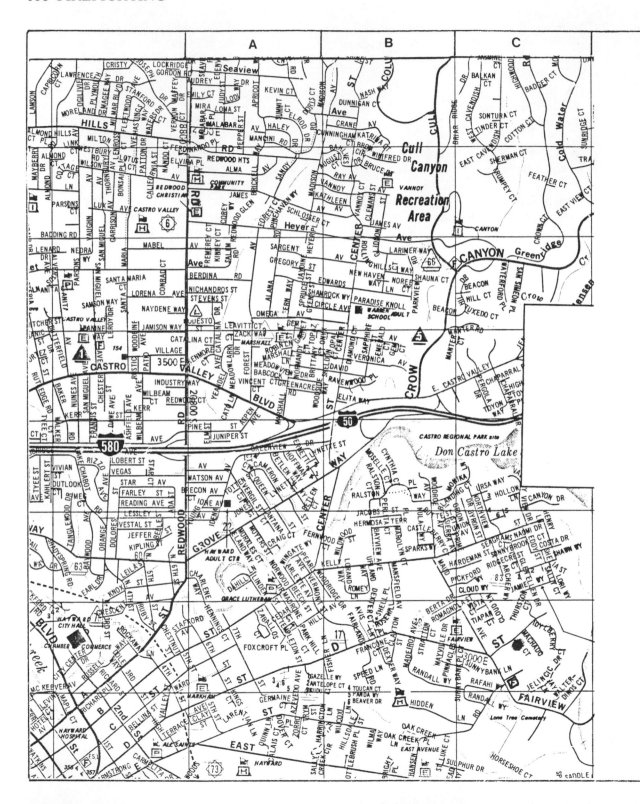

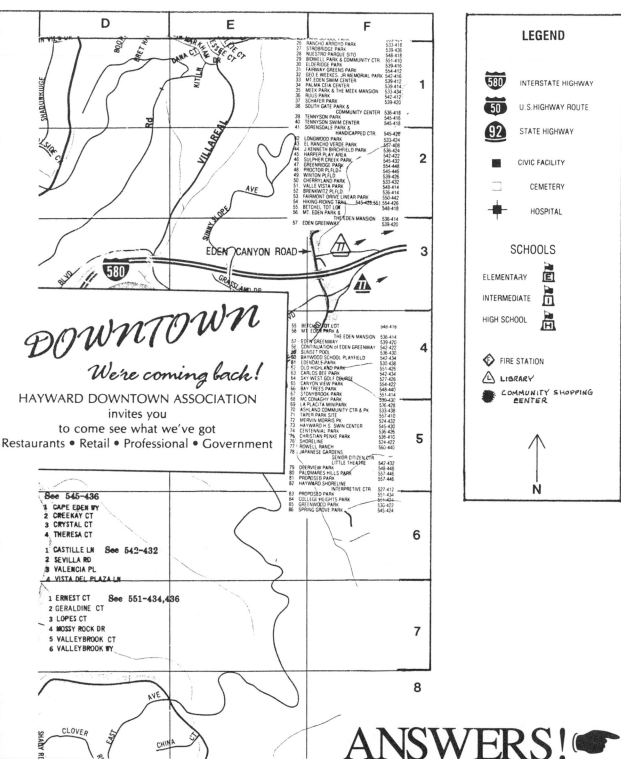

D	E	F

LEGEND

580	INTERSTATE HIGHWAY
50	U.S. HIGHWAY ROUTE
92	STATE HIGHWAY
■	CIVIC FACILITY
☐	CEMETERY
✚	HOSPITAL

SCHOOLS

ELEMENTARY	E
INTERMEDIATE	I
HIGH SCHOOL	H

F FIRE STATION

△ LIBRARY

● COMMUNITY SHOPPING CENTER

N ↑

No.	Name	Ref
26	RANCHO ARROYO PARK	533-418
27	STROBRIDGE PARK	539-436
28	NUESTRO PARQUE SITO	548-418
29	BIDWELL PARK & COMMUNITY CTR.	551-410
30	ELDERIDGE PARK	539-416
31	FAIRWAY GREENS PARK	554-412
32	GEO. E. WEEKES, JR MEMORIAL PARK	542-416
33	MT. EDEN SWIM CENTER	539-412
34	PALMA CEIA CENTER	539-414
35	MEEK PARK & THE MEEK MANSION	533-434
36	RUUS PARK	542-412
37	SCHAFER PARK	539-420
38	SOUTH GATE PARK & COMMUNITY CENTER	536-418
39	TENNYSON PARK	545-416
40	TENNYSON SWIM CENTER	545-418
41	SORENSDALE PARK & HANDICAPPED CTR.	545-420
42	LONGWOOD PARK	533-424
43	EL RANCHO VERDE PARK	557-408
44	J. KENNETH BIRCHFIELD PARK	536-424
45	HARPER PLAY AREA	542-422
46	SULPHER CREEK PARK	545-432
47	GREENRIDGE PARK	554-448
48	PROCTOR PLFLD.	545-446
49	WINTON PLFLD.	539-426
50	CHERRYLAND PARK	533-432
51	VALLE VISTA PARK	548-414
52	BRENKWITZ PLFLD.	536-414
53	FAIRMONT DRIVE LINEAR PARK	550-442
54	HIKING-RIDING TRAIL	545-428,55) 554-426
55	BETCHEL TOT LOT	548-418
56	MT. EDEN PARK & THE EDEN MANSION	536-414
57	EDEN GREENWAY	539-420
55	BETCHEL TOT LOT	548-418
56	MT. EDEN PARK & THE EDEN MANSION	536-414
57	EDEN GREENWAY	539-420
58	CONTINUATION of EDEN GREENWAY	542-422
59	SUNSET POOL	536-430
60	BAYWOOD SCHOOL PLAYFIELD	542-434
61	EDENDALE PARK	530-438
62	OLD HIGHLAND PARK	551-426
63	CARLOS BEE PARK	542-434
64	SKY WEST GOLF COURSE	527-426
65	CANYON VIEW PARK	554-422
66	BAY TREES PARK	548-440
67	STONYBROOK PARK	551-414
68	MC CONAGHY PARK	539-430
69	LA PLACITA MINIPARK	536-428
70	ASHLAND COMMUNITY CTR & PK	533-438
71	TAPER PARK SITE	557-410
72	MERVIN MORRIS PK	524-432
73	HAYWARD H.S. SWIM CENTER	545-430
74	CENTENNIAL PARK	536-426
75	CHRISTIAN PENKE PARK	536-410
76	SHORELINE	524-422
77	ROWELL RANCH	560-440
78	JAPANESE GARDENS, SENIOR CITIZEN CTR LITTLE THEATRE	542-432
79	DEERVIEW PARK	548-448
80	PALOMARES HILLS PARK	557-446
81	PROPOSED PARK	557-446
82	HAYWARD SHORELINE INTERPRETIVE CTR	527-412
83	PROPOSED PARK	551-434
84	COLLEGE HEIGHTS PARK	551-424
85	GREENWOOD PARK	530-422
86	SPRING GROVE PARK	545-424

Downtown

We're coming back!

HAYWARD DOWNTOWN ASSOCIATION
invites you
to come see what we've got
Restaurants • Retail • Professional • Government

See 545-436
1 CAPE EDEN WY
2 CREEKAY CT
3 CRYSTAL CT
4 THERESA CT

1 CASTILLE LN See 542-432
2 SEVILLA RD
3 VALENCIA PL
4 VISTA DEL PLAZA LN

1 ERNEST CT See 551-434,436
2 GERALDINE CT
3 LOPES CT
4 MOSSY ROCK DR
5 VALLEYBROOK CT
6 VALLEYBROOK WY

ANSWERS! ☞

Multiple Choice

1. B   Visualize the relationship:
2. C   You must distribute your weight
        evenly, since concentrated weight will
        break through the ice
3. E   Equations:
        If oil gas = liquid energy and liquid
        energy = a fuel source then oil gas = a
        fuel source
        If dichlorosilane = gaseous energy and
        gaseous energy = fuel for fire then
        dichlorosilane = fuel for fire
        If hay = solid energy and solid energy
        = a fuel source then hay = a fuel
        source
4. D   Visualize the relationship:
        Known:

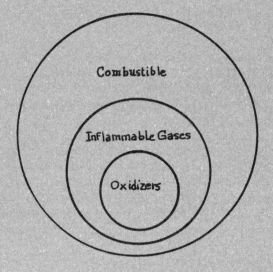

Please note: There is insufficient information to determine if any, all, or some
oxidizers are poisonous. While there is
sufficient information to know some
poisonous gases are inflammable, there
is insufficient information to know if
all poisonous gases are inflammable or
if any are oxidizers.

5. C   Note: Count your decimal   37.94
        places when multiplying.   X   .65
        The multiplicand, 37.94,   18970
        has two decimal places   22764
        plus the multiplier, .65,   246610 =
        has two decimal places;   24.661
        this gives you a total of
        four decimal places in the product.
        Similarly, .01 X .3 = .003. Since there
        are two decimal places in the multipli-
        cand plus one decimal place in the
        multiplier, you must add a zero to the
        right of the decimal to get a total of
        three decimal places.

6. D   Since 27% = 27/100, 243/x = 27/100.
        The denominator on the right of the
        equation is multiplied by the numera-
        tor on the left and vice versa.
        Thus,   27x = 243 X 100
                 27x = 24,300
                 27x/27 = 24,300/27;
        and   x = 900
        Note: If the percentage can be reduced
        to a smaller fraction, it should. For
        example, 243 is 25% of what number?
                 25% = 25/100 = ¼
        If   ¼ = 243/x then 1x = (243 X 4)
        and   x = 972

7. B   Since 12 inches = 1 foot then 5 feet, 8
        inches = 4 feet, 20 inches
        Therefore,   4 feet, 20 inches
                    − 2 feet, 10 inches
                      2 feet, 10 inches

8. B   Since the helmets were bought previ-
        ously in lots of tens and are bought
        now in lots of twelves, first you must
        determine the cost per unit:
        $80/10 = $8.00
        $111/12 = $9.25
        Second, subtract the difference
        $9.25 − $8.00 = $1.25
        Third, divide the difference by the
        original cost per unit:

$1.25/$8 = .15625 which equals 15.625%

Note: The difference is divided by the original cost whether you are calculating percent of increase or decrease.

9. D The smaller gear must rotate more times per minute in relation to the larger gear. Just as a shorter person must take more steps to cover the same distance as a taller person.

10. A It is easier to move the boulder with leverage.

11. B Both ends of hose need to be able to screw onto the device.

Reading Comprehension Hints

12. C
13. D
14. B
First, if only two or three questions are asked about the reading passage, read the questions and answers before reading the passage. Second, if several questions are asked about the passage, read the passage then answer the questions you are sure you know, then, as time allows, skim the passage for the remaining answers. Third, if time is limited, and there is no penalty for guessing, make an educated guess to the questions about which you are uncertain.

15. A You know that a shift starts at 8:00 A.M., so the shift from the previous day is on duty at 2:00 A.M. Check the symbol for the previous day to determine the correct answer.

16. D Since the 2¾" hose is at the top of the table, you need only look at the top half. Now find 600 under GPM. There are only two 600 GPMs listed for 2¾" hose. Select the one for two leads. It has 80 NP. Now follow the row across to the column for which pump pressure is needed for a 200' lead. The correct answer is the cell where the correct row and the correct column intersect.

17. A Since 3" hose is at the bottom of the chart, you need only look at the bottom half. Now find 800 under GPM. It is listed only twice with 3" hose. Select the one for three leads. It has 80 NP. Now follow the row across to the column for FL/100'; 8 PSI is in the cell.

18. A For questions 18 and 19 find the correct cell by using the letter column and number row of the section given, then see which location listed as a possible answer is in the cell where the letter column and number row intersect.

19. C
20. B Find the intersecting cell for each coordinate given, B2 and A4, then find the most direct route.

Physical Agility Events

It is important that you are in good health before taking the agility test: The test is strenuous and so is the necessary preparation. It is recommended that you check with your doctor before beginning to prepare for the agility test. Running and weight lifting may be good preparation. Women should work especially on upper body strength because this is the area in which women have most difficulty. For best results, begin preparing at least 12 weeks before the test.

The physical agility events may vary from department to department. Two physical agility (ability) tests are listed here. One is the test used by the City of Oakland, California; the other is used by the City of Seattle, Washington.

Physical Agility Test
City of Oakland

Applicants perform the tasks wearing a fire helmet, turnout coat, gloves and breathing apparatus, and regulator (weighing approximately 45 pounds). This equipment is provided for you in the various sizes offered by the manufacturer, and you will be assisted in donning it properly. If you have your own pair of work gloves, you may wear them to take the test.

1. **Hose Drag**: Candidate picks up two sections of a 150-foot length of dry, 2½ inch hose, loops them over each shoulder, and pulls it until it is straight, 150 feet out. Candidate then pulls the entire length of straightened hose 15 feet further.

2. **Hose Carry/Stair Climb**: Candidate runs to drill tower where he/she picks up a high rise bundle of hose (approximately 50 pounds) and carries it up the stairs to the fourth floor and places it on the floor.

3. **Hose Hoist**: On the fourth floor of the drill tower, candidate goes to the landing and pulls up a coil of 50 feet of 1½-inch hose, uncharged, from the ground to the fourth floor landing, using a hand-over-hand pull sequence. Candidate brings the coil up to the landing and rests it on the edge and then lowers the coil back to the ground using the same hand-over-hand technique.

4. **Smoke Ejector**: On the fourth floor, candidate goes to the hose bundle he/she carried upstairs in Event Number 2, picks it up and carries it down the stairs and places it on the ground where he/she found it. Candidate runs to the smoke ejector (on the ground), picks it up, carries it to a simulated door frame (6 feet 8 inches tall), and hangs it from the top of the frame.

5. **Citizen Rescue**: Candidate runs to the next event where he/she grasps a lifelike dummy weighing approximately 160 pounds and pulls him from a chair onto the floor, leaving the chair in an upright position. In a low position (under 3 feet in height) candidate drags the dummy 20 feet across a carpeted surface.

6. **Dry Hose Load**: Candidate proceeds to a stack of four dry hose rolls, picks up each roll one at a time and places them on a fire engine tailboard, one atop another, until all four are stacked on the tailboard. Candidate then replaces all four hose rolls in their original place, in a straight stack, and runs to the finish line thus completing the exam.

Physical Ability Test
City of Seattle

These tests are VERY strenuous. If you have had a recent illness, surgery, or are under medication, ask your doctor if it is safe for you to take the tests. If you are unable to take the tests, you may be rescheduled within a reasonable period of time.

This includes five events designed to determine your overall physical ability to enter the Fire Fighter Pre-Recruit Program. The events in this test are as follows:

1. **Fan Lift**: In 30 seconds, lift a 53-pound fan off the floor and place the hooks on the top of the fan on a door jamb that is 82 inches high, then lift the fan off the door jamb and set it on the floor.

2. **Weight Hoisting Event**: While standing on the seventh floor of the drill tower, candidates must hoist, from ground level, an 80-pound sandbag that is tied to the end of a rope. This is a timed event—40 seconds maximum.

3. **Hose Carry, Climb, and Run**: The candidate must remove an 85-pound pack of hose from a storage rack on the side of a truck and place it over the shoulder. The task is to run 100 feet to a building and up stairs to the fourth floor level. The hose pack is unloaded and a second one, just like the first, is picked up; the candidate then returns down the stairs to ground level and runs back to the finish line. This is a timed event—2 minutes maximum.

4. **Seated Steep Incline Press**: Candidate must fully press 95 pounds overhead one time while positioned on an incline board which is angled so as to be nearly vertical. To ensure correct form, the candidate will be secured to the incline board with a wide strap.

5. **Barbell Curls**: The candidate must fully curl 85 pounds one time while positioned so that the back is firmly braced against a vertical board. To ensure correct form, the candidate will be secured to the vertical board with a wide strap.

FLORAL DESIGN

Rittners School of Floral Design

Hark! hark! the lark at heaven's gate sings,
And Phoebus' gins arise,
His steeds to water at those springs
On chaliced flowers that lies,
And winking Mary-buds begin
To ope their golden eyes:
With everything that pretty is,
My lady, sweet, arise.

—William Shakespeare

"Say it with flowers."

—Patrick O'Keefe, for the
Society of American Florists,
1917

The floral designer is an artist whose media consists of flowers and allied items. His or her job involves learning the emotional needs of customers, and meeting those needs through his or her designing skills. A beautiful wedding bouquet, an impressive arrangement of flowers for a party, a natural design wishing a speedy recovery for the convalescent; all are a part of the floral artist's daily routine. Floral designers also deal with creating beautiful arrangements for the many holidays that occur throughout the year, such as Christmas, Valentine's Day, Mother's Day, Easter, and Thanksgiving.

The floral field is ideal for one who would like to work in a pleasant environment surrounded by flowers. It is an excellent career for one who enjoys people.

Floral designing is an excellent field for individuals who want to own their own business. It is a challenging and fascinating profession for one who wants to combine an artistic product with pragmatic marketing skills. When you own your own flower shop you have an opportunity to express your personality in the kinds of flowers that you carry, the mixture of gift items sold, and the styles of design that appeal to both you and your customers. The cost of owning one's own floral business is relatively inexpensive when compared to other industries.

To be a florist requires a combination of skills. One must have business knowledge as well as the critical floral designing skills. The old-fashioned way to acquire these abilities was the apprenticeship method. This was a long and arduous approach that could take well over a decade. Today the practical way to become a florist is to go to school.

The Rittners School of Floral Design in Boston, MA, has trained outstanding floral designers for over forty years. It draws students from all over the U.S. as well as from abroad. The Rittners School offers an extensive six-month training program in floral designing and shop management, an evening division in floral design, floral business skills seminars, and intensive five-week floral design workshops. The questions that follow were provided by Carl Rittner and Dr. Stephen Rittner, and are published in this collection courtesy of The Rittners School of Floral Design, 345 Marlborough St., Boston, MA 02115, tel. (617) 267-3824.

1. The term "hardening flowers" refers to
   (A) pounding them with a hammer
   (B) using a freeze-dry process
   (C) cutting the stems and putting the flowers in water and refrigeration
   (D) using older flowers

2. Which design is not a sympathy design?
   (A) Gates ajar
   (B) Spray
   (C) Cascade bouquet
   (D) Cross

3. Floral designers stylize flowers for
   (A) weddings and parties
   (B) funerals
   (C) interior decoration
   (D) all of the above

4. The most popular base used by professional florists is
   (A) foam
   (B) chicken wire
   (C) moss
   (D) broken branches stuffed into a container

5. When a florist telegraphs flowers he may *not* use which one of the following organizations
   (A) F.T.D.
   (B) Teleflora
   (C) Florafax
   (D) S.L.R.

6. The floral designer's job involves
   (A) sales
   (B) arranging flowers
   (C) advising customers
   (D) all of the above

7. Good locations for a flower shop include being near
   (A) hotels and hospitals
   (B) banks and department stores
   (C) elementary schools and hardware stores
   (D) football stadiums and movie theaters

8. The color harmony red-yellow-blue is
   (A) monochromatic
   (B) near complementary
   (C) triadic
   (D) split mutual

9. What skill is most needed by floral designers?
   (A) Growing flowers
   (B) Making wedding bouquets
   (C) Importing flowers
   (D) Programming the shop's computer

10. The most popular flower in America is the
    (A) violet
    (B) carnation
    (C) rose
    (D) lily

11. Florists commonly deliver flowers and floral designs
    (A) within four to five days
    (B) within one to two days
    (C) within seven to eight days
    (D) within two weeks

12. Flowers freeze
    (A) at 42 degrees temperature
    (B) at 31 degrees temperature
    (C) at 38 degrees temperature
    (D) they don't freeze

13. The common methods to dye or tint flowers include
    (A) spray method and absorption method
    (B) dip method and emolification technique

(C) brushing the dye on the face of the flowers

(D) by injection methodology

14. Flowers last best if
(A) they are placed in water and preservative
(B) they are placed in water and vodka
(C) they are left out of water
(D) they are put in front of an air conditioner on a hot day

15. The methods to stylize a wedding bouquet include
(A) hand method and pick method
(B) hand method and moss method
(C) hand method and blanket technique
(D) hand method and thinning-out technique

16. When selling floral designs you must know
(A) the occasion, the merchandise, and what the customer wants to spend
(B) the relationship of the sender to the recipient
(C) whether the customer is in a good mood or not
(D) the customer's profession and his/her knowledge of floral design

17. Some ways that flower shop names are picked include
(A) by location
(B) by the atmosphere of the shop
(C) by the general mood of the public
(D) A and B

18. Florists commonly advertise by all of the following except
(A) T.V. and radio
(B) newspapers and word of mouth

(C) pens, matchcovers, and key rings
(D) direct mail

19. When stylizing a corsage you should
(A) wire the flowers with number 20 wire
(B) wire the flowers with number 23 or 24 wire
(C) wire the flowers with number 30 wire
(D) use twine to hold the design together

20. When stylizing a line vase arrangement, the inverted T-shaped design is also called
(A) new convention
(B) parallelism
(C) triangle
(D) Biedermeier

21. To cut flowers properly you must use
(A) a knife
(B) a knife or a sharp scissors
(C) a hacksaw
(D) your hands

22. The least important flower holiday is
(A) Christmas
(B) Valentine's Day
(C) Halloween
(D) Mother's Day

23. The best and easiest way to learn floral design is
(A) apprenticeship
(B) on-the-job training
(C) attending a professional floral design school
(D) designing as a hobby

24. Flower shop windows should have
(A) track lighting on the ceiling and electrical outlet on a nearby wall
(B) water faucet nearby
(C) silk flowers
(D) refrigeration

25. The most important piece of equipment in a flower shop is the
    (A) cash register
    (B) refrigerators
    (C) office furniture and computer
    (D) counter display

26. The number of hours that one works in a flower shop on an average nonholiday week would be
    (A) 35 hours
    (B) 40 hours
    (C) 45 hours
    (D) 48 hours

27. The following are the two most important sections of a flower shop.
    (A) Office and bathroom
    (B) Work area and storage
    (C) Employee room and bridal consult area
    (D) Work area and sales area

28. The terms "eastern style" and "western style" refer to
    (A) funeral designs
    (B) wedding designs
    (C) flowers to wear
    (D) baby novelties

29. The visual element of a floral design with the greatest emotional impact is
    (A) shape
    (B) line
    (C) rhythm
    (D) color

30. Two of the most popular bouquets carried in weddings are
    (A) nosegay and crescent
    (B) colonial and cascade
    (C) freeform and triangular
    (D) prayerbook and fan

31. The term "personalizing a floral design" refers to the practice of
    (A) writing a personal note to accompany the design to its destination
    (B) attaching money to the design as a gift
    (C) finding the recipient's hobbies and interests and incorporating those themes into the design
    (D) incorporating the same number of flowers into a design as the recipient's age

32. Which flowers are not an appropriate combination?
    (A) Daisies and carnations
    (B) Roses and strelitzia
    (C) Peonies and anthurium
    (D) They all can be stylized together

33. When helping a customer, the floral designer should
    (A) give him a book of pictures and tell him to pick what he wants
    (B) ask questions about the occasion and offer suggestions
    (C) show the customer the refrigerator and leave him alone to leisurely make his choice
    (D) create floral designs only—the sales help should be doing the actual selling

34. Popular wedding designs for a bride or attendants to carry would include
    (A) cascade and Biedermeier bouquets
    (B) shepherd's crook
    (C) decorated musical instrument
    (D) A and B

35. Appropriate colors for sympathy flowers would be
    (A) any color at any age
    (B) bright colors for women, dark colors for men

(C) dependent upon the religious or ethnic group

(D) white for ages one through six, pastels for a child, and any color for an adult

36. The most popular way that flowers are telegraphed are by
(A) fast mail
(B) taxi
(C) phone and computer
(D) running messenger

37. When you stylize a vase arrangement, the height should
(A) be three times the length of the bottom streamer
(B) be at least one and one-half times the height or width of the container, whichever is larger
(C) depend upon how large the flowers are
(D) depend upon the setting in which the flowers will be placed

38. The sheaf or presentation bouquet is usually used for
(A) weddings, proms, and the opening of a successful stage performance
(B) baby novelties
(C) Secretary's Week and funerals
(D) A and B

39. Which of the following is not a tropical flower?
(A) Heliconia
(B) Anthurium
(C) Lily
(D) Bird of Paradise

40. Foam is used in a vase arrangement
(A) because it is a requirement of floral organizations

(B) for the green color and aesthetic purposes
(C) to feed water to flowers and hold stems in place
(D) to keep flowers lasting longer than in water

41. The proper place to wear flowers may include
(A) the shoulder
(B) the waist
(C) the wrist
(D) any place on the body

42. A floral window display featuring Mother's Day is an example of
(A) institutional window
(B) life-cycle event window
(C) holiday window
(D) educational window

43. There's a frost in Florida and the flower crop is damaged. This means that
(A) prices of flowers will remain stable everywhere but Florida
(B) prices of flowers will remain stable, then go down
(C) prices of flowers will go up everywhere
(D) prices of flowers will decrease

44. The term "servicing a wedding" refers to
(A) doing the floral designs for the wedding
(B) supervising the flowers at the actual site
(C) participating at the festivities
(D) consulting with the bride prior to the wedding

45. As a boss hiring floral design employees, one would most often look for

(A) knowledge of floral designing and a pleasant personality
(B) artistic temperament and display skills
(C) advertising and promotional abilities
(D) knowledge of growing flowers

46. The following tools are commonly used by floral designers:
(A) knife, scissors, and glue gun
(B) knife, pliers, and clippers
(C) picking machine, mallet, and hacksaw
(D) clippers, hot wire, and pliers

47. Which of the following techniques are used in floral designing?
(A) Hand method bouquet and belling technique
(B) Northern-style and western-style wedding work
(C) Pick method bouquet and eastern-style funeral work
(D) Squeezing technique and extension technique

48. A customer wants to order a blanket of flowers. What the customer means is
(A) a spray of flowers
(B) a plastic container holding flowers
(C) flowers placed in water picks
(D) something that simulates a blanket completely covered with flowers

49. The flowers that will usually last the longest in water are
(A) miniature carnations
(B) roses
(C) pompons
(D) alstroemeria

50. Corsage ribbon is normally identified as
(A) no. 40
(B) no. 3
(C) no. 9
(D) no. 100

51. It is considered unethical in the floral business to
(A) solicit wedding work
(B) tint your flowers
(C) go the deceased's home uninvited to book sympathy designs
(D) have business arrangements with caterers, interior decorators, etc.

52. The two major kinds of floral refrigerators are
(A) display and counter
(B) counter and hexagonal
(C) walk-in and storage
(D) walk-in and display

53. A vase arrangement that has been named after a famous artist is known as the
(A) Degas L
(B) Renoir round design
(C) Hogarth S Curve
(D) Van Gogh Triangle

54. Which is a very popular wedding flower, commonly grown in greenhouses along with roses?
(A) Gardenias
(B) Stephanotis
(C) Orchids
(D) Daisies

55. The proper response when handling a customer with a complaint is to
(A) show anger
(B) act as though your feelings are hurt
(C) remember the customer is always right
(D) listen carefully and judge each customer according to the situation

56. What is the best way to sell gifts in a flower shop?
(A) Sell the gift items alone
(B) Sell the gift items as a sale

(C) Sell the gift items as part of a floral design
(D) Gift items shouldn't be sold in a flower shop

57. If you work in a flower shop,
    (A) you design whatever style your artistic tastes dictate
    (B) you design whatever is in the telegraph organization manuals
    (C) you design using the style your boss likes
    (D) you design according to the popular style of the year

58. A customer comes into your flower shop whom you've never seen before. He has never made a purchase in your shop prior to this occasion. He wants to charge a floral design. You must
    (A) let him charge the design
    (B) take his credit card
    (C) accept only cash
    (D) A and C

59. Floral designing in the United States
    (A) is primarily round, mound designs
    (B) is eclectic. There are many different styles from which to choose
    (C) is only one-sided line designs
    (D) depends upon the season

60. Florists love commercial accounts. A commercial account is
    (A) someone who pays in advance
    (B) a customer who pays by check
    (C) a business account
    (D) a customer who tells all of his friends about you

61. Flowers are usually bought by florists from
    (A) local grower, broker, wholesale florist
    (B) trucker, supermarket, distant grower
    (C) street vendor, nursery, auction
    (D) flower market, gift center, garden center

62. When you design a business card for your flower shop, it should have
    (A) name of the shop, address, phone number, and your name
    (B) name of the shop, address, phone number, your name, and a list of flower occasions
    (C) name of the shop, address, phone number, your name, and your picture
    (D) name of the shop, address, phone number, your name, and any additional advertising that you feel is important

63. The most efficient size for a flower shop is
    (A) 500 sq. ft.
    (B) 1000 sq. ft.
    (C) 5000 sq. ft.
    (D) Any size shop may be efficient

64. Characteristics of most flower holidays include
    (A) customers' self-service
    (B) very busy atmosphere and a chance to make a lot of money
    (C) chaos
    (D) a vacation for the head designer

65. When you do a bridal consultation,
    (A) it should be done in the sales area of the shop
    (B) hand the bride a book and tell her to pick anything out
    (C) it should be conducted in a private area of the shop
    (D) it should be done in the bride's home

66. "Cash and carry" is a term that refers to

(A) inexpensive flowers
(B) flowers that you must pick up
(C) inexpensive flowers or floral designs that the customer must pick up
(D) inexpensive flowers or floral designs that the customer must pick up and pay for without charging

67. The best kind of traffic control in a flower shop is encouraged by
(A) allowing no running
(B) making people stay to the right when they walk down aisles
(C) using lighting, color, and display to encourage people to circulate
(D) changing the merchandise at least once a month

68. Containers or baskets used in a flower shop
(A) should be recycled
(B) should be rented
(C) should be sold new each time as part of the design
(D) all of the above

69. The proper technique for selling floral designs involves
(A) ignoring customers when they are waiting for service
(B) being assertive, taking no nonsense from the customer
(C) treating the customer the way you would want to be treated
(D) calling the customer "honey" or "dear"

70. The trade name for a vase arrangement that is relatively inexpensive is
(A) unit design
(B) bread and butter design
(C) ikebana
(D) set piece

Matching

1. Match the correct number of each description to a flower.
(A) Carnation
(B) Strelitzia
(C) Tulip
(D) Anthurium
(E) Gypsophila
(F) Statice
(G) Liatris
(H) Pompon

(1) Fill-in flower
(2) Baby's breath
(3) From Holland
(4) Workhorse flower
(5) Bird of paradise
(6) Best keeping flower
(7) Spike flower
(8) From Hawaii

2. Insert the correct number of each description to the section of a flower shop.
(A) Office
(B) Window area
(C) Storage
(D) Sales Area
(E) Work area

(1) Should be orderly and functional, but doesn't have to be elegant
(2) Should be a secured area
(3) Gives the personality of your store to the public immediately
(4) The largest amount of floor space
(5) Should never be in the front of a flower shop

Fill in the Blank

1. If you have a floral design with a wild combination of colors, the best way to blend them all together is to add _____ flowers.

2. You stylize two wedding bouquets using the exact same flowers. To make the designs appear different, _____
_____

3. The most popular sympathy floral designs include _____,

_____, _____,

and _____.

4. The most important skills in a flower shop include floral designing and

_____.

5. Florists often sell such things as gifts, balloons, stuffed animals, candles, and greeting cards. These are known as

_____ _____.

6. List 10 jobs that are commonly done in most flower shops
   (1) _____
   (2) _____
   (3) _____
   (4) _____
   (5) _____
   (6) _____
   (7) _____
   (8) _____
   (9) _____
   (10)_____

7. A basket vase arrangement may be used for _____,

_____, _____,

and _____.

8. List 10 reasons why people buy flowers
   (1) _____
   (2) _____
   (3) _____
   (4) _____
   (5) _____
   (6) _____
   (7) _____
   (8) _____
   (9) _____
   (10)_____

9. Give eight reasons why one flower shop may be more successful than another.
   (1) _____
   (2) _____
   (3) _____
   (4) _____
   (5) _____
   (6) _____
   (7) _____
   (8) _____

10. What are the six most popular means of advertising for florists?
   (1) _____
   (2) _____
   (3) _____
   (4) _____
   (5) _____
   (6) _____

Identify These Vase Arrangements

1. (A) L-shape vase arrangement
   (B) Triangle vase arrangement
   (C) S-curve vase arrangement
   (D) Crescent vase arrangement

2. (A) Massed vase arrangement
    (B) Scalene vase arrangement
    (C) Vertical vase arrangement
    (D) L-shape vase arrangement

3. (A) Inverted-T vase arrangement
    (B) S-curve vase arrangement
    (C) Horizontal vase arrangement
    (D) Vertical vase arrangement

4. (A) Parallel vase arrangement
    (B) Scalene vase arrangement
    (C) Horizontal vase arrangement
    (D) Mound vase arrangement

5. (A) Massed Vase arrangement
    (B) Scalene vase arrangement
    (C) Vegetative vase arrangement
    (D) Colonial vase arrangement

6. (A) Horizontal vase arrangement
   (B) S-curve vase arrangement
   (C) Vertical vase arrangement
   (D) Parallel vase arrangement

7. (A) Massed vase arrangement
   (B) L-shape vase arrangement
   (C) Horizontal vase arrangement
   (D) Vegetative vase arrangement

8. (A) Colonial vase arrangement
   (B) New convention vase arrangement
   (C) S-curve vase arrangement
   (D) Radiating vase arrangement

ANSWERS! ☞

Multiple Choice

1. C
2. C
3. D
4. A
5. D
6. D
7. A
8. C
9. B
10. C
11. B
12. B
13. A
14. A
15. A
16. A
17. D
18. C
19. B
20. A
21. B
22. C
23. C
24. A
25. B
26. B
27. D
28. A
29. D
30. B
31. C
32. D
33. B
34. A
35. D
36. C
37. B
38. A
39. C
40. C
41. D
42. C
43. C
44. B
45. A
46. A
47. C
48. D
49. C
50. B
51. C
52. D
53. C
54. B
55. D
56. C
57. C
58. B
59. B
60. C
61. A
62. A
63. D
64. B
65. C
66. D
67. C
68. C
69. C
70. B

Matching

1. (A): 4
    (B): 5
    (C): 3
    (D): 8
    (E): 2
    (F): 1
    (G): 7
    (H): 6

2. (A): 5
   (B): 3
   (C): 2
   (D): 4
   (E): 1

Fill in the Blank

1. white
2. use different ribbons, foliage, and other accessories
3. baskets, vase arrangements, sprays, and casket pieces
4. selling
5. allied items
6. (1) floral designing
   (2) selling
   (3) buying
   (4) care and handling of flowers and plants
   (5) telegraphing flowers
   (6) bookkeeping
   (7) wedding consultations
   (8) advertising
   (9) delivery
   (10) maintenance
7. weddings, to say congratulations, funerals, and store openings
8. (1) beauty of the flower
   (2) beauty of the floral design
   (3) good value
   (4) to express love
   (5) to express sympathy
   (6) status reasons
   (7) to make an artificial environment seem more natural
   (8) guilt
   (9) because I deserve it
   (10) to express appreciation
9. (1) better floral designing
   (2) quality merchandise
   (3) interesting product mix
   (4) good salesmanship and a personal interest in customers
   (5) personality of the owner
   (6) extra services
   (7) good value given
   (8) good reputation
10. (1) window display
    (2) storefront signs
    (3) direct mail
    (4) delivery vehicle
    (5) floral demonstrations
    (6) yellow pages

Identify These Vase Arrangements

1. B
2. D
3. A
4. C
5. B
6. C
7. A
8. D

GEOGRAPHY

National Council for Geographic Education, WNEV-TV Boston, and North Carolina University System

When asked in 1980 to give the approximate population of the United States, a statewide survey of 2200 college students conducted by the North Carolina University system revealed that 9 percent knew the answer. Incorrect answers ranged from 100,000 to 236 billion (yes, billion).

In response to a flurry of tests, surveys, and polls that show a shocking ignorance of geography among present-day Americans, educational bodies such as the National Geographic Society and the National Council for Geographic Education are pushing for reforms in our public schools' geography curriculum. According to a 1985 L.A. Times report, the consensus among geography educators is that geography was highly valued and widely taught in the exploration-crazed 1800s. Since then, the emphasis on geography has steadily declined in our school system, to the point where, by the mid-1970s, only nine percent of secondary school students took geography courses; in 1982, most upper-level high school geography teachers had never taken a college course in geography.

In this section, we have questions from three bodies of material. The first set of questions is from a test devised by the National Council for Geographic Education; in rough terms, the questions test geographic knowledge the Council believes all high school seniors should have.

The second set of questions is from a survey of 5,000 high school students in seven major cities conducted by WNEV-TV Boston and other CBS affiliates in 1987. The results of that survey included the following mind-boggling tidbits: In Dallas, 25 percent of students tested could not identify the country that borders the United States on the south; in Boston, 39 percent could not name the six New England states; in Minneapolis-St. Paul, 63 percent could not name all seven continents; in Baltimore, 45 percent could not correctly respond to the instruction, "On the attached map, shade in the area where the United States is located." In Hartford, 40 percent could not name three countries (any three) in Africa; and in Kansas City, 40 percent could not name three countries in South America.

The third set of questions is from a questionnaire created in 1984 by the Chairmen of the Departments of Geography in the North Carolina university system. It was distributed to about 2200 college students enrolled in introductory geography courses in eight schools. Again the students performed abysmally. If 70 percent is considered a passing grade, 97 percent of the freshmen and 93 percent of the upperclassmen flunked, averaging out to 95 percent for the whole sample. The highest grade was 93 percent, while almost ¾ of the students scored less than 50 percent. The details of the incorrect answers are even more disturbing than the overall results. When asked to give the approximate 1980 population of the United States, less than nine percent could give the correct answer. Proposed numbers ranged from 100,000 to 236 billion (yes, billion). When asked to list where selected cities and rivers were to be found, students placed Dublin in Ohio, Vladivostok in Germany, Lima in Italy, the Ganges in Brazil, and the Amazon in Egypt. Other answers placed the Soviet Union between Panama and Nicaragua, and identified Africa as the only country in the Americas larger than the United States. (It should be recognized that these results should by no means be interpreted as an indictment of North Carolinians in particular or the North Carolina school system; indeed, the Tar Heel State is widely regarded as having one of the better public school systems in the country.) The editors are grateful to Professor Richard J. Kopek of the Department of Geography at the University of North Carolina at Chapel Hill for this questionnaire and information about its results.

In the answer section, the percentage correct response is given along with each answer to the WNEV-TV survey and the North Carolina university questionnaire.

National Council for Geographic Education Exam

Map Skills and Locations

Questions 1–8 refer to the world map on the next page

1. Nation 13 is
    (A) Libya
    (B) Spain
    (C) Algeria
    (D) Burma

2. Nation 25 is
    (A) Cuba
    (B) the United Kingdom
    (C) Burma
    (D) Iran

3. What do nations 34 and 35 have in common?
    (A) Language
    (B) Religion
    (C) Communism
    (D) Democracy

4. Nations 29, 30, 31, and 32 are in
    (A) the Middle East
    (B) Southeast Asia
    (C) Oceania
    (D) the Indian Subcontinent

5. What is the major religion of nations 3, 4, and 5?
    (A) Protestant
    (B) Buddhist
    (C) Moslem
    (D) Roman Catholic

6. Nation 33 is
    (A) Malawi
    (B) Borneo
    (C) Pakistan
    (D) Australia

7. Nation 17 is
    (A) France
    (B) Spain
    (C) Afghanistan
    (D) Sudan

8. Which nation has the highest number of doctors per capita?
    (A) 1
    (B) 7
    (C) 13
    (D) 38

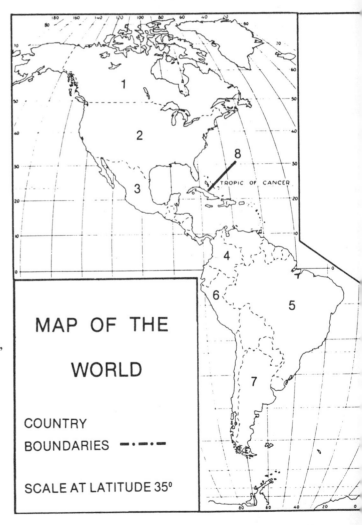

MAP OF THE

WORLD

COUNTRY
BOUNDARIES — · — · —

SCALE AT LATITUDE 35°

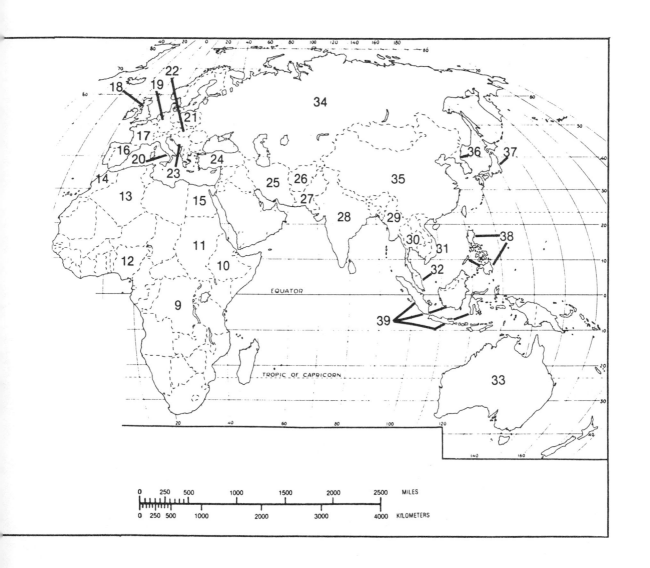

Questions 9–11 refer to the following sketch

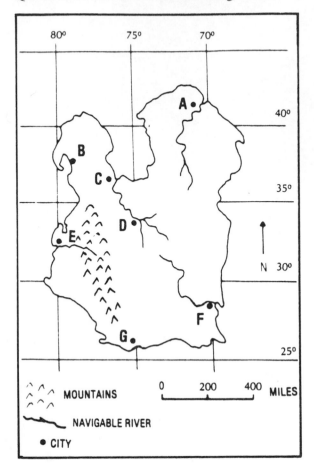

9. Approximately how far is it from B to D?
(A) 100 miles
(B) 200 miles
(C) 400 miles
(D) 600 miles

10. The 30° and 35° lines are called lines of
(A) demarcation
(B) elevation
(C) longitude
(D) latitude

11. The river near cities C and D flows
(A) south
(B) northwest
(C) southwest
(D) northeast

Questions 12–14 refer to the following sketch

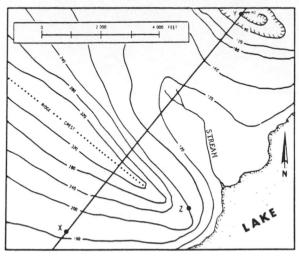

12. Point X is closest in elevation to
(A) the ridge crest
(B) Point Y
(C) Point Z
(D) the mouth of the stream

13. In what general direction does the stream flow?
(A) Northwest
(B) Northeast
(C) Southwest
(D) Southeast

14. What type of map is pictured above?
    (A) Topographic
    (B) Aerial
    (C) Political
    (D) Hachure

Physical Geography

Questions 1–3 refer to the following map of
    Africa

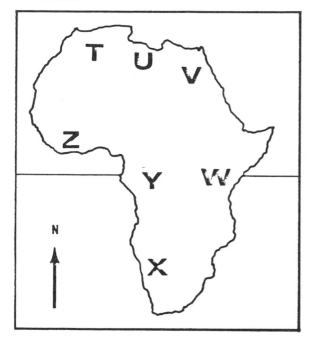

1. Which areas in Africa are most character-
   ized by tropical rainforest?
   (A) Areas T and U
   (B) Areas V and W
   (C) Areas W and X
   (D) Areas Y and Z

2. To which area of Africa do many Black
   Americans trace their roots?
   (A) Area T
   (B) Area Z
   (C) Area X
   (D) Area V

3. Which regions in Africa have the driest
   climate?
   (A) Areas T and Y
   (B) Areas U and X
   (C) Areas W and Y
   (D) Areas X and Y

4. Which is an example of a renewable natu-
   ral resource?
   (A) Petroleum
   (B) Steel
   (C) Forest
   (D) Coal

5. Most of the world is made up of
   (A) mountains
   (B) plains
   (C) deserts
   (D) oceans

6. Average temperature, humidity, and rain-
   fall describe a region's
   (A) population density
   (B) unusual weather conditions
   (C) climate
   (D) topography

7. What type of climate has heavy rainfall
   and high temperatures throughout the
   year?
   (A) Tropical savanna
   (B) Tropical rainforest
   (C) Desert
   (D) Tundra

8. The natural resources of the Soviet Union
   are
   (A) abundant and varied
   (B) severely limited
   (C) impossible to use
   (D) controlled by private owners

Question 9 refers to the following map

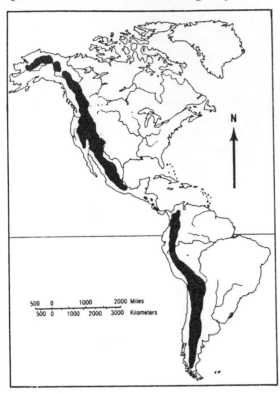

9. The shaded portions of the map above represent areas with
   (A) primarily mountainous landscapes
   (B) hot temperatures
   (C) dense populations
   (D) low annual rainfall

Questions 10 and 11 refer to the following diagram showing a cross section of landforms.

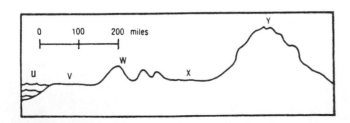

10. Which process would most likely have brought about landform Y?
    (A) Deposition
    (B) Faulting and folding
    (C) Erosion
    (D) Spreading

11. Removal of vegetation on the slopes of landform Y would likely increase
    (A) air pollution
    (B) soil erosion
    (C) earthquakes
    (D) agricultural activity

12. Industrial polluting of the world's atmosphere is of greatest concern because of its effects on
    (A) railroad transportation
    (B) the earth's temperature
    (C) soil quality
    (D) the water level of oceans

13. A process by which deserts may be changed into productive agricultural land is called
    (A) terracing
    (B) contour plowing
    (C) slash and burn agriculture
    (D) irrigation

14. Examples of natural resources are
    (A) paper and pencils
    (B) forests and minerals
    (C) lumber and boxes
    (D) steel and automobiles

15. The world's largest known oil reserves are located in
    (A) Australia
    (B) the Far East
    (C) the Middle East
    (D) South America

16. Which of these countries has the warmest climate?
(A) Canada
(B) United Kingdom
(C) Mexico
(D) U.S.S.R.

17. Most of Africa's natural resources
(A) have been used up
(B) have little value
(C) can never be used
(D) are not yet developed

Human Geography

Questions 1–3 refer to the following map showing the transportation system of nation X.

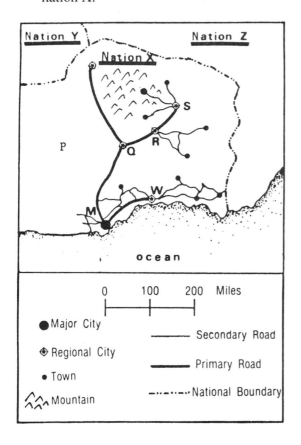

1. Where is there likely to be the greatest density of population?
(A) Between P and Q
(B) Between Q and R
(C) Between R and S
(D) Between M and W

2. City Q would most likely be a major center for
(A) recreational activities
(B) transportation
(C) environmental activities
(D) retailing

3. Which city would be the center for trade with the rest of the world?
(A) M
(B) Q
(C) R
(D) S

4. Which of the following best describes the impact of the Industrial Revolution on cities?
(A) The size of cities increased
(B) The number of cities decreased
(C) Cities became cleaner
(D) Cities declined in importance

5. Which region below was the first to have an industrial revolution?
(A) Asia
(B) Western Europe
(C) North America
(D) Africa

6. Which is one major reason why agriculture in Latin America is underdeveloped?
(A) There are too few agricultural workers
(B) There is little demand for farm products
(C) Not enough machinery and fertilizer available

(D) A high percentage of people work in factories

7. The region serviced by a city is called the city's
   (A) hinterland
   (B) zone of service
   (C) legensraum
   (D) polders

8. On which ocean would you find the least shipping?
   (A) Atlantic
   (B) Indian
   (C) Pacific
   (D) Arctic

9. Latin America refers to
   (A) the places where Latin is spoken
   (B) western hemisphere countries south of the U.S.
   (C) all countries in North and South America
   (D) only countries in South America

10. What was the major reason for the population growth of 20th-century cities?
    (A) Higher birth rates in cities
    (B) Higher death rates in cities
    (C) Movement from rural areas to cities
    (D) Immigration from other countries

11. Population density depends on the relationship between
    (A) area and population
    (B) area and income
    (C) population and income
    (D) population and natural resources

12. Which country has the most people?
    (A) Soviet Union
    (B) United States
    (C) Canada
    (D) China

Questions 13 and 14 refer to the following graph.

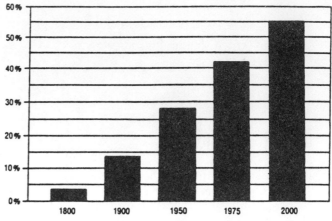

13. What made possible the trend shown on this graph?
    (A) An increase in agricultural productivity
    (B) Fear of wildlife
    (C) More efficient water transportation
    (D) Increased control of crime

14. In the year 1500, the percentage of people living in urban centers would look most similar to which date on the graph?
    (A) 1800
    (B) 1900
    (C) 1950
    (D) 2000

15. What ocean carries most of the world's trade?
    (A) Arctic
    (B) Pacific
    (C) Indian
    (D) Atlantic

16. Most of the foreign trade carried on by the Soviet Union is with
    (A) the U.S.
    (B) other communist countries
    (C) countries of western Europe
    (D) developing countries

Questions 17–19 refer to the following statement:

Juan is a subsistence farmer. He lives in Central America in a tropical rainforest area. His village is about 100 miles from a major market.

17. Juan would most likely be concerned with raising
    (A) enough to sell at the major market
    (B) enough to feed his family
    (C) crops for tax credits
    (D) crops to sell so he could buy food

18. Which of the following would best describe Juan's farm?
    (A) Over 100 acres and raising one commercial crop
    (B) Over 100 acres and raising several crops
    (C) Less than 100 acres and raising a variety of crops
    (D) Less than 100 acres and raising one commercial crop

19. If the government built a road into Juan's region, what would most likely improve his income?
    (A) Irrigating his land
    (B) Raising crops for the major market
    (C) Raising larger crops for his family
    (D) Rotating his crops

20. The exchange between two areas of raw materials and products to satisfy the needs of each area is known as
    (A) conflict
    (B) interdependence
    (C) federalism
    (D) tariff

Questions 21–23 refer to graphs X and Y.

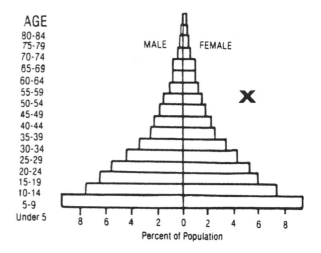

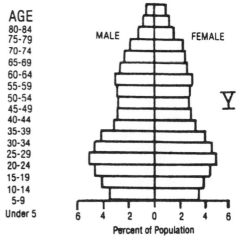

21. Graph X shows population in a
    (A) less developed country
    (B) typical western European country
    (C) highly urbanized country
    (D) highly industrialized country

22. The two countries shown are most likely to be
    (A) Britain and Germany
    (B) Japan and Canada
    (C) India and Nigeria
    (D) Mexico and the U.S.

23. Which kind of problem is least likely in a nation like X?
    (A) Unemployment
    (B) Inflation
    (C) Old-age care
    (D) Crime

24. The world's major trading regions are
    (A) North America and Europe
    (B) South America and Africa
    (C) Africa and Asia
    (D) Australia and South America

25. Among the world's top nations, Japan ranks near the top in
    (A) illiteracy
    (B) production per person
    (C) total area
    (D) mineral resources

26. With the decline of industry as a major activity in U.S. cities, which activity is expanding?
    (A) Recreational
    (B) Transportation
    (C) Residential
    (D) Service

27. The people in the United Kingdom speak the same language as the people in
    (A) the U.S.
    (B) France
    (C) the U.S.S.R.
    (D) China

28. In which area is Buddhism a major religion?
    (A) Asia
    (B) Europe
    (C) Africa
    (D) Latin America

29. Which of the following geographic regions is least heavily involved in world trade?
    (A) North America
    (B) Middle East
    (C) Sub-Saharan Africa
    (D) Europe

30. Which of the following is a major limiting factor in the economic development of Asia?
    (A) Lack of natural resources
    (B) Lack of working-age people
    (C) Lack of capital
    (D) Harsh climate

31. What do Venezuela and Iran have in common?
    (A) Oil exports
    (B) The same language
    (C) The same religion
    (D) Overall dense populations

Questions 32–35 refer to the following statement:

The transportation authority for a nearby city recently published the proposed route for the new mass transit system. One of the train stations is in a residential neighborhood just three blocks from your house.

32. The station in your neighborhood will most likely
    (A) increase the intensity of nearby land use
    (B) have no effect on the intensity of near-by land use
    (C) decrease the intensity of nearby land use
    (D) increase the intensity of nearby land use at night and decrease it during the day

33. The value of your house would most likely
    (A) decrease because of the potential noise of the trains
    (B) increase because of the nearness of auto dealerships
    (C) decrease because of the added conges-tion in the area
    (D) increase because of the increased accessibility to the transit system

34. If the area around the station did change, it would most likely change from
    (A) commercial stores to single-family housing
    (B) office buildings to single-family hous-ing
    (C) single-family housing to apartments
    (D) single-family housing to small farms

35. Generally, as the population of a city increases, so does the
    (A) percentage of people owning their own homes
    (B) frequency with which people go shop-ping
    (C) percentage of income spent on food
    (D) number of goods and services it offers

CBS Affiliates Exam

History and Social Studies
1. What president issued the Emancipation Proclamation? _____

2. Name the three branches of the U.S. gov-ernment
   (1) _____
   (2) _____
   (3) _____

3. Name the two houses of Congress
   (1) _____
   (2) _____

4. What was the historical significance of Hiroshima? _____
   _____

5. In 1975 the U.S. withdrew military forces from what Southeast Asian country?
   _____

6. What is the highest court in the American Judicial System? _____

7. What nation attacked the U.S. naval base at Pearl Harbor in 1941? _____

8. Name the Vice President of the U.S. in 1986 _____

Geography
1. Name the six New England states
   (1) _____
   (2) _____
   (3) _____
   (4) _____
   (5) _____
   (6) _____

2. Name the country that borders the U.S. on

the south _____

3. Name the country that borders the U.S. on the north _____

4. What is the imaginary line that runs around the middle of the earth? _____

5. When it is noon in Boston, what time is it in San Francisco? _____

6. Name the seven continents
   (1) _____
   (2) _____
   (3) _____
   (4) _____
   (5) _____
   (6) _____
   (7) _____

North Carolina University System Exam

1. What is the approximate 1980 population of the U.S.? _____

2. In what states will you find the following:
   (1) Mt. Mitchell _____
   (2) Grand Canyon _____
   (3) Mammoth Cave _____
   (4) Mt. St. Helens _____
   (5) Cape Cod _____

3. List the five states that border on the Pacific Ocean
   (1) _____
   (2) _____
   (3) _____
   (4) _____
   (5) _____

4. Name the five Great Lakes

(1) _____
(2) _____
(3) _____
(4) _____
(5) _____

5. How many states border the Great Lakes?

6. List, in order of size, the four oceans of the world
   (1) _____
   (2) _____
   (3) _____
   (4) _____

7. In what countries are the following cities located?
   (1) Baghdad _____
   (2) Dublin _____
   (3) Manila _____
   (4) Munich _____
   (5) Vladivostok _____

8. Name the country in the Americas that is larger than the U.S. in area

   _____

9. What country lies between Panama and Nicaragua? _____

10. Name any three African countries lying between the Sahara Desert and the Republic of South Africa
    (1) _____
    (2) _____
    (3) _____

11. In what ocean is each of the following islands or island groups found?
    (1) Falkland Islands _____
    (2) Madagascar _____
    (3) Midway Island _____
    (4) Ellesmere Island _____

ANSWERS!

National Council for Geographic Education Exam

Map Skills and Locations

1. C
2. D
3. C
4. B
5. D
6. D
7. A
8. A
9. C
10. D
11. B
12. C
13. D
14. A

Physical Geography

1. D
2. B
3. B
4. C
5. D
6. C
7. B
8. A
9. A
10. B
11. B
12. B
13. D
14. B
15. C
16. C
17. D

Human Geography

1. D
2. B
3. A
4. A
5. B
6. C
7. A
8. D
9. B
10. C
11. A
12. D
13. A
14. A
15. D
16. B
17. B
18. C
19. B
20. B
21. A
22. D
23. C
24. A
25. B
26. D
27. A
28. A
29. C
30. C
31. A
32. A
33. D
34. C
35. D

CBS Affiliates Exam

(Numbers in parentheses indicate percentage of students that answered correctly when these tests were administered. Average of all Boston-area students: 64%)

History and Social Studies

1. (49)   Abraham Lincoln
2. (51)   (1) Executive

        (2) Legislative
        (3) Judicial
3. (41)   (1) House of Representatives
        (2) Senate
4. (36)   First atomic bomb dropped on a civilian population, or first city an atomic bomb was dropped on; ended World War II between the U.S. and Japan
5. (47)   Vietnam
6. (16)   Supreme Court
7. (17)   Japan
8. (8)   George Bush

Geography

1. (39)   (1) Massachusetts
        (2) New Hampshire
        (3) Vermont
        (4) Maine
        (5) Rhode Island
        (6) Connecticut
2. (13)   Canada
3. (28)   Mexico
4. (14)   equator
5. (54)   9:00 A.M.
6. (62)   (1) North America
        (2) South America
        (3) Europe
        (4) Asia
        (5) Africa
        (6) Australia
        (7) Antarctica

North Carolina University System Exam

1. (8.37) 226 million, plus or minus 5 million
2. (38.89) (1) North Carolina
   (40.77) (2) Arizona
   (10.52) (3) Kentucky
   (69.10) (4) Washington
   (40.56) (5) Massachusetts

(1.9% got all five correct)
3. (92.43) (1) California
   (58.85) (2) Oregon
   (85.62) (3) Washington
   (26.56) (4) Hawaii
   (31.97) (5) Alaska
   (16.7% got all five correct)
4. (30.13) (1) Huron
   (45.17) (2) Ontario
   (74.67) (3) Michigan
   (68.40) (4) Erie
   (48.18) (5) Superior
   (11.9% got all five correct)
5. (3.59) eight
6. (68.67) (1) Pacific
   (66.04) (2) Atlantic
   (49.73) (3) Indian
   (28.54) (4) Arctic
   (20.3% got all four correct)
7. (10.09) (1) Iraq
   (52.68) (2) Ireland
   (27.36) (3) Philippines
   (48.87) (4) West Germany
   (46.19) (5) USSR
   (This question was shortened from the actual list containing 12 cities. Of those 12, .5% answered all correctly)
8. (47.8) Canada
9. (7.19) Costa Rica
10. (6.92) Any three of the following: Guinea, Sierra Leone, Liberia, Ivory Coast, Nigeria, Ghana, Togo, Benin, Zaire, Bourkina Fassa, Somali Republic, Equat, Gabon, Congo, Uganda, Kenya, Botswana, Rwanda, Burundi, Tanzania, Angola, Namibia, Zambia, Zimbabwe, Cent. Afr. Empire, Mozambique, Malawi, Cameroon
11. (49.25) (1) Atlantic
   (27.41) (2) Indian
   (49.20) (3) Pacific
   (6.71) (4) Arctic
   (2.3% got all correct)

GEOLOGY

California State Board of Registration for Geologists and Geophysicists

1. *A trilobite is characterized by*
    (A) three ears
    (B) three teeth
    (C) delicate biramous appendages
    (D) a soft, soothing mating trill

In general terms, geologists and geophysicists study the physical structure and composition of the earth. More specifically, they may analyze, classify, and describe minerals ("mineralogy"), study the composition, classification, and mode of origin of rocks ("petrology"), investigate the nature and distribution of chemical elements in rocks and minerals ("geochemistry"), study the causes and effects of earth processes and investigate the nature and origin of landforms ("geomorphology"), study geologic phenomena associated with volcanic activities ("vulcanology"), analyze the deformation, fracturing, and folding that has occurred within the earth's crust and the forces that produced them ("structural geology"), investigate the thickness, shape, and distribution of layered rocks and their mineral and fossil content ("stratigraphy"), study earthquakes ("seismology"), or use fossils to describe the nature and development of life through geologic time ("paleontology"). Although each subfield has its appeal, it has occurred to us that petrology has the unique advantage of allowing one to describe oneself as specializing in "hard rock" or "soft rock," depending on whether one is most interested in sedimentary or igneous and metamorphic rocks, or on whether one is talking to one's teenage nephew or one's yuppie cousin from Des Moines. All the subfields, however, qualify one to downplay the significance of human civilization or any part thereof by uttering statements beginning with the words, "Well, in geological terms...."

According to the American Geological Institute, there are about 65,000 geologists at work in the U.S. today. Most are employed by private industry. Most of these are petroleum geologists employed by oil companies. Other geologists work for mining companies to locate ore deposits and estimate reserves, for companies in the cement and ceramic industries, for sand and gravel firms, railroads, engineering companies, and in the banking industry. The largest single employer of geologists in the U.S. is the federal government. Most work for the U.S. Geological Survey; other government employers are the Soil Conservation Service, Bureau of Land Management, National Park Service, Bureau of Mines, Forest Service, and U.S. Army Corps of Engineers. In the mid-1980s graduates with bachelor's degrees in geology were receiving starting salaries of $22,000 to $28,000 in the private sector, and slightly less with federal agencies. With master's degrees typical starting salaries ranged from $28,000 to $32,000. In the petroleum industry salaries may go as high as $80,000 with bachelor's degrees and $90,000 with master's degrees. Ph.D.'s usually command much more, according to the AGI.

The questions that follow are representative of those on the registration examination for the state of California, administered by the State Board of Registration for Geologists and Geophysicists. The seven-hour exam is designed to test the applicant's ability to apply geologic knowledge and experience, together with professional judgement, to geologic problems and situations, and to demonstrate capability to assume responsible charge of professional geologic practice. Part A of the examination consists of multiple-choice and completion questions, problems, and diagrams representing a variety of the sorts of subfields described above (but not including, strangely enough, seismology—this is the *California* exam, remember). Part B consists of two mandatory and a number of optional problems. Mandatory problems are normally descriptive geometry and a geologic map exercise. The optional problems typically pertain to ground water, petroleum, mineral deposits, structural geology, earthquakes (ah!), and engineering geology. Answers were supplied by Susan Boundy-Sanders, Department of Geology and Geophysics, University of California at Berkeley.

Multiple Choice

1. Radiocarbon methods of age determination would apply to samples of the
   (A) Precambrian
   (B) Cambrian
   (C) Triassic
   (D) Pliocene
   (E) Late Quaternary

2. Most of the petroleum of the Los Angeles Basin is from rocks of the
   (A) Eocene
   (B) Miocene-Pliocene
   (C) Pleistocene
   (D) Cretaceous
   (E) Triassic

3. Characteristic faunas of the Sespe Formation should include
   (A) vertebrates
   (B) coccoliths
   (C) discoasters
   (D) foraminifera
   (E) radiolaria

4. The concept of igneous rock formation which states that a granitic magma can be derived from a basaltic magma is based upon
   (A) the concept of uniformitarianism
   (B) the law of superposition
   (C) faunal succession
   (D) Bowen's Reaction series
   (E) Eskola's Facies concept

5. Folding in the Coast Ranges (as around the San Francisco Bay Region) took place mostly during
   (A) Pleistocene
   (B) Late Pliocene
   (C) Miocene
   (D) Jurassic

6. Specific yield is found by
   (A) adding porosity to specific retention
   (B) subtracting porosity from specific retention
   (C) subtracting specific retention from porosity
   (D) getting an average output of all the wells in a given area

7. The fundamental law governing the slopes of groundwater is known as
   (A) Chezy's Formula
   (B) Darcy's Law
   (C) Gibson's Law
   (D) Toricelli's Theorem

8. Tsunamis are most frequently associated with which one of the following?
   (A) Meteorological phenomena
   (B) Earthquakes
   (C) Solar gravity attraction
   (D) Lunar gravity attraction

9. Diopside, hedenbergite, hypersthene, jadeite and riebeckite are all
   (A) anhydrous silicates
   (B) pyroxenes
   (C) found in igneous rocks only
   (D) inosilicates
   (E) minerals with essential magnesium

10. It is desired to determine the direction of principal movement on a major strike-slip fault. The most useful criterion, among those listed below, is
    (A) the slickensides
    (B) the slope of the land surface
    (C) the movement sense of minor folds within the brecciated zone
    (D) the angle made between the bedding plane and the fault plane
    (E) matching of major lithic units that occur on the two sides of the fault

11. A factor that does *not* contribute to the formation of evaporites is
    (A) solubility
    (B) aridity
    (C) concentration
    (D) humidity
    (E) environment

12. The Sierra Nevada batholith was emplaced during which of the following?
    (A) Cambrian
    (B) Pennsylvanian
    (C) Precambrian
    (D) Jurassic
    (E) Neogene

13. Shallow earthquakes occur at what depth?
    (A) Above 70 km
    (B) From 0 to 12 km
    (C) From 0 to 200 km

14. The volcanic equivalent of a granodiorite is
    (A) latite
    (B) rhyolite
    (C) dacite
    (D) phonolite

15. In the concept of plate tectonics continents are carried on rigid plates while oceanic plates disappear in the marginal trench. Continents are not carried down into the mantle because
    (A) they are centered equidistant from each side of the plates
    (B) transfrom faults carry the continents away from the marginal trenches
    (C) continents are too buoyant
    (D) none of the above

16. The most abundant constituent of sylvanite is
    (A) arsenic
    (B) mercury
    (C) silver
    (D) gold

17. In an unconfined compression test, the rock sample failed at a load of 40,000 pounds. The load was being applied over an area of 4 square inches. What is the unconfined compressive strength?
    (A) 5,000 psi
    (B) 10,000 psi
    (C) 40,000 psi
    (D) 160,000 psi

18. A rock has the following composition: 40% almandine-pyrope, 55% diopside-jadeite, 5% rutile; texture, medium, granoblastic. What is the name of the rock?
    (A) Skarn
    (B) Minette
    (C) Eclogite
    (D) Amphibolite

19. Favorable indicators for the accumulation of gas are characterized in a well log by
    (A) a reduction in SP^+ and a decrease in diagenetic value
    (B) an increase in the resistivity value
    (C) increases in the resistivity and the conductivity values
    (D) an increase in the diagenetic values

Free Answer

1. List the Geologic Map Symbol for a bed which strikes N 80°E and dips 50°NW. (It should be correctly oriented with respect to the north arrow.)

2. A bed outcrops at points A and B. Its strike is generally N-S, dip 45°E. Sketch the approximate pattern this bed should show on the topographic map below.

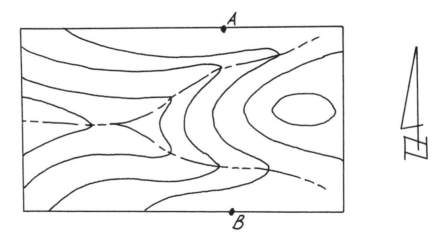

3. A groundwater basin composed of permeable sediments occupies an area of 2,000 acres. If 6,000 acre-feet of water are exported from this basin, how many feet will the water table be lowered? (Assume the basin to have vertical impermeable boundaries.)

Given: Permeability = 10,000 Meinzer's units
          Specific yield = 15%
          Porosity = 25%
          Specific retention = 10%

4. The three points given below all lie on the top, planar surface of a bed of sandstone. The figures beside each point are its elevation with respect to mean sea level. The scale is 1 inch = 200 square feet. Using a descriptive geometry technique, determine the strike and dip of the sandstone bed. Show all work.

750

900

400

5. Complete the geologic map below by either coloring or using distinctive black and white patterns.
   a. Add the proper legend along the right-hand side of the map
   b. Prepare a cross section along the line X-X', showing not only the structure, but the topographic profile that would be expected.

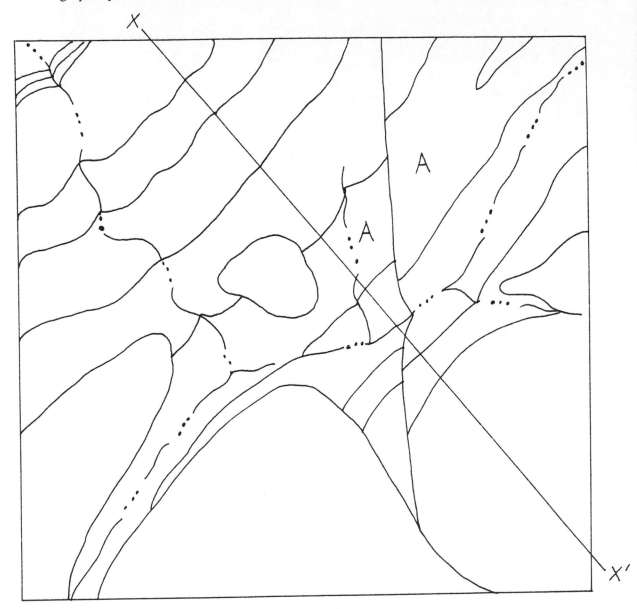

6. The top of a limestone bed (LS1) was found at outcrop A dipping due east 20°. At B the bottom of the limestone was found. The top and bottom of another bed of limestone (LS2) were found at 800- and 900-foot depths in a drill hole at A. A fault was traced along line F-F'. The movement vector of the fault is known from elsewhere to be composed of 200-foot throw (east side up) and 400-foot strike slip (left lateral).
   a. Show the complete outcrop pattern of the limestone bed (LS1).
   b. Find the thickness of the bed (LS1).
   c. A tunnel is to be driven along the line C-C' at elevation 100 feet. Draw a cross section along the line of the tunnel.

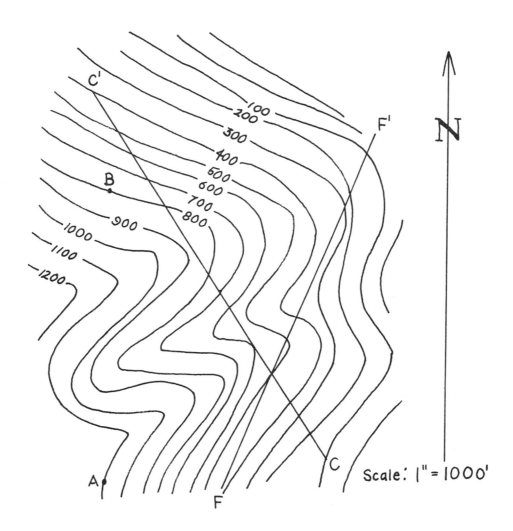

Scale: 1" = 1000'

7. A groundwater basin occupies an area of 11,000 acres. Throughout an ideal hydrologic cycle the following vegetation has existed in the basin:

Alfalfa 3,000 acres
Corn 2,000 acres
Brush 6,000 acres

Rainfall in the basin has averaged 10 inches per year; outflow from streams, 4,000 acre-feet per year; inflow from streams, 12,000 acre-feet per year.

Subsurface inflow has averaged 800 acre-feet per year and subsurface outflow has been insignificant. A water company has exported 150,000,000 cubic feet of water annually to lands outside the basin watershed. Assume the following annual consumptive use values: alfalfa, 4 feet; corn, 2 feet; brush, 0.6 feet. Specific yield of alluvial material is 13%.

a. What has been the average annual change in storage within the basin in acre feet?
b. What is the average change in water levels?

Show all work—slide-rule accuracy acceptable.

ANSWERS!

Multiple Choice

1. E
2. B
3. A
4. D
5. D
6. C
7. B
8. B
9. D
10. E
11. D
12. D
13. A
14. C
15. C
16. C
17. B
18. C
19. B

Free Answer

1.

N

2.

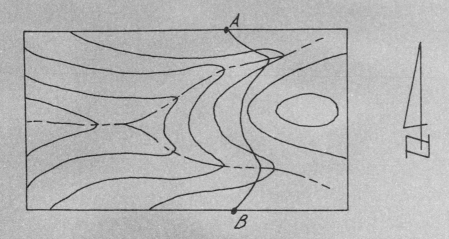

3. 6000 acre-feet = (2000 acre-feet)(x feet)(0.15 specific yield)
    x = 20 feet

4.

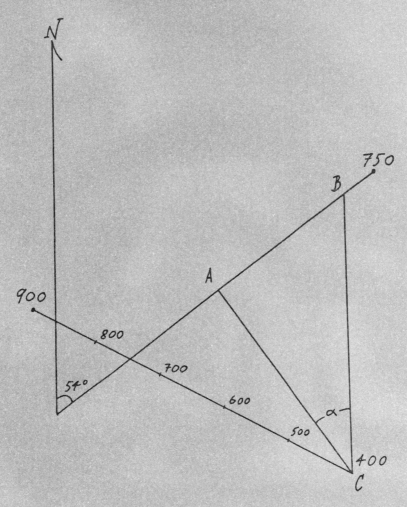

(1) Divide the distance between 400 point and 900 point into fifths, corresponding to 100-foot changes in elevation

(2) Mark the 750-foot point on this scale and connect it to the original 750-foot point. This is the 750-foot structural contour; it parallels the strike of the bed by definition. Strike is 054, or N54°E.

(3) Draw a perpendicular to the 750-foot contour through the 400 point (line AC). Mark the 750 foot contour 750 – 400 = 350 "feet" away from point A (point B). Angle α shows the dip of the bed, about 36°

Answer: bed strikes 054, dips 36°SE

5.

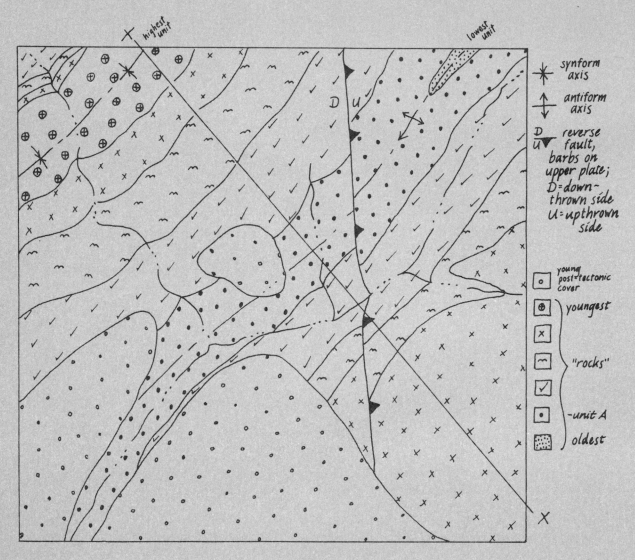

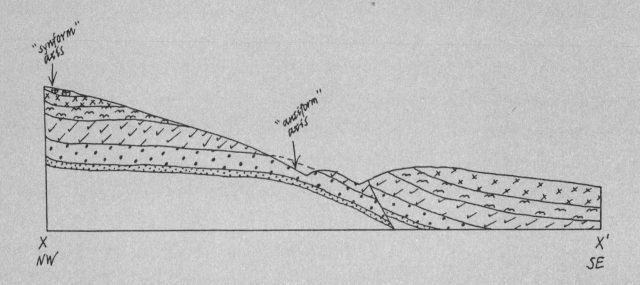

6. a:

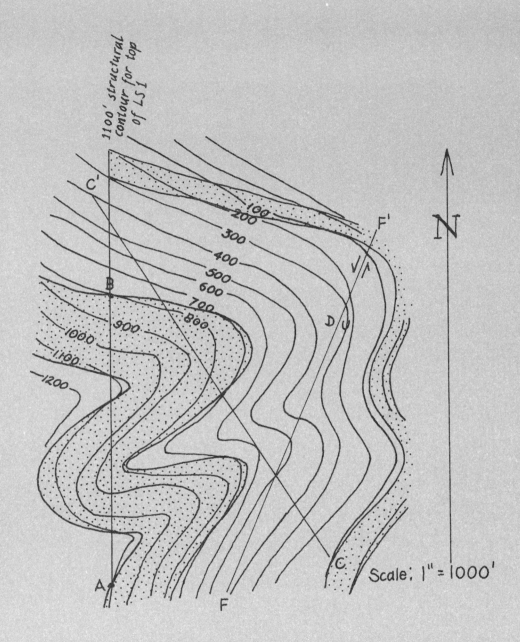

b. B is along the 1100-foot structural contour for the top of LS1. Therefore the "apparent" thickness is 300 feet and true thickness is 300 (cos 20) = 280 feet

C.

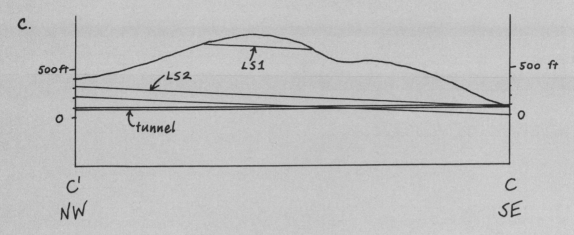

7.   OUTPUT FROM BASIN PER YEAR

$$\frac{150,000,000 \ ft^3}{46,560 \ ft^2/ac} = 3444 \ ac \cdot ft$$

4,000 ac·ft from streams
0 ac·ft from groundwater
3444 ac·ft from water company
3000 ac·4ft = 12,000 ac·ft from alfalfa
2000 ac·2ft = 4,000 ac·ft from corn
6000 ac·0.6ft = 3600 ac·ft from brush

a. INPUTS INTO BASIN PER YEAR

$\frac{10}{12}$ ft × 11,000 ac as rainfall

          = 9170 ac·ft

12,000 ac·ft from streams
  800 ac·ft from groundwater

TOTAL   21,370 ac·ft

BASIN IS BEING DEPLETED BY $(27,044 - 21,370) \approx 5700 \ ac \cdot ft/yr.$

b. Change in water level = $\dfrac{5700 \ ac \cdot ft}{11,000 \ ac \times .13 \ Specific \ yield}$

          $\approx 4 \ \frac{ft}{yr}$

GRAPHOLOGY

Handwriting Analysis

Which of the following handwriting specimens was written by an I.Q. under 65 and which by an I.Q. over 120?

Graphology—the study of personality through handwriting—is currently gaining popularity in the U.S. A painstaking science with numerous practical applications, graphology has been widely used in Europe for many years, especially by employers to screen job applicants. It is in the area of employee evaluation that the field's greatest growth is likely to occur in this country during the next decade or so.

The modern science of graphology was pioneered in the early nineteenth century by the French Abbé Jean-Hippolyte Michon, who developed a system of "fixed signs" or letter-forms which corresponded to personality traits. Although considered somewhat simplistic and one-dimensional by today's standards, Michon's work nevertheless represents the first detailed, systematic analysis in a hitherto haphazard and impressionistic field. In the late nineteenth century, Wilhelm Preyer and other German psychologists increased the sophistication and accuracy of graphological analysis by integrating into it the study of other aspects of handwriting, such as speed, pressure, and rhythm. Preyer developed a theory of what he called "brain writing," so called because he held that aspects of an individual's psyche found expression in the idiosyncrasies of his or her script, whether written with the use of the hand, the mouth, or the foot.

Present-day applications of graphology include the detection of physical and psychic illness, evaluation of I.Q., and the determination of dishonesty or criminality in writing. In an employee evaluation, the graphologist looks for similarities or discrepancies between a job description provided by the employer and characteristics of the applicant as revealed in a handwriting sample.

Some of the elements a graphologist takes into consideration when performing an analysis are slant, pressure, speed, rhythm, size, spacing, and the nature of the "connectives" used to join letters in script. Since handwriting must be viewed holistically, graphologists caution against a simplistic, atomistic analysis of individual elements as necessarily corresponding to particular personality traits. However, for the sake of illustration, we can generalize that, for example, rightward slant may indicate future or outward orientation, leftward slant roughly the opposite; heavy pressure may indicate energy and depth of feeling and emotion, light pressure sensitivity, adaptability, or passivity; a dominant lower zone (found in the descending parts of such letters as "g" and "y") may indicate strong sexual energy or athletic interest, and a dominant upper zone (in such letters as "l" and "k") may relate to mental activity, imagination, or spirituality.

One reaction graphologists often encounter from the uninitiated is skepticism that any aspect such as slant could really indicate anything about an individual's personality. After all, we are taught in school to write with a rightward slant. Also, we are all familiar with overall national differences in handwriting styles. If Germans are taught to write with a more vertical slant than Americans, does that mean that they are less outgoing or future-oriented?

The graphologist would respond that national styles are indeed taken into account in any responsible handwriting analysis. And it is undeniable that, though two people may be taught the Palmer Method in the third grade, their handwriting styles twenty years later will in all likelihood differ considerably, even to the untrained eye. It is in these deviations from Palmer that the graphologist finds significance. Even if an individual never departs from the style he or she is taught in school, such lack of originality would itself be highly revealing of his or her personality.

Those on the West Coast who are interested in pursuing a study of graphology would do well to contact Ted Widmer of the Graphological Society of San Francisco (he demystified the subject for the editors of this book). In New York City, the New School for Social Research offers good courses in graphology. Other graphologists, many of whom offer instruction, may be found in your local yellow pages under "Handwriting Analysts." You should take with a grain of salt any instructor's claim to make you a "certified graphologist," since there is as yet no meaningful process of licensing or certification.

The questions that follow represent three uses of graphology: employee evaluation, personality compatibility evaluation, and I.Q. evaluation. The analyses are abridged from *Handwriting Analysis: A Guide to Personality* by David Battan (International Resources, 1984). One of the foremost authorities in the field of graphology, Mr. Battan emphasizes the need to include all aspects of the writing sample in the analysis and utilizes worksheets to ensure a systematic approach. The worksheets, the book, and other titles in the field of graphology are available from International Resources, P.O. Box 3113, Pismo Beach CA 93449. The sections which highlight graphology methods and use Mr. Battan's examples are necessarily condensed. A thorough study of the methods, along with hundreds of examples of celebrity writing, are available in *Handwriting Analysis*.

1. Of the following eight handwriting samples, two demonstrate average intelligence (90-109 I.Q.), two would be classified as slightly above average or bright (110-119 I.Q.), two exhibit high intelligence (120-139 I.Q.) and two are indicative of genius (I.Q. of 140 or above). Analyze the eight samples and rank them in order of intelligence, from average to genius.

A.

Jack came in this took Mother to work

B.

C.

You arrive at Victoria Station go to St. Pancras Station

D.

I would suggest checking the before mailing anything as a of them are no longer in opera

a note to thank you

lovely dinner and

E.

$#$feel evening in your

F.

G.

ions. As for the specific myth work, lets face

primitive. Just as primitive artifacts are

to us lies in their direct expression of

H.

nature. You simply cannot make this

2. The owner of a small company hires you to perform a personnel evaluation of two applicants for the position of assistant to the manager. The duties of the job involve meeting the public, learning the company operation, and being able to assist the manager in his responsibilities. The skills required are flexibility and good verbal communication (both written and oral). The employer is specifically interested in organizational ability, ability to learn quickly, ability to take directions, self-confidence, ability to get along with people, and reliability. You are given the following two handwriting samples, one from each applicant, to work with. Based on these samples, which applicant would you recommend that the owner hire?

A.

B.

3. Three couples hire your services to analyze their chances of handling long-term commitments to each other. They submit to you the three pairs of handwriting samples below. Based on your analysis of characteristics displayed in their handwriting, which couple(s) would most likely be compatible, and which would not?

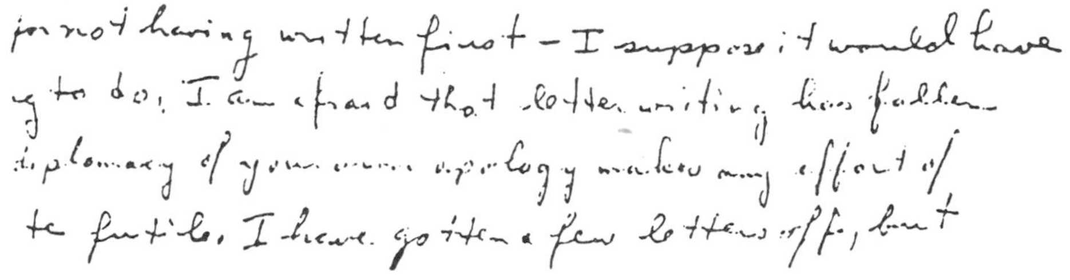

[handwriting sample: cursive]
for not having written first — I suppose it would have
to do, I am afraid that letter writing has fallen
diplomacy of your own apology makes any effort of
be futile. I have gotten a few letters off, but

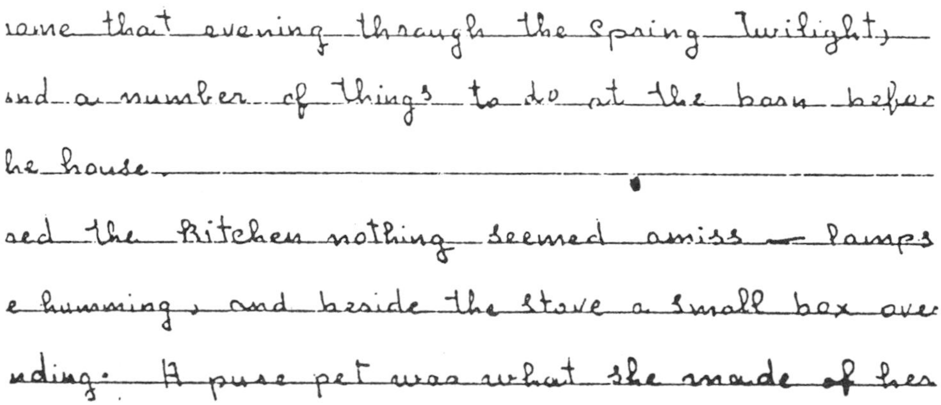

[handwriting sample: cursive]
came that evening through the spring twilight,
and a number of things to do at the barn before
he house
and the kitchen nothing seemed amiss — lamps
e humming, and beside the stove a small box over
riding. A pure pet was what she made of her

A.

Judy, I need a stateme
physician saying "it's" "OK" fo
working and how long —

Denmark to Oslo, Norwa
was very beautiful. I ha
first Class Cabin; but I
got up at 4 in the morn
to see the magnificent
sailing on the Fjor to C
P.S. 90% of the guests i
Orion are American. h

B.

country. It is extremely rare. It is a list of ships s
for his last command, HMS Director, 9 years after
the Bounty muting. It was sold several years
through Hamilton's auction at just less than 80
could be sold for much more than that.

c.

Finished her basic t
that now she's state
an air base? When she
, me, she hadn't bee
her work yet, but I

ANSWERS! ☞

1. Average intelligence (90-109 I.Q.): A and D
    Bright (110-119 I.Q.): C and E
    High Intelligence (120-139 I.Q.): F and H
    Genius (140+ I.Q.): B and G

    Analysis by category:

    Average (A and D): 48% of the population ranges from 90 to 109 I.Q. Handwriting in this range usually looks childlike or at least very conventional. The middle zone tends to be larger than the upper or lower zone. Letters are connected and often well-formed. The connecting strokes and letters are rounded. There is a general appearance that the writing is drawn rather than written. The two examples lack originality, imagination, and rhythm.

    Bright (C and E): Examples in this class show angles in the writing and signs of rhythm. The writing is still conventional but has lost the childlike quality. The middle zone is less dominant.

    High intelligence (F and H): In the 120-139 I.Q. range, the writing often becomes less conventional. The basic characteristics present are a reduction in the size of the writing, good rhythm, and many angles in the script. The writing takes on an individual character. Strokes may be used between words but with consistency and rhythm.

    Genius (B and G): I.Q. of 140 or above is seldom encountered, since this class represents only 1.5% of the population. The writing styles of two people in this range may appear to have few characteristics in common—they are highly individualized. The writing will be small, the rhythm superior, and breaks frequent between letters but in a well-defined and consistent pattern. If words are connected by strokes, the pattern will be consistent with a highly developed form. The samples here are of Ludwig van Beethoven (B) and Albert Einstein (G).

2. Recommendation: Hire A rather than B.

    Details of analysis and recommendation*:

    A: The slant is rightward with very good to superior rhythm but lacks originality. The pressure is light. The light pressure indicates sensitivity and combined with the slant indicates a responsiveness to others.

    The small middle zone and small writing indicate an ability to concentrate and a modest self-concept; confidence and persistence are shown in the firmly ending downstrokes and the fluidity of the writing. The spacing between the letters confirms interest in other people but the narrow letters indicate that he is cautious about expressing things about himself.

    There are many garlands in the writing. Considering the rightward slant and the degree of connectiveness, he is not only able to communicate with others, but he is also consistent in his thinking process. He carries through on projects logically. Some of the letters are pointed and some are rounded, showing that he grasps ideas quickly but considers the facts before taking action.

    The t-bars are of medium length and some display the conventional form typically found in the handwriting of schoolteachers. This shows a certain amount of moderation, discipline, and self-respect. I-dots are absent in the writing, but this does not show a lack of attention to detail or a lack of memory; he does not interrupt his flow of writing to go back to make the i-dots. This indicates a desire to get on with business without unnecessary interruptions. The loops are narrow and in some strokes they are absent. This demonstrates his practical nature and realistic approach.

Thus, the applicant for the position has many of the characteristics specified by the employer. He has good organizational ability and the ability to learn quickly. He is careful in checking out facts before taking action but accomplishes this with a consistent pattern. He follows through on assignments and shows both persistence and self-confidence. He has the ability to take direction from others and does not overemphasize his own importance. In this sense, he is flexible; he respects the ideas and feelings of others. He works fast and does not like to get bogged down with unnecessary detail. There is a positive tendency to respond to other people with genuine feeling, concern, and sensitivity. He can get along well with others and has the ability to communicate.

B: The slant of the writing is slightly to the right and the pressure is heavy with an uneven shading. The general rhythm of the writing is poor. A negative interpretation is given to the character traits because of the poor rhythm. He shows an emotional unevenness that allows his feelings to interfere with his judgement.

The upper zone letters dominate, but they are tall and stiff. He is bothered by conscience, and there is a suggestion that there may be conflict here. The writing is of medium size and the spacing between the letters and the width of the letters are normal. These writing characteristics indicate a struggle between what he wants to do and what he thinks he should do. The heavy, shaded, uneven pressure indicates his strong self-indulgence.

The form of connectiveness is primarily arcades, but these are moderate with some breaks in the writing. The tendency indicated by this combination is a lack of respect for others and a tendency to impose his own ideas on others. This may also show some indecision. There are some angles, but they are poorly executed, indicating tension.

The t-bar crossings are moderate in length, and there are two variations in these crossings: the first is a downward slant, indicating temper and aggressiveness, and the second is a tent-shaped t-bar crossing, indicating that he is stubborn and resents authority. The i-dots are rounded and placed high and slightly to the right. This shows good memory, but the placement of the dot over the i suggests some impatience with detail. The loops are narrow in both the upper and lower zones and have a muddy quality which shows two characteristics: a lack of imagination and a strong appetite for pleasure.

In sum, applicant B does not possess characteristics required by the employer. There are deficiencies in his organizational ability and a tendency to be indecisive and to overlook detail. At times, he would be influenced by the way he thinks things should be done rather than trying more original but consistent approaches. He can learn quickly but is indecisive in action and purpose. There may be conflict in putting into action what he has learned. The inability to take direction would present problems. He resents authority and has a strong tendency to be stubborn. He demonstrates a strong interest in himself and is concerned with satisfying his own desires. He does not demonstrate any real warmth toward people and would have a tendency to ignore others' feelings and interests.

*Although it is not usually possible to determine the sex of an individual from his or her handwriting, we may assume here that you have been given the names of the applicants for identification purposes, and that the names indicate that both applicants are male.

3.   (A) Both write with light pressure and similar slant. Both have very small hand-writing with tall strokes in the upper zone.These two individuals have similar temperaments; they are both reserved in emotional expression and would be able to talk over any problems or differences that may arise. Each enjoys time alone and can respect the other's desire to have time alone to pursue individual interests. The small writing shows an ability to concentrate, patience, and inner strengths. The tall upper strokes reveal similar values and similar degrees of intellectual interest. The lower zone loops are also similar. In sum, these two individuals are a very good match. They are both sensitive people who use logic rather than emotion to solve prob-lems; they share the need for individual creativity and in general have shared val-ues.

     (B) This couple display similar person-ality traits, but the similarity of these traits suggests potential problems. Both react emotionally, which you can determine from the rightward slant. The large, rather showy

The lower letters extend into the next line of writing below; this is a sign of getting involved in too many things at the same time. The fact that they both react impulsively makes this trait even more significant; usually the combination of these two traits results in poor financial management and impulse buying. In sum, there would be difficulty in this relationship because they are both impulsive and react emotionally, and because each wants to be the center of attention. A lasting relationship between these two would probably fail. You can be sure it would be eventful and full of fireworks!

(C) In one sample, the slant is vertical, the writing is small, and the spacing is narrow. Arcades are used in the connective form. From this we can infer strong control of emotions and a retiring personality; his or her approach is conservative and analytical. The other sample displays large writing with a large middle zone. The slant is to the right and we find initial strokes at the beginning of letters. He or she is clearly an extrovert with a strong interest in social activities. There would be a tendency to be demanding and possessive. In sum, their interests and temperaments are too far apart for a successful relationship. After a while one would probably withdraw and the other would probably feel unloved and neglected.

HISTORY AND LITERATURE

National Assessment

Eighty-five percent of 17-year-old students in the U.S. failed to answer this question correctly in an extensive survey conducted by the National Endowment for the Humanities.

1. *What is the name of the European statesman and author who traveled in the U.S. in the early years of this country's independence and wrote* Democracy in America?
   (A) *Henry David Thoreau*
   (B) *Jean Jacques Rousseau*
   (C) *Alexis de Tocqueville*
   (D) *Matthew Arnold*

In 1985, partly in response to a 50-point decline in high-school students' SAT scores between the early 1960s and the early 1980s, Congress instructed the National Endowment for the Humanities to study the state of humanities education in the public schools. As part of that study, the National Assessment of Educational Progress (see "Math" section) conducted an extensive survey of 17-year-olds' knowledge of literature and history—the first national assessment of high-school students' knowledge in those areas. In 1986, the results of the survey were one of the hottest education-related news items around, for the usual reason: students were able to answer barely more than 50% of the survey's history and literature questions correctly. In other words, assuming a score less than 60% to be failing, then this nationally representative sample of students had decisively "failed" both subjects.

In a report on the findings of the survey, the Chairman of the National Endowment for the Humanities blamed the decline in Americans' knowledge in these areas since the turn of the century on an emphasis on the "process" rather than "content" of learning, and on a replacement of the teaching of traditional offerings such as ancient history with the teaching of more practical skills. "Social studies," a subject that emphasizes the present rather than the past, has subsumed the subject of history, and "language arts" courses, stressing communication skills, have replaced more traditional literature-oriented English courses. Indeed, the single most important examination in our educational system, the SAT, painstakingly avoids assessing substantive coursework-related knowledge in favor of some more general supposed "aptitude."

The importance of the kind of knowledge tested by the NAEP survey's questions is, of course, open to debate. Those who lament the state of our educational system generally argue that our sense of nationhood is threatened by a lack of shared cultural knowledge, and that a lack of historical consciousness leaves us unable to understand or cope with our present. Of course, there are all kinds of cultural knowledge, some of which *are* shared by pretty much all of us. Organizations such as NEH, however, would claim that knowledge of contemporary or popular culture just doesn't provide adequate "civic glue" or sufficient depth of understanding of where we came from and where we're going as a nation.

It is important to explain here that the questions that follow are not exactly the same as those on the NAEP survey, since NAEP has not yet released those questions to the public. However, they *have* released paraphrases of the factual knowledge required to answer each question correctly. The questions that follow have been written so as to test that same knowledge. Along with the answer to each question, we have included the percentage of 17-year-olds in the NAEP's nationwide survey who answered the corresponding question in the survey correctly.

History

1. The light bulb was invented by
   (A) Benjamin Franklin
   (B) James Watt
   (C) Thomas Edison
   (D) Alexander Graham Bell

2. Locate the Soviet Union on the map.
   (A)
   (B)
   (C)
   (D)

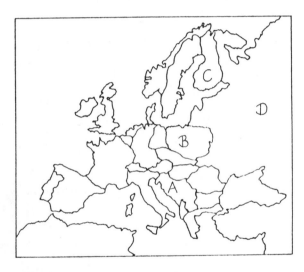

3. The inventor of the telephone was
   (A) Thomas Edison
   (B) Alexander Graham Bell
   (C) Samuel Morse
   (D) Eli Whitney

4. During which period of time was George Washington president?
   (A) 1760-1780
   (B) 1780-1800
   (C) 1800-1820
   (D) 1820-1840

5. Locate Italy on the map.
   (A)
   (B)
   (C)
   (D)

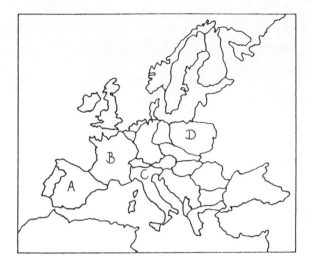

6. In the United States before 1861, the Underground Railroad was
   (A) a secret railway line built by robber baron Thomas Gould from St. Louis to California
   (B) the name given to the Chicago subway system
   (C) a system set up by opponents of slavery to help slaves escape from the South to northern states and Canada
   (D) the name given to a network of tunnels used by Confederate forces during the Civil War

7. The leader of Germany during World War II was

(A) Konrad Adenauer
(B) Otto von Bismarck
(C) Kaiser Wilhelm II
(D) Adolf Hitler

8. The main author of the Declaration of Independence was
(A) Thomas Jefferson
(B) Benjamin Franklin
(C) George Washington
(D) James Madison

9. The assembly line system was introduced by
(A) the U.S. auto industry
(B) the Japanese auto industry
(C) U.S. armaments manufacturers
(D) the U.S. steel industry

10. Locate the 13 original states of the U.S. on the map.
(A)
(B)
(C)
(D)

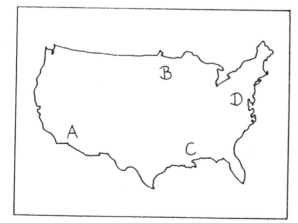

11. The Ku Klux Klan, an organization founded in the southern states after the Civil War, is best characterized by its
(A) use of violence to oppose minorities
(B) legal opposition to universal suffrage in the U.S.
(C) opposition to school prayer
(D) pacifist orientation

12. A leader in helping slaves escape from the South was
(A) George Washington Carver
(B) Harriet Beecher Stowe
(C) Harriet Tubman
(D) Nat Turner

13. Locate the Rocky Mountains on the map.
(A)
(B)
(C)
(D)

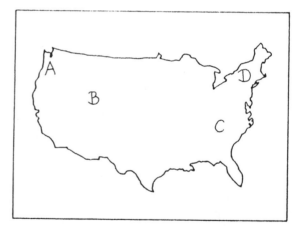

14. A guarantee of freedom of speech and religion is found in the
(A) Bill of Rights
(B) thirteenth amendment to the constitution
(C) Declaration of Independence
(D) Emancipation Proclamation

15. The event that led the U.S. into World War II was the
    (A) Axis bombing of London
    (B) German torpedoing of the passenger ship *Lusitania*
    (C) German invasion of Austria
    (D) Japanese attack on Pearl Harbor

16. The U.S. dropped the first atomic bomb on
    (A) Japan in World War II
    (B) Germany in World War II
    (C) North Korea in the Korean War
    (D) Bikini atoll in the Pacific after World War II

17. The commander of the American forces during the Revolutionary War was
    (A) Thomas Jefferson
    (B) Benedict Arnold
    (C) Patrick Henry
    (D) George Washington

18. The Prime Minister of Great Britain during World War II was
    (A) Neville Chamberlain
    (B) Sir Anthony Eden
    (C) Winston Churchill
    (D) Edward Heath

19. Television became a new feature in American homes
    (A) before 1910
    (B) between the two World Wars
    (C) during the 1940s
    (D) after 1950

20. The event that led to the resignation of Richard Nixon was
    (A) the My-Lai massacre
    (B) his failure to end the war in Vietnam
    (C) his failure to win the war in Vietnam
    (D) Watergate

21. A war in which many women worked in factories to support the war effort was
    (A) World War I
    (B) World War II
    (C) the Korean War
    (D) the Vietnam War

22. The first permanent English colony in the New World was
    (A) Jamestown
    (B) Charleston
    (C) Williamsburg
    (D) Plymouth

23. Locate West Germany on the map.
    (A)
    (B)
    (C)
    (D)

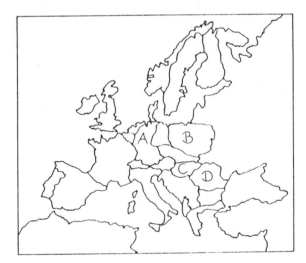

24. The first person to make a solo flight across the Atlantic was

(A) Eddie Rickenbacker
(B) Amelia Earhart
(C) Charles Lindbergh
(D) Chuck Yeager

25. The Nazi decimation of the Jewish population of Europe is referred to as
(A) the Diaspora
(B) the Holocaust
(C) the "inner migration"
(D) forced relocation

26. The Great Depression was a period of
(A) rampant inflation
(B) rapid rearmament
(C) mass unemployment
(D) persecution of suspected Communists

27. "Prohibition" refers to
(A) the emancipation of slaves
(B) the period during which women were denied the right to vote before passage of the 19th Amendment
(C) government taxes on liquor
(D) the ban on the sale and consumption of liquor

28. The war that had the strongest citizen protest movements was
(A) the Vietnam War
(B) World War II
(C) World War I
(D) the Civil War

29. The Civil Rights movement of the 1960s focused most on
(A) equality for women
(B) equality for minorities
(C) ending the war in Vietnam
(D) protection of the environment

30. A major cause of westward movement in the history of the U.S. was

(A) the discovery of gold in California
(B) the persecution of religious groups in New England
(C) overcrowding east of the Mississippi
(D) the end of the Indian Wars

31. Locate the area on the map that fought for independence from Mexico
(A)
(B)
(C)
(D)

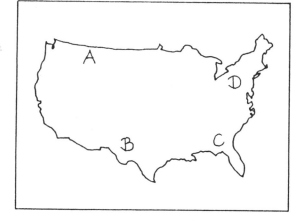

32. An invention that stimulated the plantation economy in the South was
(A) McCormick's reaper
(B) the diesel tractor
(C) the cotton gin
(D) the assembly line

33. The main opponents of the U.S. during World War II were
(A) Italy and Austria
(B) Germany and Russia
(C) Japan and Germany
(D) Russia and Japan

34. World War II ended
(A) between 1935 and 1939

(B) between 1939 and 1943
(C) between 1943 and 1947
(D) between 1947 and 1950

35. Indians were put on reservations by the U.S. government
(A) before the Revolutionary War
(B) shortly after the Revolutionary War
(C) in the early 1800s
(D) after the Civil War

36. Locate the Mississippi River on the map.
(A)
(B)
(C)
(D)

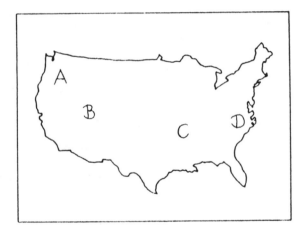

37. Susan B. Anthony was
(A) the first woman Secretary of the Treasury
(B) a Civil War hero
(C) the first woman to cross the Atlantic in an airplane
(D) a leader of the women's suffrage movement

38. Most people living in the English colonies of North America worked as
(A) farmers
(B) administrators
(C) civil servants
(D) hunters

39. The term "Secession" refers to
(A) treason against the government in wartime
(B) the withdrawal of the Southern states from the Union
(C) the meeting of the Colonial Congress before the Revolutionary War
(D) the declaration of independence from England

40. Locate Great Britain on the map.
(A)
(B)
(C)
(D)

41. Christopher Columbus discovered the New World
(A) before 1750
(B) between 1750 and 1800
(C) between 1800 and 1850
(D) after 1850

42. The Emancipation Proclamation was written by
    (A) Benjamin Franklin
    (B) Thomas Jefferson
    (C) Abraham Lincoln
    (D) John F. Kennedy

43. The signing of the Declaration of Independence took place
    (A) before 1750
    (B) between 1750-1800
    (C) between 1800-1850
    (D) after 1850

44. Locate France on the map.
    (A)
    (B)
    (C)
    (D)

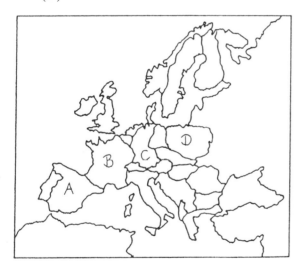

45. The Stamp Act of 1765 was
    (A) an early effort by the English to impose direct taxes on the colonies, intended to raise revenues for the support of the American army defending the colonies
    (B) a law that made it illegal for colonial postal envoys to carry or distribute letters without permission of the English Parliament
    (C) a law that levied taxes on mail delivered within the coloines
    (D) an attempt to eradicate French influence from the colonies

46. The Declaration of Independence was a document that
    (A) asserted the religious independence of the Puritans from the Church of England
    (B) declared the American colonies' break from England
    (C) declared slavery illegal in all states
    (D) set up a federal system of government, with a certain degree of power held by the individual states

47. The event that provoked the U.S. into entering World War I was
    (A) the bombing of Pearl Harbor
    (B) the German invasion of France
    (C) German expansion into the Americas
    (D) German submarine attacks

48. During what period did Watergate occur?
    (A) Before 1930
    (B) Between 1930 and 1940
    (C) Between 1940 and 1950
    (D) After 1950

49. The *Brown vs. Board of Education* decision of 1954
    (A) declared school segregation unconstitutional

(B) declared school busing
unconstitutional

(C) upheld a lower-court decision to allow the teaching of Darwin's theory of evolution in schools

(D) declared school prayer unconstitution-al

50. The name *Sputnik* was given to
(A) the Soviet space program between 1960 and 1968
(B) the first man-made satellite
(C) the period of relaxing of tensions between the superpowers during the 1970s
(D) the first Siberian labor camp in Stalinist Russia

51. The Plessy vs. Ferguson decision
(A) outlawed racial segregation in upholding a Louisiana statute requiring railroads to do away with separate accomodations for different races
(B) approved racial segregation in upholding a Louisiana statute requiring railroads operating in that state to provide "separate but equal" accomodations for whites and blacks
(C) outlawed racial segregation in schools in ruling that separate educational facilities were "inherently unequal"
(D) supported racial segregation in schools

52. The southwestern U.S. was explored and settled primarily by which European nation?
(A) England
(B) France
(C) Spain
(D) Portugal

53. When was the U.S. Constitution written?
(A) Before 1700

(B) Between 1700 and 1750
(C) Between 1750 and 1800
(D) After 1800

54. The East Coast of the U.S. was explored and settled primarily by which European nation?
(A) England
(B) France
(C) Spain
(D) Portugal

55. The U.S. president who appealed for American entry into the League of Nations was
(A) Harry Truman
(B) Franklin Roosevelt
(C) Herbert Hoover
(D) Woodrow Wilson

56. During which period of time did Japan bomb Pearl Harbor?
(A) Between 1935 and 1939
(B) Between 1939 and 1942
(C) Between 1942 and 1945
(D) Between 1945 and 1948

57. The term referring to the division of power among the different branches of the federal government is
(A) *laissez faire*
(B) federalism
(C) checks and balances
(D) socialism

58. From what areas of the world did the heaviest immigration to the U.S. come in the 1970s and 1980s?
(A) The Soviet Union and Eastern Europe
(B) Southeast Asia and Latin America
(C) Latin America and Africa
(D) Pakistan and India

59. The Articles of Confederation was the name given to
   (A) the first part of the Constitution
   (B) the southern states' declaration of independence from the Union
   (C) underground pamphlets distributed by secessionists just prior to the Civil War
   (D) the first American Constitution during the Revolution

60. Standard Oil Company was formed by
   (A) J. Paul Getty
   (B) John D. Rockefeller
   (C) Howard Hughes
   (D) John Jay Gould

61. U.S. foreign policy after World War II is characterized primarily by
   (A) isolationism
   (B) containment of Communism
   (C) protection of Latin America from the European powers
   (D) concern with human rights

62. During which period did World War II occur?
   (A) Between 1800-1850
   (B) Between 1850-1900
   (C) Between 1900-1950
   (D) Between 1950-2000

63. Which name identifies a major black leader before World War I?
   (A) Booker T. Washington
   (B) Eldridge Cleaver
   (C) Martin Luther King, Jr.
   (D) Malcolm X

64. "Prohibition" occurred during which period of time?
   (A) Between 1800-1850
   (B) Between 1850-1900
   (C) Between 1900-1950
   (D) Between 1950-2000

65. Before 1800, most immigrants to the U.S. came from
   (A) southern Europe
   (B) Africa
   (C) eastern Europe and Asia
   (D) western and northern Europe

66. Dwight D. Eisenhower was president of the U.S. during which period?
   (A) Between 1917 and 1930
   (B) Between 1930 and 1946
   (C) Between 1946 and 1963
   (D) Between 1963 and 1980

67. Which country has Israel never been invaded by?
   (A) Egypt
   (B) Syria
   (C) the Soviet Union
   (D) Lebanon

68. Which group was forced into internment camps in the U.S. during World War II?
   (A) Chinese-Americans
   (B) German-Americans
   (C) Italian-Americans
   (D) Japanese-Americans

69. Under which U.S. president's administration were relations with the People's Republic of China established?
   (A) John F. Kennedy
   (B) Richard Nixon
   (C) Gerald Ford
   (D) Jimmy Carter

70. A significant cause of population movement during the 1800s was
   (A) religious persecution

(B) overpopulation on the eastern seaboard
(C) reasonable land prices
(D) famines in the northeastern U.S.

71. The Social Security system was introduced
    (A) at the beginning of the Great Depression
    (B) during the New Deal
    (C) immediately after World War II
    (D) under Lyndon B. Johnson's administration in the 1960s

72. A significant cause of migration to California in the 1930s was
    (A) acquisiton of the territory from Mexico
    (B) the discovery of gold in the Sacramento area
    (C) the creation of the Los Angeles harbor
    (D) prolonged drought in the Dust Bowl

73. The leader of the Soviet Union during World War II was
    (A) Vladimir Lenin
    (B) Joseph Stalin
    (C) Nikita Krushchev
    (D) Leonid Brezhnev

74. The Populist Party advocated
    (A) decreases in social welfare
    (B) a withdrawal of support for the Allies in World War II
    (C) the repeal of Prohibition
    (D) government support for farmers

75. The New Deal of the Franklin D. Roosevelt administration is identified with
    (A) changes in social and economic policies
    (B) an increase in military spending
    (C) a decreased role of the federal government in education at the elementary school level

(D) monetary loans to western European nations during World War II

76. During which period was Franklin Delano Roosevelt president?
    (A) Between 1888 and 1911
    (B) Between 1911 and 1929
    (C) Between 1929 and 1946
    (D) Between 1946 and 1960

77. The quote, "Give me liberty or give me death" is attributed to
    (A) Benedict Arnold
    (B) Patrick Henry
    (C) Benjamin Franklin
    (D) John Paul Jones

78. The term denoting minimal government regulation of the economy is
    (A) checks and balances
    (B) federalism
    (C) *laissez faire*
    (D) socialism

79. The Monroe Doctrine stipulated that
    (A) the U.S. would aid any country in the Western Hemisphere if attacked by a neighbor
    (B) the European powers should not attempt to gain and/or extend their influence or control in the Western Hemisphere
    (C) any attempt by Russia to extend its territory beyond Alaska would be repulsed
    (D) any attack against England would be regarded as an attack against the U.S.

80. George Washington's farewell address warned against
    (A) concessions to special interests
    (B) placing state over national loyalty
    (C) direct power in hands of the masses
    (D) foreign alliances

81. Canada and the Mississippi Valley were first explored by which European nation?
    (A) England
    (B) France
    (C) Spain
    (D) Portugal

82. The first president of the AFL was
    (A) Samuel Gompers
    (B) Cesar Chavez
    (C) John L. Lewis
    (D) Daniel DeLeon

83. The civil rights leader who rose to prominence in the Montgomery bus boycott was
    (A) Rosa Parks
    (B) Stokely Carmichael
    (C) Malcolm X
    (D) Martin Luther King, Jr.

84. During which period did the U.S. drop the first atomic bomb?
    (A) Between 1939 and 1943
    (B) Between 1943 and 1947
    (C) Between 1947 and 1951
    (D) Between 1951 and 1954

85. The lowest point for the Americans in the Revolutionary War was
    (A) Bunker Hill
    (B) the crossing of the Delaware
    (C) Valley Forge
    (D) Yorktown

86. An issue in the War of 1812 was Britain's
    (A) continued presence in North America
    (B) interferences with American shipping
    (C) refusal to recognize the sovereignty of the U.S.
    (D) unfavorable trade balance with the U.S.

87. Andrew Carnegie was most closely associated with the development of which industry?
    (A) Oil
    (B) Steel
    (C) Automobile
    (D) Shipping

88. During which period was Thomas Jefferson president?
    (A) Between 1760 and 1780
    (B) Between 1780 and 1800
    (C) Between 1800 and 1820
    (D) Between 1820 and 1840

89. The Constitution specifies
    (A) a division of powers between the states and the federal government
    (B) a concentration of power in the federal government
    (C) a distribution of power among the states rather than in the federal government
    (D) no position with regard to state and federal powers

90. The Missouri Compromise
    (A) allowed a redrawing of the Arkansas-Missouri border in exchange for statehood
    (B) permitted Missouri a status somewhere between a slave and a free state
    (C) granted Missouri exclusive rights to trade with territories to its west in exchange for a renunciation of slavery within its borders
    (D) admitted Maine as a free state and Missouri as a slave state

91. During which period was Woodrow Wilson president?
    (A) Between 1873 and 1890
    (B) Between 1890 and 1912

(C) Between 1912 and 1929

(D) Between 1929 and 1940

92. What is Senator Joseph McCarthy most famous for?
    (A) His unsuccessful presidential bid in 1954
    (B) His opposition to U.S. involvement in the Vietnam War
    (C) The record number of times he won re-election
    (D) His role in controversies about Communism in the 1950s

93. "Nullification" refers to
    (A) states' rights to prevent the operation of a federal law within their borders
    (B) the power of the president to override Congressional decisions
    (C) the power of the Supreme Court to override lower court decisions
    (D) the power of the Supreme Court to override executive branch decisions

94. Which of the following were presidents during the Great Depression?
    (A) Warren G. Harding and Calvin Coolidge
    (B) Calvin Coolidge and Herbert Hoover
    (C) Herbert Hoover and Franklin Roosevelt
    (D) Franklin Roosevelt and Harry Truman

95. Jane Addams is known for her
    (A) work for women's suffrage in the late 19th century
    (B) founding of settlement houses for the poor in Chicago in the late 19th century
    (C) academic writings about the plight of the poor
    (D) opposition to Al Capone

96. During what period did "Reconstruction" occur?
    (A) Before 1800
    (B) Between 1800 and 1850
    (C) Between 1850 and 1900
    (D) After 1900

97. *The Federalist* advocated
    (A) armed resistance to England
    (B) rejection of the Constitution in favor of a less revolutionary document
    (C) adoption of the Constitution
    (D) separation of Church and State

98. The Supreme Court *Dred Scott* decision ruled that
    (A) a slave who moved to a free state became a citizen of that state
    (B) a slave who moved to a free state could not become a citizen of that state
    (C) a slave who moved to a free state and attained free status could not be remanded to slave status upon return to a slave state
    (D) slaves are not "property"

99. When did D-Day occur?
    (A) Between 1935 and 1939
    (B) Between 1939 and 1943
    (C) Between 1943 and 1947
    (D) Between 1947 and 1951

100. The period known as the Renaissance was characterized by
    (A) cultural and technological advances
    (B) a dramatic increase in the influence of the Roman Catholic church
    (C) a loss of interest in classical culture
    (D) the ascendance of Latin as the dominant literary language in Europe

101. Thomas Paine's tract "Common Sense" argued

(A) for reconciliation with England

(B) for colonial independence

(C) against complete colonial independence in favor of limited self-determination

(D) against tracts which denunciated British tyranny

102. The Emancipation Proclamation

(A) gave women the right to vote

(B) proclaimed the American colonies free of British rule

(C) freed slaves in the Confederacy

(D) declared all states north of the Mason-Dixon line to be "free"

103. Union membership grew in the 1930s partly because of

(A) government attempts to suppress organized labor

(B) new laws that resulted in an increase in unions' power

(C) the start of the Great Depression

(D) massive economic growth resulting in the expansion of new industries

104. When was Jamestown founded?

(A) Before 1750

(B) Between 1750 and 1800

(C) Between 1800 and 1850

(D) After 1850

105. Which of the following was *not* part of the New Deal?

(A) Creation of the Tennessee Valley Authority

(B) Price supports for agriculture

(C) Restrictions on immigration

(D) Creation of the Social Security System

106. In the U.S. Constitution, the "three-fifths compromise"

(A) limited slavery to the southern states

(B) allowed slavery to continue in states in which current slave population exceeded a certain percentage of the state's overall population

(C) declared that the national legislative body (Congress) should consist of two houses, one in which the states would have equal representation, and the other in which states would have representation according to their population

(D) represented a compromise between the southern states, which wanted slaves to have the status of "individuals," and thus be counted among the inhabitants of the state for the purpose of determining congressional representatives, and the northern states, which wanted slaves to have the status of "property"

107. From what part of the world did the greatest number of immigrants come between 1890 and 1910?

(A) Canada

(B) Mexico

(C) southern and eastern Europe

(D) northern and western Europe

108. Against what group were the Immigration Acts of 1921 and 1924 directed?

(A) Canadians

(B) Mexicans

(C) Southern and eastern Europeans

(D) Northern and western Europeans

109. The Scopes Trial concerned the issue of

(A) the teaching of the theory of evolution in public schools

(B) the use of animals in psychology laboratories

(C) the compatibility of the theory of evolution with the religious foundation of the Constitution

(D) the right of public school students to refuse to participate in the Pledge of Allegiance

110. The term "muckraker" was applied to which of the following?
(A) John Bunyan and Theodore Roosevelt
(B) Upton Sinclair, Lincoln Steffens, and Ida Tarbell
(C) Senator Joseph McCarthy and Roy Cohn
(D) various North American Indian groups

111. During which period was Theodore Roosevelt president?
(A) Between 1863 and 1878
(B) Between 1878 and 1895
(C) Between 1895 and 1913
(D) Between 1913 and 1931

112. Which of the following was a shortcoming of the Articles of Confederation?
(A) They failed to provide for a national legislative body
(B) They failed to provide sufficient protection of states' rights
(C) They failed to provide for a common treasury
(D) They failed to provide adequate taxing power

113. Who was the inventor of the polio vaccine?
(A) Albert Schweitzer
(B) Edward Jenner
(C) Jonas Salk
(D) Florence Sabin

114. Which of the following wars established the U.S. as an international power?

(A) The Revolutionary War
(B) The War of 1812
(C) The Spanish-American War
(D) World War I

115. Which of the following terms characterizes American foreign policy after World War I?
(A) Jingoistic
(B) Imperialist
(C) Expansionist
(D) Isolationist

116. During what period did the Civil War occur?
(A) Before 1800
(B) Between 1800 and 1850
(C) Between 1850 and 1900
(D) Between 1900 and 1950

117. Which phrase of Theodore Roosevelt's characterizes U.S. foreign policy in the early 1900s?
(A) "Bully! Bully!"
(B) "Speak softly and carry a big stick"
(C) "Square deal"
(D) "Lunatic fringe"

118. The purpose of the Jim Crow laws was to
(A) provide for the "equality" of "separate" facilities
(B) enforce racial segregation
(C) end racial segregation
(D) combat bootlegging during Prohibition

119. What document formed the foundation of the British parliamentary system?
(A) The Act of Union
(B) The Treaty of Westphalia
(C) The Edict of Nantes
(D) The Magna Carta

120. During what period was Andrew Jackson

president?
(A) Before 1820
(B) Between 1820 and 1840
(C) Between 1840 and 1860
(D) After 1860

121. What movement or event led to the establishment of Protestant sects?
(A) The Reformation
(B) The Counter Reformation
(C) The Western Schism
(D) The Eastern Schism

122. During what period was the United Nations founded?
(A) Before 1940
(B) Between 1940 and 1943
(C) Between 1943 and 1947
(D) After 1947

123. A document formulated during the first modern women's rights convention was
(A) the Seneca Falls Declaration
(B) the Falls Church Resolution
(C) the Muskogee Declaration
(D) the Natick Resolution

124. During what period was Abraham Lincoln president?
(A) Before 1840
(B) Between 1840 and 1860
(C) Between 1860 and 1880
(D) After 1880

125. Which of the following originated in Lyndon Johnson's term?
(A) The Vietnam War and the Civil Rights movement
(B) McCarthyism and the U.S. space program
(C) Social Security and federal aid to farmers
(D) Medicare and the Voting Rights Act

126. Which of the following were leaders of the women's movement in the 1970s?
(A) Rosa Parks and Harriet Tubman
(B) Lucretia Mott and Elizabeth Cady Stanton
(C) Betty Friedan and Gloria Steinem
(D) Geraldine Ferraro and Jean Kirkpatrick

127. The "Progressive movement" refers to reforms
(A) before World War I
(B) Between World War I and World War II
(C) between World War II and the Korean War
(D) after the Korean War

128. "Reconstruction" refers to
(A) the rebuilding of southern cities after the Civil War
(B) the readmission of Confederate states after the Civil War
(C) the rebuilding ot the economy after the Great Depression
(D) the rebuilding of Germany and Japan after World War II

129. Which of the following groups founded a colony in Boston?
(A) John Winthrop and the Puritans
(B) Ann Lee and the Shakers
(C) Loyola and the Jesuits
(D) Brigham Young and the Mormons

Literature

1. The character in the Bible who gathers pairs of creatures into the ark is
(A) Adam
(B) Moses
(C) Noah
(D) Abraham

2. In the Bible, the character who receives the 10 commandments and leads his people out of Egypt is
   (A) Adam
   (B) Moses
   (C) Noah
   (D) Abraham

3. The characters in a play by Shakespeare whose love for each other is hindered by their feuding families are
   (A) Troilus and Cressida
   (B) Hamlet and Ophelia
   (C) Antony and Cleopatra
   (D) Romeo and Juliet

4. Whose famous speech included the words, "I have a dream..."?
   (A) Abraham Lincoln
   (B) Winston Churchill
   (C) John F. Kennedy
   (D) Martin Luther King, Jr.

5. Which character in a play by Shakespeare says the following lines:

   To be, or not to be, that is the question:
   Whether 'tis nobler in the mind to suffer
   The slings and arrows of outrageous for-
   tune,
   Or to take arms against a sea of troubles
   And by opposing them to end them.

   (A) King Lear
   (B) Othello
   (C) Macbeth
   (D) Hamlet

6. Who is the stingy character who turns generous in Dickens' "A Christmas Carol"?
   (A) Ebenezer Scrooge
   (B) Uriah Heep
   (C) Tiny Tim

(D) Mr. Micawber

7. In Greek mythology, the ruler of the gods is
   (A) Hermes
   (B) Zeus
   (C) Poseidon
   (D) Kronos

8. In what book are the White Rabbit, the March Hare, and the Mad Hatter?
   (A) *Watership Down*
   (B) *Alice's Adventures in Wonderland*
   (C) *A Wrinkle in Time*
   (D) *The Hobbit*

9. What character is known for stealing from the rich and giving to the poor?
   (A) the Wizard of Oz
   (B) William Tell
   (C) Robin Hood
   (D) Captain Blood

10. What fairy tale character has her rags turn into a gown and pumpkin turn into a carriage on the night that she meets a handsome prince of her dreams?
    (A) Cinderella
    (B) Snow White
    (C) Little Red Riding Hood
    (D) Goldilocks

11. What character becomes shipwrecked on an island but survives and eventually returns to civilization?
    (A) Tom Sawyer
    (B) Robinson Crusoe
    (C) R. P. McMurphy
    (D) Jonah

12. Who was the magician who was advisor to King Arthur?
    (A) Gandalf

(B) Merlin
(C) Beelzebub
(D) Alladin

13. What book is about an orphan boy and a runaway slave and their adventures together as they travel down the Mississippi River?
(A) *Tom Sawyer*
(B) *To Kill a Mockingbird*
(C) *Incredible Journey*
(D) *The Adventures of Huckleberry Finn*

14. Which Book of the Bible includes an account of creation?
(A) Kings
(B) Genesis
(C) Numbers
(D) Deuteronomy

15. What discipline are Plato and Aristotle best known for?
(A) Philosophy
(B) Mathematics
(C) Statesmanship
(D) Music

16. What is the story about a man who falls asleep for 20 years and then wakes up to find his wife dead and himself forgotten?
(A) *Brigadoon*
(B) *Lost Horizon*
(C) "Sleeping Beauty"
(D) "Rip van Winkle"

17. Who wrote "The Pit and the Pendulum," "The Fall of the House of Usher," and "The Raven"?
(A) Herman Melville
(B) Mark Twain
(C) Edgar Allan Poe
(D) James Fenimore Cooper

18. What play by Shakespeare are the lines "Friends, Romans, countrymen, lend me your ears" from?
(A) *Hamlet*
(B) *King Lear*
(C) *Julius Caesar*
(D) *Henry IV, Part One*

19. What character in a play by Shakespeare says the lines "What's in a name? That which we call a rose/By any other word would smell as sweet"?
(A) Romeo
(B) Juliet
(C) Cleopatra
(D) Ophelia

20. Fourscore and seven years ago our fathers brought forth on this continent a new nation, conceived in liberty, and dedicated to the proposition that all men are created equal.

The above lines are from which speech or document?
(A) Washington's inaugural address
(B) the Gettysburg Address
(C) the Constitution
(D) the Declaration of Independence

21. What is the title of the novel by Mary Shelley in which a scientist creates a creature he cannot control?
(A) *Dracula*
(B) *Lord of the Rings*
(C) *The Hunchback of Notre Dame*
(D) *Frankenstein*

22. Which of the following novels helped the antislavery movement?
(A) *To Kill a Mockingbird*
(B) *Poor White*

(C) *Uncle Tom's Cabin*
(D) *Shane*

23. Which of the following is an epic that tells of the adventures of a Greek war leader on his voyage home?
(A) the *Iliad*
(B) the *Odyssey*
(C) *Oedipus Rex*
(D) *The Alexandria Quartet*

24. In whose novels do the characters Oliver, Pip, Micawber and Gradgrind appear?
(A) Charles Dickens
(B) George Eliot
(C) Jane Austin
(D) Henry James

25. Which of the following is another name for Satan?
(A) Jupiter
(B) Yahweh
(C) Jehovah
(D) Lucifer

26. What legendary king presided over the knights of the Round Table
(A) King James
(B) King Arthur
(C) King Henry
(D) King William the Conqueror

27. What character in the Bible is known for his great strength?
(A) Methuselah
(B) Solomon
(C) Samson
(D) Abraham

28. In the Bible, who does Judas betray for 30 pieces of silver?
(A) Mary Magdalena
(B) Abel

(C) Job
(D) Jesus

29. What is the moral of Aesop's fable about the tortoise and the hare?
(A) old age should be respected
(B) slow and steady wins the race
(C) money can't buy happiness
(D) only those who help with the work can enjoy its rewards

30. In the Bible, what hapens in the Cain and Abel story?
(A) Two young men have to leave the Garden of Eden
(B) Two young men have to choose a wife
(C) A generous young man helps his brother
(D) A jealous young man kills his brother

31. Who is the main character in *The Hound of the Baskervilles* and *The Sign of Four?*
(A) Leatherstocking
(B) Sherlock Holmes
(C) Sam Spade
(D) Tarzan

32. Who wrote the poems "Annabel Lee" and "The Raven"?
(A) Edgar Allan Poe
(B) William Cullen Bryant
(C) Oliver Wendell Holmes
(D) Archibald MacLeish

33. In Roman mythology, who is the goddess of love?
(A) Hera
(B) Diana
(C) Venus
(D) Aphrodite

34. We hold these truths to be self-evident, that all men are created equal, that they are endowed by their Creator with certain

unalienable Rights, that among these are Life, Liberty, and the pursuit of Happiness.

The above lines are from
(A) the Preamble to the Constitution
(B) the Gettysburg Address
(C) the Declaration of Independence
(D) Washington's inaugural address

36. The name of a play by Thornton Wilder about a typical New England village is
(A) *Our Town*
(B) *The Courtship of Miles Standish*
(C) *Main Street*
(D) *Desire Under the Elms*

37. Aesop is best known for writing
(A) novels
(B) songs
(C) fables
(D) parables

38. In Greek mythology, what escaped from Pandora's Box?
(A) The Minotaur
(B) The winged horse Pegasus
(C) An imprisoned genie
(D) A multitude of ills and evils

39. Which author wrote *For Whom the Bell Tolls* and *The Sun Also Rises?*
(A) John Dos Passos
(B) Henry Miller
(C) Ernest Hemingway
(D) William Faulkner

40. Which author wrote *Call of the Wild*, a novel about a dog in Yukon territory?
(A) Joel Chandler Harris
(B) Jack London
(C) Washington Irving
(D) Herman Melville

41. In Herman Melville's *Moby Dick,* what is Captain Ahab's obsession?
(A) Revenge against the white whale
(B) Greed for the riches of the sea
(C) Love for his ailing wife
(D) The protection of his crew

42. What is the title of the story about Lilliput, the country of little people?
(A) *The Hobbit*
(B) *Gulliver's Travels*
(C) *Of Mice and Men*
(D) *Fantastic Fables*

43. What is the theme of the novel *The Red Badge of Courage*?
(A) A young woman's infidelity
(B) A young man's struggle with his injuries after World War I
(C) A young soldier's struggle to overcome his fear in the Civil War
(D) A young soldier's headstrong behavior in World War II

44. In Greek mythology, what is the name of the divinity who has to support the heavens on his shoulders?
(A) Atlas
(B) Hercules
(C) Minerva
(D) Hydra

45. The character in the Bible who is famous for his wisdom is
(A) Methuselah
(B) King David
(C) Moses
(D) Solomon

46. Which of the following is the title of an epic poem by Homer?
(A) the *Iliad*
(B) the *Republic*

(C) *Antigone*
(D) the *Aeneid*

47. In the Bible, what happens to Jonah?
    (A) He has a dream that God wants him to kill his son
    (B) He is swallowed by a large fish
    (C) He lives very long and has many children
    (D) He kills his brother

48. What character in a Mark Twain novel is known for his clever ways of avoiding work and trouble?
    (A) Tom Sawyer
    (B) Huckleberry Finn
    (C) Jim
    (D) Oliver

49. In Greek mythology, what is the name of the king whose touch turns objects into gold?
    (A) Methuselah
    (B) Dionysus
    (C) Minos
    (D) Midas

50. Which of the following novels is about an unfaithful woman?
    (A) *Little Women*
    (B) *The Scarlet Letter*
    (C) *This Side of Paradise*
    (D) *The Courtship of Miles Standish*

51. What is the title of a novel about two children affected by community conflict when their father defends a black man in court?
    (A) *Dark Laughter*
    (B) *Main Street*
    (C) *To Kill a Mockingbird*
    (D) *The Maltese Falcon*

52. Dickens' novel *A Tale of Two Cities* takes place during what period?
    (A) The French Revolution
    (B) The Civil War
    (C) The American Revolution
    (D) The Renaissance

53. What American poet wrote a poem about Paul Revere that includes the lines "One if by land, Two if by sea"?
    (A) Conrad Aiken
    (B) Ogden Nash
    (C) John Greenleaf Whittier
    (D) Henry Wadsworth Longfellow

54. What statesman said, "The only thing we have to fear is fear itself," and "Yesterday, December 7, 1941—a date which will live in infamy..."?
    (A) Franklin D. Roosevelt
    (B) Winston Churchill
    (C) Joseph Stalin
    (D) Harry Truman

55. In addition to plays, what literary forms did Shakespeare work with?
    (A) Novels
    (B) Sonnets
    (C) Novellas
    (D) Short stories

56. In Roman mythology, the god of war is named
    (A) Vulcan
    (B) Mercury
    (C) Mars
    (D) Saturn

57. What public figure said, "I have nothing to offer, but blood, toil, tears, and sweat," and, "From Stettin in the Baltic to Trieste in the Adriadic, an Iron Curtain has descended across the continent"?
    (A) Neville Chamberlain

(B) John F. Kennedy
(C) Queen Elizabeth II
(D) Winston Churchill

58. What playwright wrote *Death of a Salesman* and *The Crucible*?
(A) Arthur Miller
(B) Clare Booth Luce
(C) Oscar Wilde
(D) Tennessee Williams

59. What statesman said, "And so, my fellow Americans, ask not what your country can do for you; ask what you can do for your country"?
(A) Abraham Lincoln
(B) John F. Kennedy
(C) Franklin D. Roosevelt
(D) Ronald Reagan

60. In Greek mythology, who traveled in quest of the Golden Fleece?
(A) Hercules
(B) Ulysses
(C) Jason
(D) Odysseus

61. Who wrote *The Great Gatsby,* a novel about the pursuit of wealth and status in the 1920s?
(A) Henry Miller
(B) F. Scott Fitzgerald
(C) Ernest Hemingway
(D) Somerset Maugham

62. What is the name of the character in an ancient Greek play who murders his father and marries his mother?
(A) Achilles
(B) Sophocles
(C) Oedipus
(D) Heroditus

63. From the Greek epic Iliad, we have the expression "Achilles heel." What is the meaning of the expression?
(A) Someone who complains too much
(B) Someone who doesn't take responsibility for himself or herself
(C) A nagging source of irritation
(D) A weak point in a strong person

64. In Greek mythology, what happens to Icarus and his father Daedalus?
(A) They anger Zeus by playing a practical joke and are exiled on the island of Corinth
(B) They make wax-and-feather wings to escape their prison, but Icarus flies too close to the sun, his wings melt, and he falls into the sea and drowns
(C) They ride the winged horse Pegasus so far and long that Zeus becomes furious and turns them into statues
(D) They free their townspeople from the Hydra, but Icarus makes the mistake of looking into the Hydra's eyes and he is turned to stone

65. What is the name of the mythical hero whose journey home after the Trojan War is described in a famous Greek epic?
(A) Achilles
(B) Odysseus
(C) Alexander the Great
(D) Hercules

66. What are the literary figures Byron, Keats, and Wordsworth chiefly known as?
(A) Playwrights
(B) Novelists
(C) Short-story writers
(D) Poets

67. What is the name of the knight in a famous Spanish romance who attacks

windmills, thinking they are giants?
(A) Don Quixote
(B) Sancho Panza
(C) Cervantes
(D) La Mancha

68. What is the name of a play about a man whose ambition to be king leads him to murder?
(A) *The Crucible*
(B) *Romeo and Juliet*
(C) *Faust*
(D) *Macbeth*

69. "To every thing there is a season, and a time to every purpose under the heaven: a time to be born, and a time to die..."

From what book is the above quote from?
(A) *The Sun Also Rises*
(B) *Things Fall Apart*
(C) the Rig-Veda
(D) The Bible

70. What is the name of the epic poem in which the hero battles the monster Grendel?
(A) *Lord of the Rings*
(B) the *Odyssey*
(C) *Beowulf*
(D) the *Aeneid*

71. Which poet wrote *The Waste Land*, "The Love Song of J. Alfred Prufrock," and "The Hollow Men"?
(A) Ezra Pound
(B) T. S. Eliot
(C) Babette Deutsch
(D) Robert Frost

72. In Greek mythology, what is the cause of the Trojan War?
(A) Paris of Troy kidnaps Helen, a beautiful Greek woman
(B) Paris of Troy steals the golden apple of discord from Zeus
(C) The Trojans refuse the gift of a large wooden horse from the Greeks
(D) The Trojans steal the golden apple of discord from the Greeks

73. What collection contains the maxims "A penny saved is a penny earned" and "A small leak will sink a great ship"?
(A) Jefferson's diary
(B) *Poor Richard's Almanack*
(C) The Proverbs section of the Old Testament
(D) Aesop's fables

74. Who wrote "The Minister's Black Veil," "Young Goodman Brown," and "Rappaccini's Daughter"?
(A) Ambrose Bierce
(B) Washington Irving
(C) Nathaniel Hawthorne
(D) Walt Whitman

75. What is the title of a novel about a man who battles a great fish?
(A) *The Old Man and the Sea*
(B) *The Sea Wolf*
(C) *Ship of Fools*
(D) *You Can't Go Home Again*

76. What is the name of the epic poem by John Milton about the rebellion of Satan and fall of Adam and Eve?
(A) *This Side of Paradise*
(B) *Paradise Lost*
(C) *The Guardian Angel*
(D) *East of Eden*

77. What is John Steinbeck's novel *The Grapes of Wrath* about?
(A) The struggles of labor leader Cesar

Chavez
(B) The power of wealth to corrupt
(C) A family that migrates from the Dust Bowl to California
(D) A man who travels around the country with his dog

78. What is the name of a Greek play about a woman who defies the orders of a king to honor her dead brother?
(A) *Mourning Becomes Electra*
(B) *Antigone*
(C) *Oedipus Rex*
(D) *Troilus and Cressida*

79. Turning and turning in the widening gyre
The falcon cannot hear the falconer;
Things fall apart; the center cannot hold;
Mere anarchy is loosed upon the world...

What work are the above lines from?
(A) "The Love Song of J. Alfred Prufrock" by T. S. Eliot
(B) *Things Fall Apart* by Chinua Achebe
(C) The Bible
(D) "The Second Coming" by William Butler Yeats

80. In Greek mythology, who is punished for stealing fire by being chained to a rock and having a vulture eat his liver?
(A) Hercules
(B) Pericles
(C) Prometheus
(D) Thucydides

81. What is the name of the novel about a character named Heathcliff's obsessive love of Catherine?
(A) *Pride and Prejudice*
(B) *Middlemarch*
(C) *Great Expectations*
(D) *Wuthering Heights*

82. Who wrote *Pygmalion, Arms and the Man,* and *Saint Joan*?
(A) George Bernard Shaw
(B) Eugene O'Neill
(C) Oliver Wendell Holmes
(D) Oscar Wilde

83. Who in the Bible is known for his great patience during suffering?
(A) Cain
(B) Job
(C) King David
(D) Solomon

84. What poet of the Harlem Renaissance wrote *Not Without Laughter*?
(A) Langston Hughes
(B) Le Roi Jones
(C) William Du Bois
(D) Ralph Ellison

85. Who wrote *The Canterbury Tales*?
(A) Andrew Marvell
(B) William Shakespeare
(C) Geoffrey Chaucer
(D) Francis Bacon

86. Who wrote *Billy Budd,* "Benito Cereno,"and "Bartleby the Scrivener"?
(A) Stephen Crane
(B) Herman Melville
(C) James Fenimore Cooper
(D) Jack London

87. What is the name of the novel by George Orwell about a dictatorship that watches everyone in order to stamp out individuality?
(A) *A Clockwork Orange*
(B) *Brave New World*
(C) *1984*
(D) *This Perfect Day*

88. What is the name of a novel about children stranded on an island who try but fail to lead a civilized life?
    (A) *Robinson Crusoe*
    (B) *Tom Sawyer*
    (C) *Treasure Island*
    (D) *Lord of the Flies*

89. In the Bible, what cities are destroyed because of the wickedness of their inhabitants?
    (A) Galilee and Jerusalem
    (B) Sodom and Gomorrah
    (C) Bethlehem and Babylon
    (D) Tigris and Euphrates

90. What is the name of the work by Dante about a journey through Hell, Purgatory, and Heaven?
    (A) *the Divine Comedy*
    (B) *Paradise Lost*
    (C) *the Decameron*
    (D) *Don Giovanni*

91. What black American writer wrote *Native Son,* about black life in Chicago, and *Back Box*?
    (A) Langston Hughes
    (B) Richard Wright
    (C) Ralph Ellison
    (D) Eldridge Cleaver

92. What is the name of the English author who wrote "The Rocking Horse Winner," *Women in Love,* and *Sons and Lovers*?
    (A) Lawrence Durell
    (B) Virginia Woolf
    (C) D. H. Lawrence
    (D) Geoge Eliot

93. What is the name of the American novelist and short-story writer who celebrated pioneer traditions of the Nebraska prairies and the deserts of the Southwest in works such as *My Antonia, Death Comes for the Archbishop*, and *O Pioneers!*?
    (A) Josephine Preston Peabody
    (B) Willa Cather
    (C) Ellen Glasgow
    (D) Harriet Elizabeth Prescott Spofford

94. What American playwright wrote *A Streetcar Named Desire* and *The Glass Menagerie*?
    (A) Tennessee Williams
    (B) Arthur Miller
    (C) George Abbott
    (D) Eugene O'Neill

95. What American novelist and short-story writer wrote "In Another Country," "The Short Happy Life of Francis Macomber," and "The Killers"?
    (A) Henry Miller
    (B) Ernest Hemingway
    (C) Robert Herrick
    (D) Stephen Crane

96. What English novelist wrote *The Return of the Native, Tess of D'Urbervilles*, and *The Mayor of Casterbridge*?
    (A) Charles Dickens
    (B) Geoge Eliot
    (C) Thomas Hardy
    (D) Charlotte Bronte

97. What is the title of the novel about a 16-year-old boy who is expelled from prep school, goes to New York for the weekend, and has an emotional breakdown?
    (A) *The Bell Jar*
    (B) *Addie Pray*
    (C) *Catcher in the Rye*
    (D) *East of Eden*

98. What author wrote about the encounters of

American heroines with European culture in *Daisy Miller* and *Portrait of a Lady*?
(A) Ezra Pound
(B) T. S. Eliot
(C) Thomas Wolfe
(D) Henry James

99. Who is the author of *Hedda Gabler, A Doll's House*, and *An Enemy of the People*?
(A) Marcel Proust
(B) Honore de Balzac
(C) Henrik Ibsen
(D) Robert Browning

100. Who wrote *Heart of Darkness, Lord Jim*, and *The Secret Sharer*?
(A) Joseph Conrad
(B) Henry James
(C) Henry Fielding
(D) James Joyce

101. What novel by black American writer Ralph Ellison is abut a young man who grows up in the South and moves to Harlem?
(A) *A Tree Grows in Brooklyn*
(B) *Invisible Man*
(C) *The Souls of Black Folk*
(D) *All God's Chillun Got Wings*

102. What Russian author wrote *Crime and Punishment* and *The Brothers Karamazov?*
(A) Pushkin
(B) Tolstoy
(C) Dostoevsky
(D) Nabokov

103. What is the name of the Irish author who wrote *Ulysses, A Portrait of the Artist as a Young Man*, "Araby," and "Eveline"?

(A) Flannery O'Connor
(B) James Joyce
(C) George Bernard Shaw
(D) W. B. Yeats

104. What is the name of the European statesman and author who traveled in the U.S. in the early years of this country's independence and wrote *Democracy in America?*
(A) Henry David Thoreau
(B) Jean Jacques Rousseau
(C) Alexis de Tocqueville
(D) Matthew Arnold

105. _____! _____! burning bright
In the forests of the night,
What immortal hand or eye
Could frame thy fearful symmetry?

What does William Blake refer to in the above poem?
(A) A forest fire
(B) A tiger
(C) A demon
(D) A goddess

106. What is the name of the novel about the temptations that Christians face in life?
(A) Geoffrey Chaucer's *The Canterbury Tales*
(B) Jonathan Swift's *Gulliver's Travels*
(C) Henry Fielding's *Tom Jones*
(D) John Bunyan's *Pilgrim's Progress*

ANSWERS! ☞

Numbers in parentheses represent the percentage of high-school students who answered that question correctly.

History

1. C (95.2)
2. D (92.1)
3. B (91.1)
4. B (87.9)
5. C (87.7)
6. C (87.5)
7. D (87.4)
8. A (87.4)
9. A (87.2)
10. D (84.8)
11. A (83.9)
12. C (83.8)
13. B (81.3)
14. A (81.3)
15. D (80)
16. A (79.9)
17. D (79.2)
18. C (78.1)
19. D (78.1)
20. D (77.4)
21. B (77.3)
22. A (76.1)
23. A (76.1)
24. C (76.1)
25. B (75.8)
26. C (75.1)
27. D (74.6)
28. A (72.1)
29. B (71.7)
30. A (71.3)
31. B (71.0)
32. C (70.7)
33. D (70.7)
34. C (70.7)
35. D (70.7)
36. C (70.3)
37. D (68.9)
38. A (69.7)
39. B (69.7)
40. B (70.2)
41. A (68.1)
42. C (68)
43. B (67.8)
44. B (65.8)
45. A (67.3)
46. B (67.6)
47. D (64.6)
48. D (64.5)
49. A (63.7)
50. B (62.7)
51. B (61.4)
52. C (61)
53. C (60.9)
54. A (60.6)
55. D (60.2)
56. B (60)
57. C (59.9)
58. B (59.5)
59. D (59.4)
60. B (57.8)
61. B (57.7)
62. C (57.3)
63. A (57.1)
64. C (56.4)
65. D (56.3)
66. C (55.6)
67. C (55.4)
68. D (55.2)
69. B (55.1)
70. C (54.7)
71. B (54.7)
72. B (53.8)
73. B (53.6)
74. D (52.8)
75. A (52.3)
76. C (52)
77. B (51.1)
78. C (51)
79. B (50.9)
80. D (50.3)
81. B (50.3)
82. A (49.8)
83. D (48.9)
84. B (48.6)
85. C (47.9)
86. B (47)
87. B (46.9)
88. C (45.6)
89. A (43.8)
90. D (43)
91. C (42.9)
92. D (42.6)
93. A (42.4)
94. C (41.1)
95. B (41)
96. C (40.2)
97. C (40.1)
98. B (39.5)
99. C (39.5)
100. A (39.3)
101. B (38.3)
102. B (38.2)
103. B (38.2)
104. A (38)
105. C (37.8)
106. D (37.7)
107. C (37.6)
108. C (37.3)
109. A (37.2)
110. B (37.1)
111. C (36.9)
112. D (36.8)
113. C (34.3)
114. C (33)
115. D (32.3)
116. C (32.2)
117. B (31.6)
118. B (30.7)
119. D (30.6)
120. B (29.9)
121. A (29.8)

122. C (25.9)
123. A (25.8)
124. C (24.7)
125. D (23.9)
126. C (22.8)
127. A (22.6)
128. B (21.4)
129. A (19.5)

Literature

1. C (94)
2. B (92.3)
3. D (89.7)
4. D (88.1)
5. D (87.8)
6. A (87.2)
7. B (86.7)
8. B (86.1)
9. C (85.7)
10. A (85.1)
11. B (83.6)
12. B (80.5)
13. D (80.5)
14. B (79.5)
15. A (79)
16. D (76.3)
17. C (75.2)
18. C (74.9)
19. B (74.2)
20. B (73.9)
21. D (73.8)
22. C (73.4)
23. B (73)
24. A (72.7)
25. D (72.3)
26. B (72)
27. C (71.8)
28. D (69.5)
29. B (67.7)
30. D (67.3)
31. B (67.2)
32. A (67)

33. C (66.5)
34. C (65.7)
35. A (65.7)
36. A (65.6)
37. C (65.3)
38. D (64)
39. C (63.2)
40. B (62.5)
41. A (61.8)
42. B (61.7)
43. C (61.6)
44. A (61.1)
45. D (61)
46. A (60.6)
47. B (60.2)
48. A (59.8)
49. D (59.5)
50. B (59.4)
51. C (59.1)
52. A (59)
53. D (58.8)
54. A (57.2)
55. B (57)
56. C (56.2)
57. D (55.7)
58. A (53.7)
59. B (52.7)
60. C (52.5)
61. B (51.7)
62. C (51.7)
63. D (51.5)
64. B (50.2)
65. B (49.8)
66. D (48.1)
67. A (47.9)
68. D (47.3)
69. D (46.7)
70. C (45.8)
71. B (45.4)
72. A (45.4)
73. B (43.6)
74. C (43.3)
75. A (43)

76. B (41.2)
77. C (39.7)
78. B (39.1)
79. D (38.1)
80. C (38.5)
81. D (37.9)
82. A (37.5)
83. B (37.2)
84. A (36.2)
85. C (36.1)
86. B (35.9)
87. C (35.5)
88. D (35.3)
89. B (33.4)
90. A (32.8)
91. B (32.3)
92. C (28.7)
93. B (28.2)
94. A (27.6)
95. B (27.3)
96. C (24.4)
97. C (22.5)
98. D (21.9)
99. C (20.3)
100. A (19.3)
101. B (18.3)
102. C (17.1)
103. B (15.6)
104. C (15.5)
105. B (13.6)
106. D (13.4)

INTERIOR DECORATING

Academy of Art College

Decorator: "But, darling, are you sure you want me to install track shelving over the walnut paneling in the dining room so you can display Andy's cookie jars?"

Client: "Just because you didn't buy them for me, darling, doesn't mean they aren't worth looking at."

An interior decorator or designer, according to the National Council for Interior Design Qualification, is someone who: "identifies, researches, and creatively solves problems pertaining to the function of the interior environment; performs services relative to interior spaces, including programming, design analysis, space planning, and esthetics, using specialized knowledge of interior construction, building codes, equipment, materials, and furnishings; and prepares drawings and documents relative to the design of interior spaces in order to enhance and protect the health, safety, and welfare of the public." The interior designer thus requires much more than an esthetic sensibility and familiarity with fabrics; he or she must have acquired much of the technical knowledge commonly associated with the field of architectural design.

In several states, it is illegal to call yourself an interior designer without first acquiring a license, for which the primary requirement is passing the NCIDQ examination; the exam is also a prerequisite to joining one of the professional organizations in the field, such as the American Society of Interior Designers and the Institute of Business Designers. To qualify for taking the exam, you have to have had several years of relevant professional experience, some of which may be substituted by schooling in a university-level interior design program. The exam itself consists of two parts: a 3½-hour multiple-choice section, testing knowledge of such areas as interior design theory, building construction, materials, and history of the field; and a 10-hour design section consisting of a jury-scored realistic design problem involving a design concept statement, space planning, and furniture selection and arrangement.

The questions that follow should give you a fairly clear picture of the sort of knowledge required in the field and on the exam. We've left out questions pertaining to drier, more technical aspects such as drawing up contracts and knowledge of building codes. The questions were provided by Nancy Brown, ASID, a faculty member of the Academy of Art College in San Francisco, which has one of the most highly ranked interior design programs in the country; for information about the courses and degrees they offer, contact the Interior Design Department, Academy of Art College, 2300 Stockton Street, Suite 300, San Francisco CA 94133, tel. (415) 673-4200.

Multiple Choice

1. The science that seeks to adapt the environment to its users is called
   (A) metamerism
   (B) ergonomics
   (C) anthropometrics

2. What one element helps to give balance to a room?
   (A) A window on every wall
   (B) A fireplace
   (C) Matching wallpaper and draperies
   (D) Furniture of varied heights

3. In a formal living room, which two are out of place?
   (A) Damask sofa
   (B) A lambrequin
   (C) Windsor chair
   (D) Bergere chair
   (E) Pewter wall sconces

4. Which two elements are typical of Queen Anne style?
   (A) Cabriole leg
   (B) Straight tapered legs
   (C) Bee motif
   (D) Shell carving

5. Which two elements are typical of Thomas Chippendale's furniture?
   (A) Extensive use of oak
   (B) Chinese fretwork
   (C) Gothic design motifs
   (D) Shield-shaped motifs

6. Which two could be found in a Victorian living room?
   (A) Antimacassers
   (B) Marquetry table
   (C) Eames chair
   (D) Belter chair

7. Where was hard-paste porcelain first successfully produced in Europe?
   (A) England
   (B) France
   (C) Saxony
   (D) Holland

8. What two contributions has India made to Western design?
   (A) Batik fabric
   (B) Copper pots
   (C) Dhurrie rugs
   (D) Paisley prints

9. Three leaders of the Bauhaus School were
   (A) William Morris
   (B) Walter Gropius
   (C) John Goddard
   (D) Le Corbusier
   (E) Mies van der Rohe
   (F) Frank Lloyd Wright

10. Which two would not be seen in a Roman villa?
    (A) Ceramic tile
    (B) Trompe l'oeil
    (C) A triptych
    (D) A vitrine
    (E) Hot water pipes

11. Two items that could be found in an informal living room include
    (A) a pine armoire
    (B) an Aubusson carpet
    (C) a plaid loveseat
    (D) a torchier

12. Which architectural element would best divide a wall?
    (A) Cornice
    (B) Dado
    (C) Soffit
    (D) Corbel

13. What is the best lighting for a dining room?
    (A) Chandelier
    (B) Recessed ceiling lights
    (C) Spots and uplights
    (D) All of the above

14. Which two materials conduct most heat and cold?
    (A) Brick
    (B) Glass
    (C) Metal
    (D) Wood
    (E) Cork

15. Which two design elements can add drama to a room?
    (A) Deep wall color
    (B) A lot of accessories
    (C) One well-lighted piece of art
    (D) A variety of patterns

16. Which three are natural fibers?
    (A) Silk
    (B) Rayon
    (C) Cotton
    (D) Ramie
    (E) Acetate

17. Choose three ways to make a room seem larger.
    (A) Paint walls a cool color
    (B) Use a lot of pattern
    (C) Use several large upholstered pieces
    (D) Upholster main pieces in light, solid-colored fabric
    (E) Use some mirror

18. What two events influenced 17th-century European furniture styles and decorative arts?
    (A) Versailles became a royal residence
    (B) Edict of Nantes revoked

(C) Dutch East India Company founded
(D) England established a colony in Virginia

19. What two events influenced 18th-century European furniture styles and decorative arts?
    (A) Formula for hard-paste porcelain perfected
    (B) Louis XVI and Marie Antoinette beheaded
    (C) Industrial Revolution
    (D) American Revolution

20. What two events influenced 19th-century furniture styles and decorative arts?
    (A) Napoleon's conquest of Egypt
    (B) Source of Ganges River discovered
    (C) Excavations at Pompeii
    (D) Italian Republic established

21. What one invention has had the greatest influence on 20th-century furniture and decorative arts?
    (A) Invention of atomic power
    (B) Invention of plastics
    (C) Invention of frequency modulation

22. One way to identify a Persian rug is
    (A) shag pile
    (B) lack of human form as a design element
    (C) pastel coloring

23. The best light to read by is
    (A) ambient lighting
    (B) shielded task lighting
    (C) track lighting

24. Which two color combinations stimulate us to be active?
    (A) Pastel pink and white
    (B) Lemon chiffon and celadon green

(C) Candy apple red and forest green
(D) Orange and mustard yellow

25. Which two statements are *not* true?
(A) Warm hues are restful
(B) The only true neutral colors are black, white, and gray
(C) Complementary hues are directly opposite on the color wheel
(D) Objects appear smaller against a dark wall

26. What three factors are important to discuss with a client during the first interview?
(A) Client's lifestyle
(B) Client's education
(C) Client's budget restrictions
(D) Site restrictions
(E) City codes

27. What three factors would be considered when laying out a furniture plan for a living room?
(A) Which existing pieces of furniture will be used
(B) What color does client prefer
(C) What is circulation pattern
(D) Where will television be placed
(E) What window treatment will be used

28. What one factor is most important when mixing patterns?
(A) You must like them all
(B) Patterns must vary in size
(C) All patterns should be made of the same fabric

29. New laws require contract designers to consider what three areas?
(A) Energy efficiency
(B) Color codes
(C) The handicapped
(D) Hazardous materials
(E) Maintenance standards

30. What two pieces of furniture are uniquely American?
(A) Handkerchief table
(B) Hitchcock chair
(C) Hunt table
(D) Pembroke table

31. The two best qualities of wool carpet are its
(A) resistance to soil
(B) resistance to insects
(C) resistance to static
(D) durability

32. Since the 1950s most carpet has been manufactured on
(A) a tufting loom
(B) a Jacquard loom
(C) an Axminster loom

33. Japanning is
(A) furniture made in the Japanese style
(B) a technique of applying a lacquer finish to furniture
(C) Japanese calligraphy

34. Two important factors when planning a new kitchen include
(A) task and ambient lighting
(B) traffic patterns
(C) wine storage
(D) display space

35. Three 20th-century furniture designers are
(A) Eero Saarinen
(B) Henry Belter
(C) Michael Thonet
(D) Duncan Phyfe
(E) Marcel Breuer
(F) John Goddard

36. Three 20th-century architects are
(A) Frank Lloyd Wright

(B) Andrea Palladio
(C) Philip Johnson
(D) Michael Graves
(E) Christopher Wren
(F) James Hoban

37. Who was the first American interior decorator?
    (A) Nancy McClelland
    (B) Elsie de Wolfe
    (C) Letitia Baldrige
    (D) Diana Vreeland

38. Two factors that determine the successful design of a room are
    (A) using all of the client's furniture
    (B) the color scheme
    (C) the furniture arrangement
    (D) the placement of windows and doors

39. What three factors are important in the furniture arrangement of a room?
    (A) Balance
    (B) Style
    (C) Scale
    (D) Budget
    (E) Proportion

40. Balance in furniture arrangement is defined as
    (A) good distribution of weight, height, and size
    (B) good distribution of colored objects
    (C) good distribution of client's own furniture

41. Which is not a good utilization of space in a dead corner?
    (A) A decorative screen
    (B) An important object of art
    (C) Conversation grouping
    (D) A specimen plant

42. What one factor must be considered when laying out the plan for a living room?
    (A) Book storage
    (B) Conversation grouping
    (C) Display of art collection
    (D) Entertainment center

43. Three ways to achieve color harmony include
    (A) use equal areas of contrasting colors
    (B) contrast light against dark
    (C) use equal amounts of warm and cool colors
    (D) contrast bright against dull
    (E) use bits of white, no matter what the scheme
    (F) use equal amounts of shades

44. Which two medical environments should be painted in a cool color?
    (A) Pediatric area
    (B) Orthopedic ward
    (C) Physiotherapy room
    (D) Psychiatric ward

45. To practice interior design in most states one needs
    (A) a contractor's license
    (B) an architect's license
    (C) a resale or sales tax number
    (D) a college degree

46. Which two are not part of the styling of a sofa?
    (A) Knife edge
    (B) Kick pleat
    (C) Jabot
    (D) Dovetail
    (E) Welting

47. Which three are not part of detailing of a breakfront?

(A) Gallery
(B) Escutcheon
(C) Dado
(D) Chevel glass
(E) Broken pediment
(F) Gimp

48. The National Trust for Historic Preservation was founded by
(A) the Daughters of the American Revolution (the DAR)
(B) the American Institute of Architects (AIA)
(C) the Congress of the United States

49. In textile weaving, which two statements are *incorrect?*
(A) Warp threads run lengthwise on the loom
(B) A damask pattern is woven on a Jacquard loom
(C) Jacquard weaves produce a smooth, glossy fabric
(D) Twill weaves show definite horizontal lines
(E) Pile weaves make a three-dimensional fabric

50. Three decorative objects unique to France are
(A) a Chinese export porcelain
(B) a Sevres figurine
(C) a Gobelin tapestry
(D) a silver epergne
(E) a trumeau
(F) a Capo di Monte bowl

51. Three decorative objects unique to America are
(A) scrimshaw
(B) a banjo clock
(C) salt-glazed stoneware
(D) Moravian fancywork
(E) painted tinware

Matching

1. Match best use of following types of lighting:
(A) halogen
(B) fluorescent
(C) incandescent

(1) warm, soft, low light level
(2) special effects
(3) energy efficient, high light level

2. Match material with typical style:
(A) marble
(B) gold leaf
(C) chrome
(D) wrought iron

(1) Louis XV
(2) Jacobean
(3) Victorian
(4) Art deco

3. Match what is ideal distance between
(A) sofa and coffee table
(B) occupied dining chair
(C) occupied desk chair

(1) 3 feet
(2) 1 foot
(3) 1½ to 2 feet

4. Match style/period with typical wood used in furniture making:
(A) black walnut
(B) mahogany
(C) pine
(D) teak
(E) satinwood
(F) oak

(1) Louis XVI
(2) Queen Anne
(3) Colonial American
(4) Victorian
(5) Arts and Crafts
(6) Ming

5. Arrange the following pieces of furniture on the plan below, keeping in mind balance, traffic patterns, conversational groupings, and television viewing. The room is 19 by 15 feet and one square equals one foot. Furniture sizes are given in inches.

(1) sofa (84 wide by 30 deep)
(2) coffee table (60 by 24)
(3) 2 club chairs (30 by 30)
(4) occasional table (18 by 28)
(5) chest (34 by 18 by 28 high)
(6) cabinet with doors (42 by 20 by 72 high)
(7) ottoman (30 by 24)
(8) round occasional table (30 by 30)
(9) wing chair (30 by 34)
(10) floor lamp with tray table (12 by 12)
(11) three table lamps

6. Match decorative object with period or style:

   (A) stained-glass lamp
   (B) Wedgewood urn
   (C) faience bowl
   (D) wrought-iron weathervane
   (E) lacquer screen

   (1) French Provincial
   (2) Art Nouveau
   (3) Pennsylvania Dutch
   (4) Chinese
   (5) Georgian

7. Match the following color term with the definition:

   (A) tint
   (B) hue
   (C) chroma
   (D) value

   (1) degree of intensity of a color
   (2) a hue to which white is added
   (3) degree of lightness or darkness of a color
   (4) a specific tint or shade

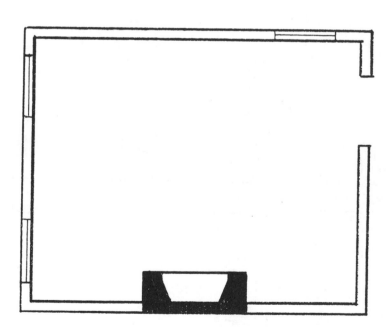

8. From the sketch below, match the chair
   back and legs to the appropriate period or
   style.
   (A) Ming
   (B) Hepplewhite
   (C) Chippendale
   (D) French Provincial
   (E) Louis XVI
   (F) Thonet bentwood
   (G) Queen Anne
   (H) Bauhaus/Breuer

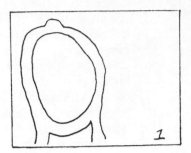

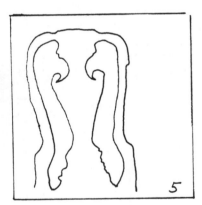

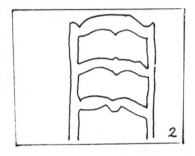

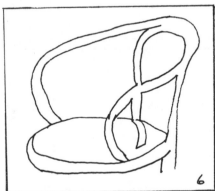

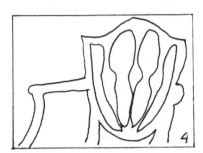

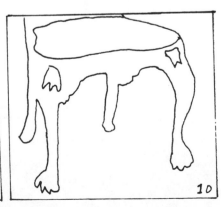

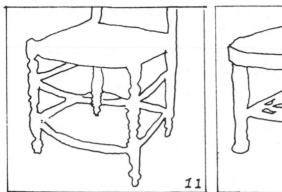

11

12

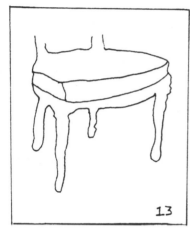

13

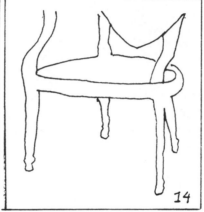

14

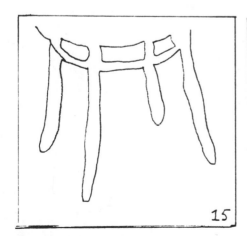

15

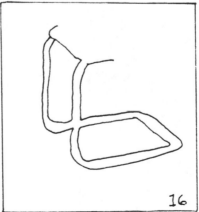

16

ANSWERS!☞

Multiple Choice

1. B
2. D
3. C and E
4. A and D
5. B and C
6. A and D
7. C
8. C and D
9. B, D, and E
10. C and D
11. A and C
12. B
13. D
14. B and C
15. A and C
16. A, C, and D
17. A, D, and E
18. B and C
19. A and C
20. A and C
21. B
22. B
23. B
24. C and D
25. A and D
26. A, C, and D
27. A, C, and D
28. B
29. A, C, and D
30. A and B
31. A and D
32. A
33. B
34. A and B
35. A, C, and E
36. A, C, and D
37. B
38. B and C
39. A, C, and E
40. A
41. C

42. B
43. B, D, and E
44. C and D
45. C
46. C and D
47. C, D, and F
48. C
49. C and D
50. B, C, and E
51. A, B, and D

Matching

1. A: 2
    B: 3
    C: 1
2. A: 3
    B: 1
    C: 4
    D: 2
3. A: 2
    B: 3
    C: 1
4. A: 4
    B: 2
    C: 3
    D: 6
    E: 1
    F: 5
5. See two answers on next page
6. A: 2
    B: 5
    C: 1
    D: 3
    E: 4
7. A: 2
    B: 4
    C: 1
    D: 3
8. A: 7 and 9
    B: 4 and 14
    C: 3 and 12
    D: 2 and 11

E: 1 and 13
F: 6 and 15
G: 5 and 10
H: 8 and 16

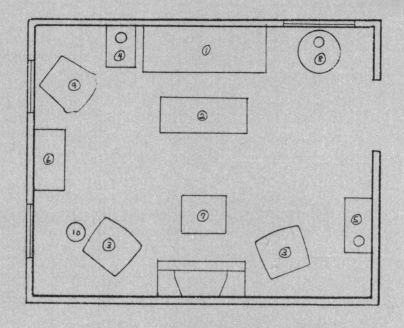

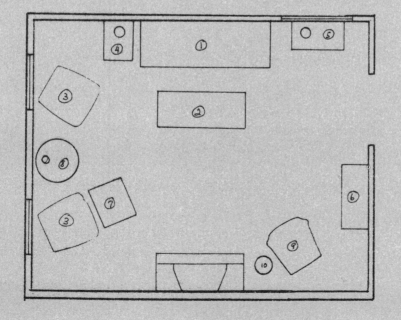

JAPANESE UNIVERSITY ADMISSIONS EXAM

Kyotsu Ichiji

たかが入試、されど入試！

One of the most notorious elements of the Japanese educational system is the *Kyotsu Ichiji*, or national university entrance exam. Unlike the SAT exam, the Japanese university exam is a test not so much of aptitude as of substantive knowledge that one is expected to acquire in high school. Actually, no one is expected to acquire all of the knowledge tested in the exam in the normal course of high school, and realistically no one does. Hence, even the best students may hire tutors, at fees of perhaps $40 an hour at the current exchange rate, for periods of a year or maybe even two, to help them perform well on the exam.

A number of students each year commit suicide because of this test, either worn out from the stress of preparing for it, or because of the loss of face in failure. The one consolation for the student is that, once he or she gains admission to a university, all the hard work is pretty much over. In the U.S., we're used to high school being a typically frivolous affair, with college being somewhat more demanding, and grad school being downright grueling. In Japan, the system is more or less reversed. While high school is stressful and demanding, college is a time to drink copious amounts of beer and *sake* and maybe do a little schoolwork on the side; the job one gets afterward is determined much more by where one goes to school than how one does *in* school.

The exam consists of about a dozen subjects, of which the student is required to take seven. Of those seven, three (Math, English, and Japanese) are obligatory; the remaining four must be chosen from the natural and social science categories.

From the exam, we have chosen 10 from the World History section and 5 from a section that could be translated roughly as Social Relations. These questions are from the most recent *Kyotsu Ichiji*.

World History

As the characteristics of war differ according to place and time, so too peace has had different meanings throughout history.

The so-called "Pax Romana" (Roman Peace) was synonymous with domination by Rome. In medieval Europe, "peace by God" came to be advocated by the Church to prohibit fighting among secular leaders as a means of settling disputes. At the same time, however, the Church did involve Europe in warfare against "heathens" or "heretics." At the time of the Crusades, the Pope _____, who
1
achieved the Church's greatest power—of which the humiliation of the English King John was one manifestation—instituted severe anti-Semitic policies.

In Asia, too, various conceptions of peace emerged. In China, for example, among the thinkers of the ancient time, _____ proclaimed absolute aversion to
2
war, appealing to mercy, charity, and love of one's fellow man and to pacifism, while Meng-tsu urged the unification of China under peace by the "Royal (or Divine) Conduct."

1. Of the following statements, select the wrong one.
   (A) The period of "Pax Romana" usually refers to the time between Augustus and the Five Good Emperors
   (B) The territory of the Roman Empire was largest at the time of Trajan
   (C) Roman citizenship was gradually granted to the nearby people under their domination
   (D) Christianity, which called for the liberation of slaves, became the Empire's religion and slavery disappeared

2. Select the name of the Pope who fits (**1**) in the passage above:
   (A) Gregory VII
   (B) Urban II
   (C) Innocent III
   (D) Boniface VIII

3. Select the name of the thinker who fits (**2**) in the passage above:
   (A) Mo-tzu
   (B) Sun-tzu
   (C) Shang Yang
   (D) Hsün-tzu

Due to the Reformation and the rise of absolutist nations, the old orders of medieval Europe collapsed. As a result, numerous wars took place in modern Europe. In the 17th century, as a reaction to the calamities of war, new measures for maintaining peace were formulated, including international laws. As a consequence, "peace" often stood for the maintenance of a balance of power among the major powers. The balance of power during the period of absolutism, however, suffered serious damage from the French Revolution and the Napoleonic Wars at the turn of the 19th century. To repair this balance, the Congress of Vienna was held. From then until the 1870s, peace was maintained by the British hegemony, with the potential oppositions among the major powers unresolved.

4. Of the following statements about Grotius, the "Father of International Law," select the correct one.
   (A) He wrote "On the Law of War and Peace" during the Dutch Republic's revolt against Spain

(B) He advocated the reconstruction of the medieval order with the Pope at its center

(C) He considered rational international relations to be based on the natural laws

(D) He said that the foundation of peace lies in the unity of each nation under a strong monarch

5. The principle of "balance of power" was adopted at the Congress of Vienna. Of the following statements about the balance of power at the time of the Congress, select the wrong one:

(A) England adopted an anti-continental policy to prevent any single nation from becoming a superpower

(B) To achieve a balance of power, it was agreed that small countries like Poland should become independent

(C) Major powers yearned for the expansion of their territories, so the meeting was merely a scrambling for new land by the powers

(D) In order to justify the changing of national borders at the major powers' will, a policy of "substitutionism" was adopted, and Austria renounced the Netherlands to acquire Northern Italy

6. With regard to the British hegemony, the situation of general world peace at this time was designated "Pax Britannica." Of the following statements about Pax Britannica, select the correct one:

(A) Under the peace, England did not have wars overseas, and expanded free international trade

(B) What disturbed the power balance of Europe was Russia's advancement into Balkan territories, taking advantage of the decline of the Ottoman Empire

(C) Bismarck, having unified Germany, attempted the expansion of its power, and consequently international tension increased

(D) Because the United States proclaimed the Monroe Doctrine, the English capitalists were not able to advance into Central and South America

World War I brought overwhelming human and material losses. In view of this, the demand for peace and order was strongly made after the war. In this context, the League of Nations was established as the international organization for maintaining peace by collaboration. Among its activities, international meetings were held on disarmament and international security. However, despite such efforts, another war broke out. After World War II, in October 1945, the United Nations was organized to maintain peace despite differences of political systems and individual beliefs, and various organizations were created to promote international collaboration and communication in such areas as security, economics, social affairs, and culture. At the same time, facing such situations as regional disputes and the Cold War, movements of non-alliance and positive neutralism arose, involving independence from the Soviet Union and the United States and anti-colonialism. Yet there were still many international disputes, and many difficulties for the establishment of real international peace.

7. Select the correct combination of countries that were not affiliated with the League of Nations when it was established:

(A) the United States, the Soviet Union,

and Germany
(B) the United States, England, and Japan
(C) China, Vietnam, and India
(D) Germany, France, and England

8. Select the correct statement about the result of the Washington Conference held during 1921-1922:
   (A) the reduction of the annual reparations of Germany was endorsed
   (B) the Japan-England alliance was abrogated
   (C) the maintenance of the Rheinland and mutual security were promised
   (D) warfare as a means for settling international disputes was denounced

9. With regard to the United Nations, select the correct statement from the following:
   (A) the permanent members of the Security Council are the United States, the Soviet Union, England, France, and Japan
   (B) to settle international disputes, the U.N. established NATO
   (C) its headquarters are in Geneva, Switzerland
   (D) UNESCO was established by the U.N. to promote free cultural exchange throughout the world

10. Select the one person who is not an appropriate representative of the movement of non-alliance and neutralism mentioned above:
    (A) Nehru
    (B) Tito
    (C) Franco
    (D) Sukarno

Social Relations

Questions 1–5 refer to the following dialogue:

Student A: The *Kyotsu Ichiji* will be over today. How are you doing so far?

Student B: Not too bad, but I hate to take exams. With all this pressure, I feel like the "right to receive education" that our Constitution assures is the "duty to receive education."

A: You really shouldn't say things like that. There are many people who cannot afford to go to university even though they want to.

B: Right, the right to receive education is one of the fundamental human rights, and sure I know it's important...

A: And also, the right to receive education is a kind of social right, so it has a positive aspect, that is, we are entitled to petition the government for an improvement in the education provided to us.

B: I think it's true, yes. However, take, for example, the problem of textbook authorization. People are arguing that it is virtually a censorship on education by the government. Isn't there another level of consideration which is distinct from the issue of social rights?

A: Yeah, you may be right. After all, there are two kinds of relation between the government and education, one being, say, the right to have freedom, and the other being social rights. And I think this duality makes the issues associated with education especially complicated.

B: Besides, the present system of college entrance, you know, these awful exams, is badly influencing education in general. Of course, we don't have time to argue about it right now.

A: But see, we shouldn't be indifferent to the

real social issues by being too preoccupied with our entrance exam.

B: Well, maybe. Anyway, let's do our best on the rest of the subjects today.

1. Select the statement which is inappropriate as a reason for respecting fundamental human rights:
   (A) the fundamental human rights have been obtained through the struggle against injustice done by the national government
   (B) all individuals live within society, and thus must always act by giving priority to the public welfare of society as a whole
   (C) in order to achieve administration for the people based on the principle of democracy, the assurance of the fundamental human rights is an indispensible prerequisite
   (D) people have rights given by nature, and must be treated equally and assured freedom in terms of them

2. Select the one statement which is inappropriate as an explanation of social rights:
   (A) they were proposed to solve social and economic problems that came about as a result of the development of capitalism
   (B) they were first formulated in the Weimar Constitution, where it also was stated that the right to own property is accompanied by duties
   (C) people suffering from poverty are entitled to request living expenses from the government by making an apppeal to the court, directly on the basis of the social rights defined in Article 25 of the Constitution
   (D) to respond to the social rights, the government must promote the social welfare, social security, and public health

3. It has been debated whether the system of textbook authorization, whereby only those books that are authorized by the Ministry of Education can actually be used as textbooks in elementary and high schools, might be in violation of the Constitution,a and certain Articles of the Constitution are typically cited. Of the following three Articles of the Constitution, mark the invariably-cited one(s) with (1), and mark the one(s) that has (have) no relevance to the issue with (2).
   (A) Prohibition of censorship (Article 21, Section 2)
   (B) Rectification (Article 29, Section 3)
   (C) Freedom of learning (Article 23)

4. Select the government's proper educational policy with regard to the right to liberty:
   (A) the government provides textbooks used in elementary and junior high schools (i.e. at the level of mandatory education) free of charge
   (B) in order to establish rich and varied opportunities for education, the government establishes vocational high schools as well as ordinary ones
   (C) the government enlarges school libraries and enhances accessibility to them
   (D) the government defines the curriculum and demands that teachers follow it
   (E) the government provides scholarships for those who are unable to go to school for financial reasons

5. Select the statement which best describes the social problems representing viola-

tions of fundamental human rights:

(A) the system of public access to information, which is at work at various levels of local government, is not provided for by any national law

(B) the Supreme Court has passed judgement several times on the issue of the ratio of representatives to the Diet. However, the government hasn't yet made any changes in the ratio

(C) even though bodies like Japan National Railways, the Telecommunications Agency, and the Tobacco Agency have become private, the workers in these companies, like public servants, are denied the right to strike due to the highly public nature of their occupation

(D) the government takes the position that giving prayers in an official capacity at the Yasukuni Shrine* might violate the Constitution, which stipulates the separation of church and state; thus, no Prime Ministers have ever given prayers at the shrine

*The Yasukuni Shrine is a highly sacred monument where all those killed in war are symbolically buried. (In Japanese society, dying in war also qualifies one for deification.)

ANSWERS!

World History

1. A
2. C
3. A
4. C
5. B
6. B
7. A
8. B
9. D
10. C

Social Relations

1. B
2. C
3. A: 1
   B: 2
   C: 1
4. D
5. A

MASSAGE THERAPY

Atlanta School of Massage

"Uhh! Oh! Uggh! Whew!"
"That will be $..."
"Uhh! Oh! Uggh!"

Eager to shed its outdated image, the new massage profession has wasted no time in cutting a path for itself as a serious preventive health care option. No longer using the titles masseur and masseuse, the modern-day massage therapist is much more than a manipulator of muscles. He or she has probably had extensive training in a variety of massage techniques in addition to a host of other subjects including anatomy and physiology, hydrotherapy, pathology, and injury repair.

Today, massage therapists entering the field find a great variety of career options from which to choose. Some work closely with the medical field, possibly in tandem with a doctor, chiropractor, or physical therapist. Others may work in health clubs, hotels, and resorts. Others may find they like the privacy of working in their homes, or the independence of setting up their own office or clinic. Massage is also making its way into the corporate world. "On-site" massage has become popular with executives who turn themselves over to the massage therapist for a brief 10- or 15-minute stress-reducing break. Possibly the biggest growth in the massage industry has come in the rapidly expanding field of sports massage.

Training in the massage field can take a variety of different forms. There are around 500 schools teaching massage nationwide. However, of these, there are only 55 in the U.S. and 3 in Canada with their curricula approved by the American Massage Therapy Association, the largest professional organization and regulating body for massage education and practice.

Upon completion of their training, massage therapists may be required to pursue state licensure in order to practice. There are currently only 13 states with statewide massage practitioner-based laws. The majority of states have no statewide laws regulating massage practice, while a few others have laws which regulate establishments only. There is also a great deal of variance between states regarding what constitutes proper training.

The questions that follow were provided by the Atlanta School of Massage, an AMTA-approved school in Atlanta, GA. They are similar to questions that might appear on a licensing exam. Questions 1–9 refer to anatomy and physiology, questions 10–25 to massage theory, practice, and history, and questions 26–32 to hydrotherapy. For more information about courses, contact the Atlanta School of Massage at 2300 Peachford Road, Suite 3200, Atlanta GA 30338, tel. (404) 454-7167.

Anatomy and Physiology

1. An inflammation of a vein is known as
   (A) a varicose
   (B) phlebitis
   (C) nephritis
   (D) venules

2. The prevention of the backflow of blood in the veins is caused by
   (A) vesicles
   (B) venules
   (C) valves
   (D) all of the above

3. Muscle action where the muscle remains the same length and increases in tension is called
   (A) isotonic
   (B) isometric
   (C) tetanic
   (D) both A and B

4. What type of joint is between the thumb and hand?
   (A) saddle
   (B) ball and socket
   (C) hinge
   (D) pivot

5. Lateral refers to
   (A) a plane divided between upper and lower halves of the body
   (B) towards the midline of the body
   (C) away from the midline of the body
   (D) movement in a superior direction

6. What muscle originates on the sternum and inner border of the clavicle?
   (A) Splenius capitis
   (B) Scalenes
   (C) Semispinalis
   (D) Sternocleidomastoid

7. The following muscles help stabilize the scapula for movement of the arm:
   (A) anterior serratus and rhomboids
   (B) trapezius and triceps
   (C) rhomboids and gluteles
   (D) levator scapulae and pectoralis major

8. The four basic types of tissue are
   (A) muscle, nervous, epithelial, and connective
   (B) nervous, squamous, muscle, and connective
   (C) simple, compound, complex, and stratified
   (D) none of the above

9. What effect will stimulation of the parasympathetic nervous system have on heart rate?
   (A) It will decrease heart rate
   (B) It will increase heart rate
   (C) It will have no effect
   (D) None of the above

Massage Theory

1. The semimembranosus is located in the
   (A) posterior arm
   (B) posterior thigh
   (C) posterior leg
   (D) hand

2. Through which of the following does lymph drain from the arms and breasts?
   (A) Axillary nodes
   (B) Superficial inguinal glands
   (C) Superficial inguinal nodes
   (D) Submaxillary group

3. What type of effleurage is used to encourage lymphatic flow?
   (A) Light and soothing
   (B) Fast and vigorous

(C) Alternating fast and slow
(D) Slow and rhythmic

4. What is the purpose of petrissage?
   (A) To spread lubricant
   (B) To "milk" the muscle of waste products
   (C) To help the patron go to sleep
   (D) All of the above

5. Massage deep into joint spaces or around bony prominences is known as
   (A) vibration
   (B) effleurage
   (C) friction
   (D) petrissage

6. When a client is laying face-up, this position is known as
   (A) prone
   (B) extended
   (C) supine
   (D) none of the above

7. Exercises in which the client does not assist the therapist are known as
   (A) active
   (B) passive
   (C) coordinated
   (D) resistive

8. To whom is the first organized system of massage credited?
   (A) Boll
   (B) Ling
   (C) Johnson
   (D) Kamenetz

9. Which of the following is a contraindication for massage?
   (A) Poor circulation
   (B) Sore muscles
   (C) Severe fatigue
   (D) Severe hypertension

10. When should a massage therapist diagnose clients?
    (A) On the phone
    (B) In the office
    (C) After the massage
    (D) Never

11. Nerve strokes are applied
    (A) with deep pressure
    (B) toward the heart
    (C) away from the heart
    (D) with circular friction

12. The movement of the skeletal structure increasing or decreasing the angle of articulation is known as
    (A) vibration
    (B) palpation
    (C) joint manipulation
    (D) tapotement

13. A continuous shaking or trembling movement is known as
    (A) friction
    (B) palpation
    (C) vibration
    (D) joint manipulation

14. What is the manipulation which involves stretching a joint?
    (A) Flexion
    (B) Circumduction
    (C) Traction
    (D) Chiropractic

15. The best form of heat to produce relaxation prior to a massage is what type?
    (A) electric
    (B) dry
    (C) prolonged
    (D) moist

16. The application of hands and fingers on the surface of the body to detect abnormalities of tissue structure is known as
    (A) vibration
    (B) tapotement
    (C) friction
    (D) palpation

Hydrotherapy

1. Underwater exercises are performed in a
   (A) hydrocollator
   (B) contrast bath
   (C) Hubbard tank
   (D) Russian bath

2. The area of the body for which a sitz bath is used is the
   (A) foot
   (B) pelvis
   (C) knee
   (D) back

3. In Hydrotherapy, the most important effect of water is
   (A) thermal
   (B) sedative
   (C) stimulative
   (D) none of the above

4. The local application of cold produces a condition known as
   (A) hypocontraction
   (B) autoreflex
   (C) vasoconstriction
   (D) vasodilation

5. A medicated pack used externally or internally is called a
   (A) salt glow
   (B) fibre pack
   (C) hydrocollator pack
   (D) poultice

6. What is a chemical pack of silica gel called?
   (A) An atomizer
   (B) A hydrocollator
   (C) A lesion reducer
   (D) A paraffin bath

7. In the early treatment of sprains, contusions, and soft tissue injuries, as well as acute bursitis, the normal procedure is to use
   (A) hot packs
   (B) ice packs
   (C) whirlpool baths in excess of 103 degrees
   (D) exercise

ANSWERS!☛

Anatomy and Physiology

1. B
2. C
3. B
4. A
5. C
6. D
7. A
8. A
9. B

Massage Theory

1. B
2. A
3. D
4. B
5. C
6. C
7. B
8. B
9. D
10. D
11. C
12. C
13. C
14. C
15. D
16. D

Hydrotherapy

1. C
2. B
3. A
4. C
5. D
6. B
7. B

MATH

National Assessment

"I say it's spinach and the hell with it!"

It seems, according to a flurry of recent studies, that America has once again grown complacent after the Sputnik-inspired flowering of science and math programs in our school curricula in the early 60s. Now, however, the foreign threat most often mentioned is Japan. Did you hear about the Japanese semiconductor company that opened a plant in the Southeastern U.S. and was forced to use American grad students to do the same jobs that were done by high-school graduates back home? Or that the *average* Japanese high school student has a higher level of math ability than the top 5 percent of American students enrolled in college prep courses? Such stories and tidbits of information will probably multiply in direct proportion to our perceived loss of economic ground to the Japanese.

The National Assessment of Educational Progress (a federally funded project that has been testing American students regularly since 1969 in such areas as math, reading, literacy, science, and citizenship) is one particularly prominent critic of our educational system in general, and math instruction in particular. According to investigations conducted by NAEP since 1973, our secondary school system is failing to teach high-school students the level of mathematical ability required by our colleges and by the workplace. If things continue this way, warns NAEP, our economic, technological, and scientific growth will suffer.

Actually, there are some encouraging trends over the period of time chronicled by the NAEP assessments. For example, groups that showed poor performance in the early surveys have improved significantly (for example, Blacks, Hispanics and those in the Southeast). Thus, average performance has improved. But the gains are mostly confined to what are referred to as "lower-order skills," with performance in more complex skills showing no improvement in any group. So-called "multistep problems" were handled by a mere 6 percent of high-school students, even though the ability to solve such problems is essential for a wide variety of tasks in the workplace, such as keeping track of inventory in the company warehouse and as a basis for more advanced instruction in our universities.

In the section that follows, the questions from the most recent (1986) NAEP assessment are grouped according to their level of difficulty, from "simple arithmetic facts" to "multistep problem solving and algebra." In the answer section, figures are given for the percentage of students in three age groups—9, 13, and 17—able to handle those levels of difficulty. The questions from the 1982 assessment were chosen by us for their difficulty—none was answered correctly by more than 60 percent of the 17-year-olds. The answer section includes for each question the percentage of 17-year-olds able to provide the correct answer. So if you are able to answer the one that only 5 percent of high-school seniors got right, you might justifiably feel good about yourself—or bad about our educational system.

1986 Assessment Questions

Simple Arithmetic Facts

1. Which of these numbers is closest to 30?
   (A) 20
   (B) 28
   (C) 34
   (D) 40

2. Add
   $$35$$
   $$+\,42$$

Beginning Skills and Understanding

1. Subtract
   (A) 39 – 26 =
   (B) 79 – 45 =

2. Each bag has 10 marbles in it. How many marbles are there in all?
   (A) 10
   (B) 15
   (C) 25
   (D) 140
   (E) 150
   (F) 160
   (G) I don't know

3. Which coins are the same amount of money as a quarter?
   (A) 2 dimes
   (B) 3 nickels and 1 dime
   (C) 3 dimes
   (D) 4 nickels
   (E) I don't know

4. Find the quotient

   $$5\overline{)15}$$

5. Which animal is heavier than a lion?
   (A) Fox
   (B) Seal
   (C) Alligator
   (D) Sheep

6. The animals that weigh less than 100 pounds are
   (A) alligator, sheep, lion
   (B) monkey, sheep, lion
   (C) fox, beaver, monkey
   (D) fox, lion, seal

Basic Operations and Beginning Problem Solving

1. Which is worth the most?
   (A) 11 nickels
   (B) 6 dimes
   (C) 1 half dollar
   (D) I don't know

2. Subtract
   $$604$$
   $$-207$$

3. There are 10 airplanes on the ground. 6 take off and 4 more land. How many are on the ground then?
   (A) 4
   (B) 8
   (C) 14
   (D) 20

4. At the store, the price of a carton of milk is 40¢, an apple is 25¢, and a box of crackers is 30¢. What is the cost of an apple and a carton of milk?
   (A) 55¢
   (B) 65¢
   (C) 70¢
   (D) 95¢

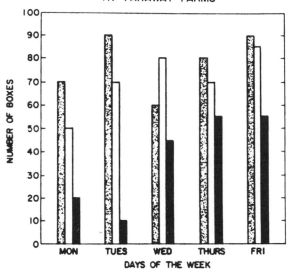

BOXES OF FRUIT PICKED
AT FARAWAY FARMS

ORANGES
LEMONS
GRAPEFRUIT

5. How many boxes of oranges, lemons, and grapefruit were picked on Tuesday?
   (A) 10
   (B) 90
   (C) 170
   (D) 400
   (E) 940
   (F) 1700
   (G) I don't know

6. Find the product
   21
   x 3

7. Sam has 68 baseball cards. Juanita has 127. Which number sentence could be used to find how many more cards Juanita has than Sam?
   (A) 127 – 68 = _____
   (B) 127 + _____ = 68
   (C) 68 – _____ = 127
   (D) 68 + 127 = _____
   (E) I don't know

Moderately Complex Procedures and Reasoning

1. Which of the following is true about 87% of 10?
   (A) It is greater than 10
   (B) It is less than 10
   (C) It is equal to 10
   (D) Can't tell
   (E) I don't know

2. If $7x + 4 = 5x + 8$, then $x =$
   (A) 1
   (B) 2
   (C) 4
   (D) 6

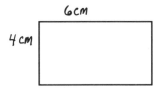

6 CM

4 CM

3. What is the area of this rectangle?
   (A) 4 square cm
   (B) 6 square cm
   (C) 10 square cm
   (D) 20 square cm
   (E) 24 square cm
   (F) I don't know

Refer to the following graph. This graph shows how far a typical car travels after the brakes are applied.

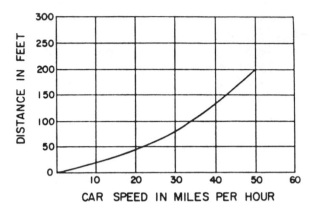

4. A car is traveling 55 miles per hour. About how far will it travel after applying the brakes?
   (A) 25 feet
   (B) 200 feet
   (C) 240 feet
   (D) 350 feet
   (E) I don't know

Questions 5 and 6 refer to the following illustration.

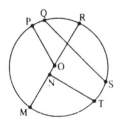

5. Which of the following is a radius of the circle?
   (A) Line OP
   (B) Line QS
   (C) Line RM
   (D) Line NT

6. Which points are the end points of an arc?
   (A) O, P
   (B) Q, S
   (C) N, T
   (D) N, M

Multi-step Problem Solving and Algebra

R	S	40
35	25	15
T	V	W

1. In the figure above, R, S, T, V, and W represent numbers. The figure is called a magic square because adding the numbers in any row or column or diagonal results in the same sum. What is the value of R?
   (A) 30
   (B) 40
   (C) 50
   (D) Can't tell

2. Suppose you have 10 coins and have at least one each of a quarter, a dime, a nickel, and a penny. What is the *least* amount of money you could have?
   (A) 41¢
   (B) 47¢
   (C) 50¢
   (D) 82¢

3. If $f(x) = x^3 - x^2 + x - 4$, what is $f(-3)$?
   (A) –43
   (B) –37
   (C) –1
   (D) 17

4. Christine borrowed $850 for one year from the Friendly Finance Company. If she paid 12% simple interest on the loan, what was the total amount she repaid?

5. Which of the following are equivalent equations?
(A) x + 2 = 9 and x − 2 = 9
(B) y − 3 = 7 and y + 5 = 15
(C) z − 6 = 3 and z = 3
(D) 1 + 2 = w and w + 1 = 2

6. The number of tomato plants (t) is twice the number of pepper plants (p). Which equation best describes the sentence above?
(A) t = 2p
(B) 2t = p
(C) t = 2 + p
(D) 2 + t = p

1982 Assessment

1. Suppose you want to bake some cakes for a party. Two cake recipes require the following amounts of flour:

Pineapple Swirl Cake	Chocolate Velvet Cake
2⅓ cups flour	2½ cups flour

How much flour will be needed to make three Pineapple Swirl Cakes and two Chocolate Velvet Cakes?
(A) 4 $5/6$ cups
(B) 7 cups
(C) 10 $5/6$ cups
(D) 12 cups
(E) 12 $1/6$ cups
(F) I don't know

2. The length of a table measured to the nearest inch is 42 inches. What does this mean about the length of the table?
(A) It is exactly 42 inches
(B) It may be anywhere between 41 inches and 43 inches
(C) It may be anywhere between 41½ inches and 42½ inches
(D) I don't know

3. Which decimal is equal to $5/6$?
(A) .375
(B) .428571
(C) .66
(D) .77
(E) .83
(F) I don't know

4. Linda's new bike cost $159.99 and the sales tax was 5%. How much did she pay including tax?
(A) $164.99
(B) $167.99
(C) $172.98
(D) $177.99
(E) I don't know

5(a). $x^5 \cdot x^7 =$
(A) x^{-2}
(B) x^2
(C) x^{12}
(D) x^{35}
(E) $12x$
(F) $35x$
(G) I don't know

5(b). $\dfrac{x^5}{x^{15}}$
(A) $x^{1/3}$
(B) x^{-3}
(C) x^{-10}
(D) x^{10}
(E) x^{20}
(F) $1/3$
(G) $1/3x$
(H) I don't know

6.
  (A) $6
  (B) $12
  (C) $20
  (D) $25
  (E) $50
  (F) I don't know

ESTIMATE the answer to each of the next two problems. You will not be given enough time to calculate each answer using paper and pencil. Fill in the oval next to the answer CLOSEST to your ESTIMATE.

7(a). 347.0 + 938.0 + 1.327
  (A) 100
  (B) 1,000
  (C) 10,000
  (D) 100,000
  (E) I don't know

7(b). .01 + .0001 + .0000009
  (A) 1
  (B) .01
  (C) .00011
  (D) .1
  (E) I don't know

8. Which one of the following is a quadratic equation?
  (A) $3x^3 + 4x^2 = 8$
  (B) $x^2 + 7x + 9 = 0$
  (C) $ax + b = c$
  (D) $3x + 46 = 17$
  (E) I don't know

9. How many pints are in one quart?
  (A) 2
  (B) 4
  (C) 6
  (D) 8
  (E) I don't know

10. The integers are the numbers
    ...−3, −2, −1, 0, 1, 2, 3...
    If a and b are integers, then a ÷ b is an integer
  (A) always
  (B) sometimes
  (C) never
  (D) I don't know

11. If $y = {}^5/_x$, what happens to y as x increases?
  (A) y increases
  (B) y decreases
  (C) y remains the same
  (D) I don't know

12. A store is offering a discount of 15 percent on fishing rods. What is the amount a customer will save on a rod regularly priced at $25.00?

13. Ms. Robinson spent $2.48 on stamps. She bought some 10¢ stamps and some 16¢ stamps. If she bought 23 stamps, how many 10¢ and 16¢ stamps did she get?

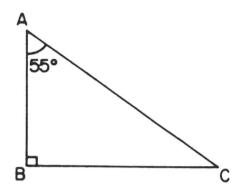

14. ABC is a right triangle. What is the measure of < ABC?
    (A) 35°
    (B) 45°
    (C) 55°
    (D) 90°
    (E) Not enough information given
    (F) I don't know

Income and Expenses of Metro, Co. 1967-1971

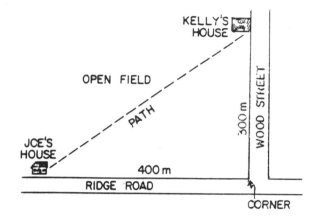

15. According to the graph, in which year did the Metro Company make the largest dollar amount of profit?
    (A) 1967
    (B) 1968
    (C) 1969
    (D) 1970
    (E) 1971

16. On the same day, the highest temperature at Nome, Alaska was 28 degrees below zero, and the highest temperature at Miami, Florida was 78 degrees above zero. What was the difference between the two temperatures?

17. How many pint-sized containers could be filled from a half-gallon carton of milk?

18. Joe's house on Ridge Road is 400 meters from the corner of Ridge Road and Wood Street. Kelly's house is on Wood Street and is 300 meters from the same corner. When Joe goes to Kelly's house, he walks through the open field. How many meters does he walk?
    (A) 450
    (B) 500
    (C) 550
    (D) 600
    (E) I don't know

19. An ALTITUDE of a triangle always
    (A) bisects an angle
    (B) bisects a side
    (C) is perpendicular to a side or its

extension
(D) divides the triangle into two congruent triangles
(E) I don't know

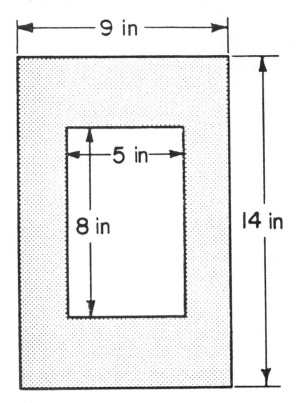

20. What is the area of the shaded part of the figure?

21. Write in decimal form: Forty-two ten-thousandths

22. How is 3,482,000 written in scientific notation?
(A) 3×10^6
(B) 3482×10^3
(C) 3.482×10^6
(D) 3.482×10
(E) I don't know

23. George had $3/4$ of a pie. He ate $3/5$ of that. How much did he eat?
(A) $3/20$
(B) $3/10$
(C) $9/20$
(D) $6/9$
(E) $5/4$

24. Suppose you are playing a game. If you toss a coin and it lands tails you win $3, but if it lands heads you lose $2. If you toss the coin 100 times you will
(A) probably win more money than you lose
(B) be equally likely to win or lose money
(C) probably lose more money than you win
(D) I don't know

25. Which of the following numbers could be written in the form 4m + 3 where m is a counting number?
(A) 25
(B) 28
(C) 31
(D) 80
(E) I don't know

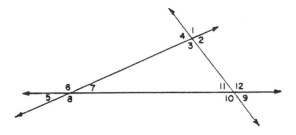

26. What is the sum of the measures of angles 1, 3, 5, 7, 9, 11?
   (A) 180°
   (B) 360°
   (C) 720°
   (D) Not enough information given
   (E) I don't know

27. Arrange the numbers from LEAST to GREATEST: 0.07, 0.4, 0.23, 0.009, 0.1

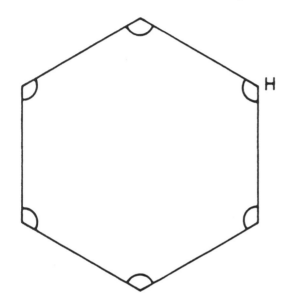

28. The figure above is a regular hexagon. What is the measure of angle H?
   (A) 60°
   (B) 90°
   (C) 115°
   (D) 120°
   (E) 150°
   (F) I don't know

29. Solve this equation for x: ax + b = c + 2

30. A pound of grass seed will cover an area of 400 square feet. How many pounds of grass seed are needed to cover a rectangular yard that is 120 feet long and 90 feet wide?

31. In a coordinate plane a rectangle has vertices at the points (−2,3), (−2, −2), (12, −2) and (12, 3). What is the area of this rectangle?
   (A) 38
   (B) 50
   (C) 70
   (D) 84
   (E) I don't know

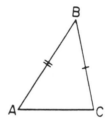 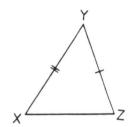

32. In triangles ABC and XYZ, side AB is congruent to side XY, and side BC is congruent to side YZ. Which statement would NOT guarantee that the triangles are congruent?
   (A) Angle A is congruent to angle X, and angle C is congruent to angle Z
   (B) Angle B is congruent to angle Y
   (C) Angle A is congruent to angle X
   (D) Side AC is congruent to side XZ
   (E) I don't know

Amount of Sale	Total
10.19 to 10.51	$.93
10.52 to 10.84	.96
10.85 to 11.18	.99
11.19 to 11.51	1.02
11.52 to 11.84	1.05
11.85 to 12.18	1.08
12.19 to 12.51	1.11

33. Using the sales tax collection chart given on the previous page, find the amount of tax to be added to a sales transaction totaling $12.35.

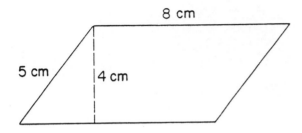

34. The dotted line is an altitude of the parallelogram. What is the area of the parallelogram?

35. Construct a line perpendicular to line A at point P. Use the ruler as a straightedge and the compass. Be sure to show your work.

36. Five people belong to the Tiger Club. No person may hold two offices. How many ways can the club elect a president and secretary?
    (A) 5
    (B) 9
    (C) 10
    (D) 15
    (E) 20
    (F) I don't know

37. Dick drove his parent's car from his house to his grandfather's farm at 40 mph. He returned by bicycle at 8 mph. If the entire trip took three hours, how far is it from his house to his grandfather's farm?

ANSWERS! ☛

1986 Assessment Questions

Simple Arithmetic Facts

Age 9	Age 13	Age 17
97.8	100.0	100.0

1. B
2. 77

Beginning Skills and Understanding

Age 9	Age 13	Age 17
73.8	98.5	99.9

1. (A) 13
   (B) 34
2. E
3. B
4. 3
5. B
6. C

Basic Operations and Beginning Problem Solving

Age 9	Age 13	Age 17
20.8	73.1	96.0

1. B
2. 397
3. B
4. B
5. C
6. 63
7. A

Moderately Complex Procedures and Reasoning

Age 9	Age 13	Age 17
0.6	15.9	51.1

1. B
2. B
3. E
4. C
5. A
6. B

Multi-step Problem Solving and Algebra

Age 9	Age 13	Age 17
0.0	0.4	6.4

1. A
2. B
3. A
4. $952
5. B
6. A

1982 Assessment

Numbers in parentheses indicate the percentage of 17-year-old students that answered correctly.

1. D   (60%)
2. C   (59.3%)
3. E   (58%)
4. B   (57.2%)
5. (A) C (54.2%)
   (B) C (19.5%)
6. C   (53.9%)
7. (A) B (51.3%)
   (B) B (32.6%)

8. B (50.6%)
9. A (49.8%)
10. B (46.8%)
11. B (44.4%)
12. $3.75, 3.75, or 375¢ (44%)
13. Twenty 10¢ and three 16¢ stamps
    (43.6%)
14. A (43.6%)
15. E (43.4%)
16. 106 (43.3%)
17. 4 (41.3%)
18. B (39%)
19. C (36.9%)
20. 86 sq. in. (35.6%)
21. .0042 (32.8%)
22. C (32%)
23. C (29.9%)
24. A (29.2%)
25. C (27.9%)
26. B (27.7%)
27. 0.009, 0.07, 0.1, 0.23, 0.4 (27.2%)
28. D (25.5%)
29. x = $\dfrac{C + s - B}{A}$ (24.8%)

30. 27 (22.9%)
31. C (22.7%)
32. C (22.4%)
33. $1.11 (21.1%)
34. 32 sq. cm (19.2%)
35.

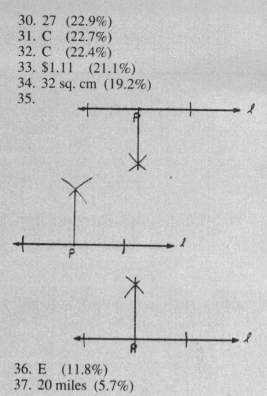

36. E (11.8%)
37. 20 miles (5.7%)

The duties a notary public most often performs are ones of "acknowledgment" and "jurat." In the acknowledgment, the notary certifies:
—that the signer personally appeared before the notary public on the date indicated in the county indicated;
—that the signer's identity is as claimed; and
—that the signer acknowledged signing the document.
The notary must personally know the signer or have "satisfactory evidence" that the signer's identity is as claimed and notarized. "Satisfactory evidence," as defined in the California notary public lawbook, means the absence of any information, evidence, or other circumstances which would lead a "reasonable person" (not defined in the lawbook) to believe that the signer is not the individual he or she claims to be *and* any one of the following:
—the oath or affirmation of a credible witness personally known to the notary that the signer is personally known to the witness;
—reasonable reliance on the presentation to the notary of a valid state DMV identification card or driver's license, U.S. passport, or state inmate identification card; or
—reasonable reliance on the presentation of a foreign passport, other state's or Canadian or Mexican driver's license, other state's DMV identification card or identification card issued by any branch of the U.S. armed forces.

The jurat is identified by the wording, "Subscribed and sworn to" immediately above the place where the notary public signs his or her name. In the jurat, the notary certifies;
—that the signer personally appeared before the notary public on the date and in the county indicated;
—that the signer signed the document in the presence of the notary; and
—that the notary public administered an oath such as, "Do you swear or affirm that the statements in this document are true?" In the jurat, the notary public is not certifying to the identity of the signer.

For his or her services, the notary is permitted to charge fees ranging from $2 to $10, depending on various details of the service performed. It is the *duty* of a notary public to provide notary services to anyone who presents a proper request and pays the required fees. Not providing services when asked could cause the notary to be liable if any damages resulted from the refusal. A notary is also liable for all damages sustained because of official misconduct or neglect. Thus, a notary public who performs an "acknowledgment" for someone with whom he or she is not acquainted and whose identity is not satisfactorily proven will be held liable for any consequent damages.

In order to provide some protection to the public, states require notaries public to be bonded. The amount of the bond in California is $10,000. The bond represents a limited fund for paying claims against the notary, and is not an "insurance policy"; the notary remains personally liable for any damage.

Besides getting together the money for the bond, the process of becoming a notary is fairly simple. In California, any interested party has simply to pass the short open-book test on the following page. Thirteen out of fifteen answered correctly is considered a passing score. The answers must only be notarized to prove that they were indeed supplied by the applicant.

The following examination must be answered before a notary public and certified to by such notary public who shall be entitled to a fee not to exceed $5 for the service. Read and respond to each of the following statements. While taking this examination, you may refer to the booklet containing the laws of the State of California relating to notaries public for assistance in determining whether the following statements are true or false. However, you may not be assisted by any person once you begin reading and responding to the examination. You must answer at least 13 statements correctly. If you fail to answer at least 13 statements correctly, you may not reapply for a commission until the calendar month following the month that you are notified that you failed to pass.

True or False

_____ 1. A notary public who is an immigration specialist cannot advertise that he or she is a notary public

_____ 2. Any duly commissioned notary public is authorized to certify copies of deeds

_____ 3. The statement that a document was signed and sworn to before a notary public is known as a venue

_____ 4. A person who makes a sworn statement is called an affiant

_____ 5. Notaries public may act as such anywhere in the state

_____ 6. The records of a deceased notary public are kept by the county clerk for a minimum of five years

_____ 7. When a document is not acknowledged, proof of execution may be made by a credible witness

_____ 8. "Satisfactory evidence" of identity can be established by a birth certificate

_____ 9. A certificate of acknowledgment must be completely filled out when the notary public signs and seals the document

_____ 10. The form prescribed for acknowledgments is set forth in the Code of Civil Procedure

_____ 11. The form most frequently completed by a notary public is an acknowledgment

_____ 12. The law that contains the requirements to become a notary public is the Business and Professions Code

_____ 13. The forms of identification allowed to establish the identity of persons whose signatures are acknowledged are prescribed by the Secretary of State

_____ 14. The fee for administering an oath to a deponent is $2.00

_____ 15. Documents must be complete before they are notarized

I the undersigned notary public, hereby certify under penalty of perjury, that the applicant named in the foregoing application for a notary public commission personally appeared before me and completed the above examination in my presence.

Executed at_____, California, on_____,19_____

_____
(Signature of Notary Public)

_____
(Type or print name under signature)

POSTAL SERVICE

Clerk and Carrier Exam

A first-class stamp is the biggest bargain in the western world. For that I can't even hire my four-year-old to lick it.

It may come as a surprise to those who think of the postal service in terms of those scowling faces behind bulletproof barriers at the midtown post office, but employment with the USPS is actually about as sought-after as tenure-track positions at Harvard. The pay is good, and the job security and benefits are excellent, so there are often hundreds of eager applicants for each clerk or mail-carrier job opening. Since increased automation more than keeps pace with population growth, positions open up only when existing employees quit, retire, or trundle their mail cart up to heaven (where, it is said, there is only one ZIP code, and hence no need to sort).

For the positions of clerk and carrier, there is a two-part written examination. The first part tests clerical accuracy by requiring the examinee to proofread one column of addresses against another, and the second part tests ability to memorize mail distribution systems. Applicants who score highest are chosen first to fill vacancies, with preference given to veterans.

We have also included Number Series questions, which are part of the Letter Sorting Machine Operator Exam. LSM operator is a salary level 6 position, generally filled from within the postal service organization by salary level 5 clerks and carriers.

Directions: The five boxes below are labelled A, B, C, D, and E. In each box are three sets of number spans with names, and two names which are not associated with numbers. In the next three minutes, you must try to memorize the box location of each name and number span. The position of a name or number span within its box is not important. You need only remember the letter of the box in which the item is to be found. You will use these names and numbers to answer test questions.

A	B	C	D	E
5300-5399 Ford Doyer	1100-3299 Ford Ardsley	3600-3799 Ford School	5800-6099 Ford Church	4500-4799 Ford Arnhem
8500-9199 Ames Popham	6800-8699 Ames Childs	9900-9999 Ames Bryant	2400-2899 Ames Gaines	7600-8699 Ames Kramer
7200-8499 Hilton	2000-2099 Hilton	6100-7299 Hilton	4100-4899 Hilton	1300-1599 Hilton

Memory for Addresses Test
Time Limit: 5 Minutes (88 Questions)

You are NOT permitted to look at the boxes above. Cover them so they are not visible and work from memory, as quickly and as accurately as you can. Number your paper from 1–88. For each of the following addresses write the letter of the box that the address would be found in. Start your timer and begin.

1. 9900-9999 Ames
2. 1300-1599 Hilton
3. 7200-8499 Hilton
4. 1100-3299 Ford
5. Childs
6. Kramer
7. 6100-7299 Hilton
8. 2400-2899 Ames
9. 4500-4799 Ford
10. School
11. Gaines
12. 5300-5399 Ford
13. 7600-8699 Ames
14. 8500-9199 Ames
15. 5800-6099 Ford

16. 2000-2099 Hilton
17. Popham
18. Doyer
19. 3600-3799 Ford
20. 4100-4899 Hilton
21. 6800-8699 Ames
22. Ardsley
23. Arnhem
24. Bryant
25. 8500-9199 Ames
26. 1300-1599 Hilton
27. 5800-6099 Ford
28. Church
29. 5300-5399 Ford
30. 9900-9999 Ames
31. 3600-3799 Ford
32. 6100-7299 Hilton
33. School
34. Childs
35. 2000-2099 Hilton
36. 2400-2899Ames
37. 7600-8699 Ames
38. 7200-8499 Hilton
39. 1100-3299 Ford
40. Kramer
41. Popham
42. 6800-8699 Ames
43. 4100-4899 Hilton
44. 5800-6099 Ford
45. Doyer
46. Ardsley
47. Gaines
48. 4500-4799 Ford
49. 2000-2099 Hilton
50. 9900-9999 Ames
51. 1300-1599 Hilton
52. 5300-5399 Ford
53. Bryant
54. Church
55. 7600-8699 Ames
56. 8500-9199 Ames
57. 1100-3299 Ford
58. 2400-2899 Ames

59. 6100-7299 Hilton
60. Arnhem
61. Popham
62. Kramer
63. 7200-8499 Hilton
64. 6800-8699 Ames
65. 4100-4899 Hilton
66. 5800-6099 Ford
67. 3600-3799 Ford
68. 6100-7299 Hilton
69. 8500-9199 Ames
70. Gaines
71. Doyer
72. 7600-8699 Ames
73. 5300-5399 Ford
74. 4100-4899 Hilton
75. Popham
76. Ardsley
77. 9900-9999 Ames
78. 4500-4799 Ford
79. 7200-8499 Hilton
80. 5800-6099 Ford
81. Church
82. Bryant
83. Kramer
84. 1100-3299 Ford
85. 2400-2899 Ames
86. 2000-2099 Hilton
87. 1300-1599 Hilton
88. 3600-3799 Ford

Address Checking Test
Time Limit: 6 Minutes (95 Questions)

Directions: For each question, compare the address in the left column with the address in the right column. If the two addresses are ALIKE IN EVERY WAY, answer "A." If the two addresses are DIFFERENT IN ANY WAY, answer "D."

1. 4326 NE Ridge Rd   4326 NW Ridge Rd
2. 5182 Sarles Ln   5182 Saries Ln
3. 8490 Roaring Brk Lk   8490 Roaring Brk Lk
4. 2576 Van Cortlandt Pk Ave   2756 Van Cortlandt Pk Ave
5. 5234 Chateau Lorraine   5234 Chateau Larraine
6. Pocatello ID 83209   Pocatello ID 82309
7. 9081 Siscowit Rd   9081 Siscowit Rd
8. 7585 138th Cir Dr   7585 138th Cir Dr
9. 5159 Coachlight Sq Apts   5159 Coachlight Dr Apts
10. 1869 Sprout Brook Pky   1869 Sprout Brook Rd
11. 1445 Riverview Ave   1455 Riverview Ave
12. 2588 Somerstown Ctr   2588 Somerston Ctr
13. 1864 W Lefurgy Ave   1864 N Lefurgy Ave
14. 8297 Fort Hill Village   8297 Fort Hill Village
15. 6070 Timberland Pass   607 Timberland Pass
16. 3423 Moseman St   3423 Moselman St
17. 5526 Forbes Blvd   5526 Forbes Blvd
18. La Jolla CA 92093   La Jolla CA 92093
19. 4606 Muchmore Rd   4406 Muchmore Rd
20. 825 Bullet Hole Way   825 Bullet Hole Way
21. 5871 Guion Pl So   5871 Guion Pl No
22. 1027 Rolhus Pt   1027 Rolhus Pt
23. 2182 Buena Vista Dr   2128 Buena Vista Dr
24. 4570 Halstead Ave   4570 Halsted Ave
25. Poughkeepsie NY 12601   Poughkeeppsie NY 12601
26. 1939 Riverdale Blvd   1939 Riverside Blvd
27. 2275 Jefferson Valley Rd   2257 Jefferson Valley Rd
28. 8719 Shenorock Houses   8719 Shenorock Houses
29. 9426 Elisa Lane   9426 Elissa Lane
30. 7203 Montefiore Pky   7203 Monteforte Pky
31. Carbondale IL 62901   Carbondale IL 62901
32. 4144 Stonegate Apts   4144 Stonegate Apts
33. 6576 Hortontown Hill Rd   6576 Hortontown Hill Rd
34. 3965 W Palmer Ave   3956 W Palmer Ave
35. 8973 W Mountain Rd S   8973 S Mountain Rd W
36. 2358 Cowles Ave   235A Cowles Ave
37. Lynchburg VA 24503   Lynchberg VA 24503

38.	3481 Poningo Pt	3481 Poningo Pt
39.	8762 Mile Square Rd	8762 Miles Square Rd
40.	1441 Massachsuetts Ave NE	1441 Massachusetts Ave NW
41.	2214 Quaker Bridge Hwy	2214 Quaker Ridge Hwy
42.	2776 Babbit Rdg Dr	2776 Babbitt Rdg Dr
43.	Albuquerque NM 87131	Albuquerque NH 87131
44.	8268 Bronxville River Rd	8628 Bronxville River Rd
45.	1100 Ehrbar Ave	1100 Ehrbar Ave
46.	2143 Leather Stocking Ln	2143 Leatherstocking Ln
47.	Gainesville FL 32611	Gainesville FL 23611
48.	6224 Scarborough Manor	6224 Scarborough Manor
49.	6785 Scenic Circle	6785 Scenick Circle
50.	5416 Crossbar Rd	5416 Crossbar Rd
51.	9162 E 145th Crescent Rd	9162 E 145th Crescent Dr
52.	6048 Administration Ave	6048 Administrative Ave
53.	8588 Quintard Dr Pt	8558 Quintad Dr Pt
54.	Bethlehem PA 18015	Bethlehem PA 18015
55.	6456 Attitash Pl	6456 Attitash Pz
56.	135 Sixth No	1355 Sixth No
57.	4461 Doansbridge St	4461 Doonsbridge St
58.	9296 Hollowbrook Ct	9296 Hollowbrook Ct
59.	3907 Middle Patent Val	3097 Middle Patent Val
60.	Lincoln NE 68508	Lincoln NB 68508
61.	2756 Nepperhan Av	2756 Neperhan Av
62.	4365 Cadillac Dr	4365 Cadillac Rd
63.	5176 Tanglewylde Wy	5176 Tanglewood Wy
64.	8429 Grey Rock Terr	8429 Grey Rock Terr
65.	Boulder CO 80302	Boulder CO 80302
66.	852J Depew Dr N	852J Depuw Dr N
67.	1571 Kissam Rd	1571 Kissam Rd
68.	8858 Albany Post Rd	8558 Albany Post Rd
69.	4274 S Winchester Oval	4274 E Winchester Oval
70.	2606 Gleneida Ave	2606 Glenieda Ave
71.	Grinnell IA 50112	Grinnell IA 50122
72.	3125 Lakeshore Dr	3125 Lake Shore Dr
73.	1075 Central Park Ave NW	1075 Central Park Ave NE
74.	6422 Borcher Ave	6422 Borcher Ave
75.	9832 Brooklands Blvd	9832 Brooklands Blvd
76.	3521/2 Village Green Center	3521/2 Village Green Centre
77.	3611 W 361st Ave NE	3611 W 361st Ave NE
78.	6368 Woodlea Dr	6368 Woodlea Dr
79.	Lawrence KS 66045	Laurence KS 66045
80.	5656 Heritage Hills Dr	5656 Heritage Hills Dr

81.	6579 Olcott Ave	6579 Alcott Ave
82.	7587 Koerner St	7857 Koerner St
83.	222E Skytop Hill Wy	222E Skytop Hill Wy
84.	2271 Old Knollwood Dr	2271 Knollwood Dr
85.	Granville OH 43023	Granville OH 43023
86.	4913 Pythian Pl	4913 Phythian Pl
87.	5784 Birch Brk Blvd	7584 Birch Brk Blvd
88.	6276 Dogwood Lk Ln	6276 Dogwood Ln Lk
89.	5083 Ellendale Ave	5083 Ellendale Ave
90.	Bronx NY 10458	Bronx NY 10485
91.	5614 Theodore Fremd Ave	5614 Theodore Freud Ave
92.	3798 Augustine Ave So	3798 Augustine Ave, So
93.	9421 Reyna Ln	9421 Reyna Ln
94.	8205 Martling Ave Ext	8205 Martting Ave Ext
95.	9278 Sabbathday Hill Rd S	9278 Sabbathday Hill Rd S

Number Series Test

Directions: Each number series question consists of a series of numbers which follows some definite order. The numbers progress from left to right according to some rule. One lettered pair of numbers comprises the next two numbers in the series. Study each series to try to find a pattern to the series and to figure out the rule which governs the progression. Choose the answer pair which continues the series according to the pattern established.

1. 12 26 15 26 18 26 21...
   (A) 21 24
   (B) 24 26
   (C) 21 26
   (D) 26 24
   (E) 26 25

2. 72 67 69 64 66 61 63...
   (A) 58 60
   (B) 65 62
   (C) 60 58
   (D) 65 60
   (E) 60 65

3. 81 10 29 81 10 29 81...
   (A) 29 10
   (B) 81 29
   (C) 10 29
   (D) 81 10
   (E) 29 81

4. 91 91 90 88 85 81 76...
   (A) 71 66
   (B) 70 64
   (C) 75 74
   (D) 70 65
   (E) 70 63

5. 22 44 29 37 36 30 43...
   (A) 50 23
   (B) 23 50
   (C) 53 40
   (D) 40 53
   (E) 50 57

6. 0 1 1 0 2 2 0...
   (A) 0 0
   (B) 0 3
   (C) 3 3
   (D) 3 4
   (E) 2 3

7. 32 34 36 34 36 38 36...
   (A) 34 32
   (B) 36 34
   (C) 36 38
   (D) 38 40
   (E) 38 36

8. 26 36 36 46 46 56 56...
   (A) 66 66
   (B) 56 66
   (C) 57 57
   (D) 46 56
   (E) 26 66

9. 64 63 61 58 57 55 52...
   (A) 51 50
   (B) 52 49
   (C) 50 58
   (D) 50 47
   (E) 51 49

10. 4 6 8 7 6 8 10 9 8...
    (A) 7 9
    (B) 11 12
    (C) 12 14
    (D) 7 10
    (E) 10 12

11. 57 57 52 47 47 32 37...
    (A) 32 32
    (B) 37 32
    (C) 37 37
    (D) 32 27
    (E) 27 27

12. 13 26 14 25 16 23 19...
    (A) 20 21
    (B) 20 22
    (C) 20 23
    (D) 20 24
    (E) 22 25

13. 15 27 39 51 63 75 87...
    (A) 97 112
    (B) 99 111
    (C) 88 99
    (D) 89 99
    (E) 90 99

14. 2 0 2 2 2 4 2 6 2 8...
    (A) 2 2
    (B) 2 8
    (C) 2 10
    (D) 2 12
    (E) 2 16

15. 19 18 18 17 17 17 16...
    (A) 16 16
    (B) 16 15
    (C) 15 15
    (D) 15 14
    (E) 16 17

16. 55 53 44 51 49 44 47...
    (A) 45 43
    (B) 46 45
    (C) 46 44
    (D) 44 44
    (E) 45 44

17. 100 81 64 49 36 25 16...
    (A) 8 4
    (B) 8 2
    (C) 9 5
    (D) 9 4
    (E) 9 3

18. 2 2 4 6 8 18 16...
    (A) 32 64
    (B) 32 28
    (C) 54 32
    (D) 32 54
    (E) 54 30

19. 47 43 52 48 57 53 62...
    (A) 58 54
    (B) 67 58
    (C) 71 67
    (D) 58 67
    (E) 49 58

20. 38 38 53 48 48 63 58...
    (A) 58 58
    (B) 58 73
    (C) 73 73
    (D) 58 68
    (E) 73 83

21. 12 14 16 13 15 17 14...
    (A) 17 15
    (B) 15 18
    (C) 17 19
    (D) 15 16
    (E) 16 18

22. 30 30 30 37 37 37 30...
    (A) 30 30
    (B) 30 37
    (C) 37 37
    (D) 37 30
    (E) 31 31

23. 75 52 69 56 63 59 57...
    (A) 58 62
    (B) 55 65
    (C) 51 61
    (D) 61 51
    (E) 63 55

24. 176 88 88 44 44 22 22...
    (A) 22 11
    (B) 11 11
    (C) 11 10
    (D) 11 5
    (E) 22 10

ANSWERS!

Memory for Addresses Test

1. C
2. E
3. A
4. B
5. B
6. E
7. C
8. D
9. E
10. C
11. D
12. A
13. E
14. A
15. D
16. B
17. A
18. A
19. C
20. D
21. B
22. B
23. E
24. C
25. A
26. E
27. D
28. D
29. A
30. C
31. C
32. C
33. C
34. B
35. B
36. D
37. E
38. A
39. B
40. E
41. A

42. B
43. D
44. D
45. A
46. B
47. D
48. E
49. B
50. C
51. E
52. A
53. C
54. D
55. E
56. A
57. B
58. D
59. C
60. E
61. A
62. E
63. A
64. B
65. D
66. D
67. C
68. C
69. A
70. D
71. A
72. E
73. A
74. D
75. A
76. B
77. C
78. E
79. A
80. D
81. D
82. C
83. E
84. B

85. D
86. B
87. E
88. C

Address Checking Test

1. D
2. D
3. A
4. D
5. D
6. D
7. A
8. A
9. D
10. D
11. D
12. D
13. D
14. A
15. D
16. D
17. A
18. A
19. D
20. A
21. D
22. A
23. D
24. D
25. D
26. D
27. D
28. A
29. D
30. D
31. A
32. A
33. A
34. D
35. D
36. D

37. D
38. A
39. D
40. D
41. D
42. A
43. D
44. D
45. A
46. D
47. D
48. A
49. D
50. A
51. D
52. D
53. D
54. A
55. D
56. D
57. D
58. A
59. D
60. D
61. D
62. D
63. D
64. A
65. A
66. D
67. A
68. D
69. D
70. D
71. D
72. D
73. D
74. A
75. A
76. D
77. A
78. A
79. D

80. A
81. D
82. D
83. A
84. D
85. A
86. D
87. D
88. D
89. A
90. D
91. D
92. A
93. A
94. D
95. A

Address Checking Error Analysis Chart

Type of Error	Tally	Total Number
Number of addresses which were alike and you incorrectly marked "different"		
Number of addresses which were different and you incorrectly marked "alike"		
Number of addresses in which you missed a difference in NUMBERS		
Number of addresses in which you missed a difference in ABBREVIATIONS		
Number of addresses in which you missed a difference in NAMES		

Self-Evaluation Chart

Test	Excellent	Good	Average	Fair	Poor
Memory for Addresses	75–88	60–74	45–59	30–44	1–29
Address Checking	80–95	65–79	50–64	35–49	1–34

Number Series Exam

1. D
2. A
3. C
4. E
5. B
6. C
7. D
8. A
9. E
10. E
11. B
12. C
13. B
14. C
15. A
16. E
17. D
18. C
19. D
20. B
21. E
22. A
23. D
24. B

RESTAURATEUR, HOTELIER

American College of Hotel and Restaurant Management

*There's not supposed to be an "n" in Restaurateur.
It's French. We can charge more for this book that
way.*

With the food service industry expected to grow faster and steadier than just about anything else in the U.S. economy into the next century, it's no wonder that more and more people are entering culinary academies and restaurant schools to learn about catering, preparing food, serving food and wine, and managing a restaurant business. Systematic training in restaurant management is strongly recommended not only for those who are interested in seeking a managing position with an existing restaurant or other food service operation, but also—perhaps more important-ly, considering whose nest egg may be on the line—for those who want to start their own business. That dream of running your own cozy little tapas bar can quickly go sour if you approach it too naively, that is, merely as a romantic notion and not as a business endeav-or. Nothing wrong with romance—it just won't cover the overhead.

Restaurant management programs typically stress not only such hard-core business details as cost control, labor laws, and marketing, but also knowledge which bears on all the other aspects of running a restaurant, such as cooking, dining room service, and wine service, storage, and purchasing. The American College of Hotel and Restaurant Manage-ment, which supplied the questions that follow, has courses in all those areas and more—business law, computer technology, and conversational French (so you don't embarrass yourself when offering the customer an *hors d'oeuvre chaud*). As you might guess from the name of the school, ACHRM also has programs in hotel management—another rapidly growing facet of the so-called "hospitality" industry. In fact, you may notice that there are some hotel-related questions sprinkled in with the restaurant ones, just to keep you on your toes. If you're interested in pursuing a study of hotel or restaurant management or in finding out more about the program, you can contact the American College of Hotel and Restaurant Management at 555 Universal Terrace Parkway, Suite 467, Universal City CA 91608, tel. (818) 505-9800.

Multiple Choice

1. The employees of which department are often in a better position to embezzle assets than most other employees?
   (A) The accounting department
   (B) The housekeeping department
   (C) The marketing department
   (D) The personnel department
   (E) The food and beverage department

2. In a well-run housekeeping department, of every dollar spent for floorcare
   (A) .30 goes for labor; .70 goes for equipment and chemicals
   (B) .10 goes for labor; .90 goes for equipment and chemicals
   (C) .85 goes for labor; .15 goes for equipment and chemicals

3. In general, the most productive advertising for restaurants comes from listings in
   (A) local publications
   (B) national publications
   (C) airline publications
   (D) travel guides

4. As the inventory turnover rate decreases for a food and beverage operation
   (A) stock-outs are more likely to occur
   (B) more money is being invested in inventory
   (C) guests may become dissatisfied
   (D) cash becomes available for other purposes

5. If a hotel sold 240 rooms, and the income from room sales equaled $10,636.00, the daily rate would be
   (A) $43.42
   (B) $143.28
   (C) $23.44
   (D) $44.32

6. Which of the following types of chemical poisonings is controlled by washing all fruits and vegetables to be used fresh?
   (A) Lead poisoning
   (B) Copper poisoning
   (C) Antimony poisoning
   (D) Zinc and cadmium poisoning
   (E) Ptomaine poisoning

7. The dollar value used to calculate inventory turnover is taken from the
   (A) requisitions
   (B) physical inventory
   (C) receiving clerk's daily reports
   (D) perpetual inventory

8. An in-house document used by small properties to record informal orders is a
   (A) purchase order
   (B) purchase record
   (C) purchase requisition
   (D) storeroom requisition

9. Which is a major factor in quality grading of beef?
   (A) Amount of marbling
   (B) Outside fat covering
   (C) Conformation of the animal
   (D) Aging of the beef
   (E) Color of the meat

10. The way to find the number of rooms to be cleaned is by
    (A) consulting room attendants' schedules
    (B) doing morning room check
    (C) consulting rooms division
    (D) reviewing the invoices

11. The phrase "X the machine" refers to
    (A) indicating to the manager that the machine needs to be replaced
    (B) replacing smaller bills for larger denominations
    (C) returning the cash register tally to a zero balance
    (D) interfacing the cash register with the companion precheck register
    (E) reading the amount of sale rung on the machine without returning the balance to zero

12. Which of these usually includes three meals a day?
    (A) South American Plan
    (B) American Plan
    (C) European Plan
    (D) Neopolitan Plan
    (E) Family Plan

13. Differentiated marketing means
    (A) positioning a firm in the largest market segment
    (B) trying to attract all market segments
    (C) developing concepts positioned in each marketing segment
    (D) presenting unique, innovative advertising
    (E) learning how to shop for the best prices

14. Which of the following records are to be kept in Housekeeping?
    (A) employee driving records
    (B) invoices for chef's supplies
    (C) lost and found; room histories
    (D) room status
    (E) check-in status

15. The best prospects for direct mail campaigns are
    (A) lists developed by mail houses
    (B) people who have made inquiries
    (C) people recommended by former guests
    (D) former guests
    (E) friends and families of employees

16. The hotel assures the guest that a room will be held until the guest's arrival or check-out time the next day if the guest holds a
    (A) guaranteed reservation
    (B) nonguaranteed reservation
    (C) nonguaranteed confirmed reservation
    (D) confirmed acknowledgement
    (E) same-day acknowledgement

17. Which of the following is an unacceptable method for thawing frozen foods?
    (A) under cold running water
    (B) under refrigeration
    (C) as part of a conventional cooking process
    (D) at room temperature

18. The details of the order placed with a supplier are contained on the
    (A) menu
    (B) food sample data sheet
    (C) standard purchase specification
    (D) information request sheet

19. Pork and pork products are potentially hazardous foods and must reach a minimum internal temperature of _____ during cooking.
    (A) 165°F/75°C
    (B) 150°F/66°C
    (C) 140°F/60°C
    (D) 130°F/54°C

(E) It doesn't really matter as long as you cook it for 15 minutes or more

20. All of the following information would typically be found on a wine bottle label except
    (A) varietal labeling
    (B) name of winery
    (C) vintage date
    (D) type of wine
    (E) blending process

21. A theme weekend is a
    (A) self-contained promotion
    (B) merchandising technique
    (C) full destination promotion
    (D) trip to an amusement park
    (E) none of the above

22. Budgeting exact amounts for promotional spending should be based on
    (A) an established percentage of income
    (B) industry averages
    (C) the job to be done
    (D) the cost of the marketing staff's salaries
    (E) a percentage of the profits

23. The type of hotel that features guest accommodations which consist of a separate bedroom and living room is called a
    (A) resort hotel
    (B) commercial hotel
    (C) business hotel
    (D) suite hotel
    (E) executive hotel

24. Fresh fish should have all of the following traits EXCEPT
    (A) sunken eyes
    (B) elastic flesh
    (C) red gills
    (D) tight scales

25. Seat turnover is calculated by dividing the number of customers who are served in a meal period by
    (A) the number of hours in the meal period
    (B) the number of seats available
    (C) the number of service employees which have been used
    (D) the number of income dollars which have been generated
    (E) the number of employees working

True or False

1. _____Planning and controlling are two of the functional concepts of management

2. _____The possibility of rebooking a convention into a given property or area is in direct relationship to customer satisfaction

3. _____Housekeeping involves management of people, equipment, and supplies; preservation of building, finishes, fabrics, and furnishings; controlling costs

4. _____Since not all crime is preventable, a security program should stress the apprehension of criminals over the prevention of crimes

5. _____Two goals of the hotel's sales promotion effort are to attract more people from the existing market and to motivate new people to try the property's services

6. _____The way a menu looks is more important than the way it is worded

7. _____The process of accounting involves recording, classifying, and summarizing financial information

8. _____There is little relationship between the extent to which employees are involved and whether or not they are motivated to better perform work

9. _____The primary reason many supervisors are ineffective relates to problems with communications

10. _____The hospitality market must be identified before the product image can be developed

11. _____The marketing concept proposes that customer satisfaction is the means to increasing profits

12. _____Satisfying hunger and thirst are the only reasons a guest visits a dining service operation

13. _____Dining room managers are rarely seen by the guests

14. _____If a guest becomes angry during the complaint handling process, the desk clerk should try to match the guest's level of anger

15. _____A key control system is essential to the security of any hotel

16. _____In order to maintain guest relations, the manager should train the host/hostess to underestimate the length of waiting time when guests' names are placed on a waiting list

17. _____If a credit card company will not allow credit to its cardholder, the front desk clerk should immediately summon the local police to the hotel

ANSWERS! ☛

Multiple Choice

1. E
2. C
3. A
4. B
5. D
6. A
7. B
8. B
9. A
10. B
11. E
12. B
13. C
14. C
15. D
16. A
17. D
18. D
19. B
20. E
21. A
22. C
23. D
24. A
25. A

True or False

1. T
2. T
3. T
4. T
5. T
6. F
7. T
8. F
9. T
10. T
11. T
12. F
13. F
14. F
15. T
16. F
17. F

SECURITIES

Securities Training Corporation

"But where are the customers' yachts?"

The securities and commodities industries are governed by specific regulatory bodies. These include the Securities and Exchange Commission (SEC) and the National Association of Securities Dealers (NASD) for securities and the Commodities Futures Trading Commission (CFTC) for commodities. These agencies require the registration of individuals whose jobs involve interaction with the public and those involved in supervision and management of brokerage activities.

In order to obtain registration, an individual must pass a qualification examination. These examinations are divided into two areas: registered representative examinations and principal examinations. The registered representative examinations are for those individuals involved in selling or trading securities or commodities and the principal examinations are for those involved with supervision and management.

These examinations require extensive preparation on the part of the individual. The most efficient way to prepare for these exams is to enroll in a training program designed for the specific exam that must be taken.

The questions that follow were provided by Securities Training Corporation, which offers a wide range of programs to prepare individuals for the various securities and financial industry examinations. Each STC program is available on a classroom or correspondence basis. STC has its headquarters in New York City and has branch offices in San Francisco, California, Fort Lauderdale, Florida, Chicago, Illinois, and Minneapolis, Minnesota. For a schedule of classes and information on in-house programs, you may contact the STC office nearest you or call (800) STC-1223.

1. Two customers ask their account executive to combine an odd-lot order for each of them. They want the orders combined into one round lot of 100 shares and entered on one order ticket in order to save the odd-lot differential. This:
   (A) would require approval of only one of the customers
   (B) would require the approval of both of the customers
   (C) would require approval of the NYSE
   (D) cannot be done

2. An order entered with a brokerage firm will be processed in which order of priorities?
   I.   Cashier's department
   II. Margin department
   III. Purchase and sale (P&S) department
   IV. Wire room (order department)

   (A) I, II, III, and IV
   (B) I, III, II, and IV
   (C) IV, III, II, and I
   (D) II, III, I, and IV

3. The basic difference between an open-end investment company and closed-end investment company is:
   (A) the capitalization of the investment companies
   (B) how the net asset value is computed
   (C) the type of stocks purchased by these investment companies
   (D) the type of bonds purchased by these investment companies

4. How long after a new issue is registered for sale will it be shown on the NASDAQ system?
   (A) On the effective date
   (B) 10 days after the effective date
   (C) 30 days after the effective date
   (D) 45 days after the effective date

5. A customer wishes to create a spread position. This transaction must be executed
   (A) in the cash account
   (B) in the margin account
   (C) as two separate transactions, with the long position in the cash account and the short position in the margin account
   (D) as two separate transactions, with the short position in the cash account and the long position in the margin account

6. Each of the following broker-dealers are violating Rule 15c3-1 except
   (A) a clearing broker-dealer with aggregate indebtedness of $500,000 and net capital of $34,000
   (B) a clearing broker-dealer with aggregate indebtedness of $280,000 and net capital of $20,000
   (C) a fully disclosed broker-dealer with aggregate indebtedness of $16,000 and net capital of $4,000
   (D) a fully disclosed broker-dealer with aggregate indebtedness of $80,000 and net capital of $5,000

7. Which of the following broker-dealers is in violation of Rule 15c3-1?

   I.   Clearing broker-dealer also doing best efforts underwriting with aggregate indebtedness of $100,000 and net capital of $12,000
   II. Fully disclosed broker-dealer in his first year of operation with aggregate indebtedness of $80,000 and net capital of $8,000
   III. Broker-dealer handling only mutual funds and variable annuities plus an occa-

sional trade for his own account with no aggregate indebtedness and net capital of $3,000

(A) II only
(B) I and II
(C) III only
(D) I, II, and III

8. A broker-dealer has a common stock position totaling $50,000. If there are two market-makers in the security, the amount of the haircut is:
(A) $50,000
(B) $25,000
(C) $20,000
(D) $15,000

9. Fails to deliver for common stock are subject to a haircut if they are
(A) 5 days or more old
(B) 10 days or more old
(C) 15 days or more old
(D) 30 days or more old

10. A broker-dealer has an aged fail to deliver for a common stock totaling $20,000. The haircut is
(A) $2,000
(B) $3,000
(C) $5,000
(D) $6,000

11. A trader has a regulated futures account and a securities account at a member firm. The trader receives a margin call in his securities account. There is excess equity in his regulated futures account. The member firm in this case

I. could transfer the money from the regulated futures account to the securities account unless the customer gave specific instructions that this could not be done
II. could not transfer money from the regulated futures account to the securities account even if the customer requests that this be done
III. could make the transfer only by obtaining written consent from the customer each time a transfer is to be made
IV. could make the transfer if the customer has signed an agreement that authorizes the firm to make such transfers from the regulated futures account to the securities account

(A) I and II
(B) II and III
(C) III and IV
(D) I and IV

12. The term "demand elasticity" refers to a situation whereby
(A) a change in the price will result in a change in the amount of the commodity that is produced
(B) a change in the price will result in a change in the amount of the commodity that is purchased
(C) a shortage of the cash commodity will result in a greater production in the future
(D) the amount of the commodity that is in storage exceeds the amount that is currently being purchased

13. An exporter of soybean oil can effectively hedge against all of the following except
(A) increases in the cost of soybeans
(B) decreases in the demand for soybean oil leading to falling prices
(C) fluctuations in the foreign exchange rates in the countries where he sells his product
(D) increases in ocean freight rates

14. If the price of near futures is below the price of deferred futures and a spreader thinks the spread will narrow, he will buy the near month and sell the deferred month.
    (A) True
    (B) False

15. Included in the term "offer" or "offer to sell" are all of the following except
    (A) a solicitation to buy a security for value
    (B) a solicitation to sell a security for value
    (C) a gift of nonassessable securities
    (D) an offer or attempt to dispose of a security for value

16. A client is in a low tax bracket and desires a conservative investment strategy. The agent recommends the purchase of a municipal bond. This recommendation would be considered
    (A) too risky
    (B) unsuitable
    (C) suitable
    (D) fraud

17. As an agent, which of the following is prohibited?
    (A) Stating facts relating to material inside information to a client
    (B) Stating facts relating to material in a final prospectus to a client
    (C) Stating facts relating to a firm's current financial statements to a client
    (D) Stating facts relating to a market letter published by your firm to a client

18. Which of the following would be considered a prohibited business practice?
    (A) Giving a quote for a security that is not the current market price
    (B) Soliciting orders for unregistered non-exempt securities
    (C) Creating transactions that give the misleading appearance of active trading in a security
    (D) All of the above

19. An "agent" would be considered:

    I. a trust company, bank, or any savings institution
    II. a sales assistant authorized to accept customer orders
    III. any person other than a broker-dealer who acts on behalf of a broker-dealer or issuer in effecting sales or purchases of securities

    (A) I, II, and III
    (B) III only
    (C) II only
    (D) II and III only

20. An investor writes one XYZ April 35 call at 18½ and buys one XYZ April 40 call at 14¼. XYZ is selling at 50. If the investor does not own XYZ stock, the amount of cash he must deposit would be
    (A) $75.00
    (B) $500.00
    (C) $2,600.00
    (D) $4,025.00

21. An investor has sold stock short at 60. The current market price of the stock is 40 and the investor believes the stock will recover somewhat before going lower. He should
    (A) buy a put
    (B) buy a call
    (C) write a call
    (D) write a straddle

22. An investor who receives a maintenance call may do all of the following *except*
    (A) deposit cash
    (B) deposit stock with a loan value equal to the call
    (C) liquidate the position on which he is getting the call
    (D) request an extension if he has a valid reason

23. A customer who wishes to purchase securities in a restricted margin account
    (A) must deposit payment in advance
    (B) must deposit payment by the next business day
    (C) must deposit payment within the time prescribed for regular-way margin purchases, which is seven business days
    (D) may not purchase securities in a restricted margin account

24. The opening of a discretionary account requires which of the following documentation?

    I.   Written authorization
    II. A limited power of attorney
    III. A full power of attorney
    IV. An account agreement

    (A) I only
    (B) I and IV
    (C) I, II, and IV
    (D) I, III, and IV

ANSWERS!☞

1. (B). Odd-lot orders on the NYSE can be combined into one round-lot to save the ⅛-point odd-lot differential. The order is entered as one round-lot but each customer will receive a separate odd-lot confirmation. However, this requires the approval of both of the customers.

2. (C). When an order is entered by a customer, it is processed first in the wire room or order room, then in the P&S department, then the margin department, and then the cashier's department.

3. (A). The basic difference between an open-end and closed-end investment company is the capitalization. An open-end investment company can issue only common stock, whereas a closed-end investment company (like a corporation) may issue common stock, preferred stock, and bonds.

4. (A). A new issue will appear on the NASDAQ system on the effective date of the issue. The effective date, which is determined by the SEC upon completion of the registration process, is the first date that the securities may be sold to the public.

5. (B). Spread positions are executed in the margin account. A spread position is created when a customer simultaneously buys and sells the same class of option on the same underlying stock with different series.

6. (A). A broker-dealer must maintain a minimum dollar amount of net capital, depending upon the nature of his business, or a minimum percentage (1/8th or 1/15th of his aggregate indebtedness), whichever is greater.

   The broker-dealer in answer (A) is a clearing firm and therefore requires $25,000. 1/15th of his aggregate indebtedness is $33,333. As he has $34,000, he is in compliance with the rule.

   The clearing broker-dealer in answer (B) has only $20,000 of net capital. As he requires a minimum of $25,000, he is in violation of the rule by $5,000.

   The broker-dealer in answer (C) is operating on a fully disclosed basis and therefore requires a minimum net capital of $5,000. As he has only $4,000 of net capital, he is in violation of the rule by $1,000.

   The broker-dealer in answer (D) is operating on a fully disclosed basis and requires a minimum net capital of $5,000, which he has. However, his aggregate indebtedness is $80,000. 1/15th of the aggregate indebtedness equals $5,333. Therefore, he is in violation of the rule by $333.

7. (B). The broker-dealer in answer (I) is a clearing firm and therefore requires a minimum net capital of $25,000. Therefore, as his net capital is only $12,000, he is in violation of the rule by $13,000.

   The broker-dealer in answer (II) is in his first year of operation. His aggregate indebtedness may not exceed 800% (8 times) his capital. As his net capital is $8,000, he may not have aggregate indebtedness exceeding $64,000.

   The broker-dealer in answer (III) is in compliance with the rule as he requires a minimum net capital of $2,500.

8. (C). The haircut on common stock is 30%. However, common stock that has a "limited market" is subject to a higher haircut. A limited market exists when there are less than three market makers in an over-the-counter security. In this case, the haircut is 40%.

9. and 10. The correct answer for question 9 is (A) and for 10 (D). Fails to deliver represent an asset of a broker-dealer. They represent the dollar value of securities that the broker-dealer owes to another broker-dealer but has not yet delivered. This might

occur because he sold stock short or because he sold stock for a customer and the customer has not yet delivered the stock. When the stock is delivered, the broker-dealer will receive cash equal to the sales price.

If a broker-dealer has fails to deliver for common stock that are over four days old, he is required to treat the stock as he would treat stock that he owned in his own investment or trading account. As common stock is subject to a 30% haircut, the same haircut would apply to fails to deliver that are over four days old.

In question 10, the haircut of 30% on stock with a value of $20,000 would equal $6,000.

11. (C). Transfers from a regulated commodities account to a securities account may be accomplished only if the customer specifically requests that a transfer be made or if he signs the transfer consent form authorizing that such transfers be made automatically.

12. (B). The term "demand elasticity" describes a condition where changes in price will cause changes in the amount purchased. As the price rises, purchases decrease; as the price declines, purchases increase.

The term "supply elasticity" describes a condition where changes in price will cause changes in the amount produced. As the price rises, production increases; as the price declines, production decreases.

13. (D). A user of soybeans may hedge against an increase in the cost of soybeans by the purchase of soybean futures. A producer of soybean oil can hedge against falling prices by the sale of soybean futures. An individual who fears a devaluation of a foreign country's currency may hedge that country's currency in the futures market.

However, it is not possible to hedge against increases in freight rates as there are no transportation futures.

14. (A). If a spreader anticipates that a spread will narrow, he will always buy the lower-priced futures and sell the higher-priced futures.

15. (C). An "offer" or an "offer to sell" is any attempt to buy or sell a security for value. A gift of nonassessable securities would not be considered a sale or an offer to sell. Nonassessable means there are no tax ramifications upon disposal. A gift of a security to a charitable organization would be nonassessable.

16. (B). Recommending the purchase of a municipal bond to an investor in a low tax bracket would not be suitable since the federal tax exemption on municipal bond interest income would not have a significant impact on the investor's overall tax liability. Corporate bonds with higher yields would be more advantageous to investors in lower tax brackets.

17. (A). An agent is prohibited from relating material inside information to anyone except his immediate supervisor.

18. (D). All of the choices listed would be considered a prohibited business practice.

19. (D). Authorized sales assistants and individuals who effect transactions for broker-dealers or issuers (normally charging a commission) are considered to be agents.

20. (A). On a call spread, no margin is required if the long position expires at the same or a later date than the short position and the long position has the same or a lower exercise price. If the long position has a higher exercise price, margin is required.

In this question, the long position expires at the same time as the short position and has a higher exercise price. The margin requirement is therefore the difference between the exercise prices ($500) or the margin on the short position, whichever is lower. The short position is in-the-money by $1,500. The margin requirement on the short call is 15% of the market price of $5,000 ($750) plus the premium of $1,850, which totals $2,600. The difference in exercise prices is $500. Therefore, the lower margin requirement of $500 is required. The total dash requirement would be computed as follows:

Margin on the short position:	500.00
Plus premium on long position:	1425.00
	1925.00
Minus premium received on short position:	1850.00
Total cash requirement:	75.00

21. (B). The stock is currently trading at 40 and the investor thinks the price will rise. An investor who is bullish on an underlying stock will buy a call.

22. (D). A maintenance call (as opposed to a Regulation T call) may be met with any type of deposit. A liquidation is also permitted in the case of a maintenance call. The member firm is not required to freeze the account. The only time that the member firm must freeze an account is when an investor liquidates a position to meet an initial Regulation T call, not a maintenance call. An extension may not be requested for a maintenance call, which must be met promptly.

23. (C). A restricted margin account is one in which the equity is below the Regulation T margin requirement. For example, on 50% margin, if an investor has securities with a market value of $10,000 and a debit balance of $6,000, his equity is $4,000. This is less than the Regulation T mini- mum. There are no penalties associated with a restricted account. An investor could make a new purchase and would be required to deposit cash within the prescribed time in the same manner as a purchase in a nonrestricted account.

24. (C). In order to open a discretionary account, the member firm requires written authorization from the customer granting limited power of attorney to the person exercising discretion. The limited power of attorney grants the person power to buy and sell securities without reference to the customer. An account agreement is required for any type of account that a member firm opens.

STUDENT vs. TEACHER CHALLENGE

Rutgers New Jersey Bowl

We do not recommend this quiz show format for daytime TV. Most educators without advanced degrees would be disqualified because they couldn't even understand the rules. For the students, though, brought up in the computer age, they were a snap. Have you ever tried to dope out a computer software manual?

The 1986 kickoff of the New Jersey Network's "Rutgers New Jersey Bowl" television quiz show featured a match between four students from past New Jersey Bowl championship high school teams and four award-winning high school teachers. The face-off ended in a resounding victory for the students, who, after a slow start, came from behind to overtake the teachers and win by a score of 220 to 105.

The Rutgers New Jersey Bowl, now in its eighth season, is a single elimination-style tournament consisting of 31 games that run from November into June. Every year, the kick-off show is a special event that is not part of the regular 31-part series. The first 30 episodes are a half-hour in length; the final is an hour long and is broadcast live in June.

The series is produced by Rutgers, the State University of New Jersey, in an effort to promote a sense of pride in the state's educational system and to reward academic excellence—in fact, the show is partially funded by the New Jersey Department of Higher Education. Todd Hunt, a communications professor at Rutgers, hosts the program. The series airs twice-weekly on New Jersey Network, the state's PBS-affiliate.

Thirty-two New Jersey high schools compete in the tournament each year. Each team consists of four members, an alternate, and a faculty advisor. Each of the four members of the championship team receives a $1,000 scholarship, made possible by New Jersey Power and Light Company, a local utility.

The questions that follow are from the 1986 special kick-off episode. The format of the show is roughly as follows: The first round consists of ten-point "toss-ups," that is, as each question is read by the quiz-show host, whichever team hits the buzzer first gets to try to answer it. If one team answers the question correctly, that team gets a "bonus opportunity," which means that it gets exclusive rights to an extra question. There is no penalty for answering a question incorrectly, but hitting the buzzer before the question is read through in its entirety means that important clues in the rest of the question might be missed. The second and third rounds are ten-point "challenge rounds," one for each of the two teams. In each challenge round, one team gets exclusive rights to the questions, but no discussion between team members is allowed. The reward for hitting the buzzer and answering the questions quickly is that the team gets the chance to answer more questions before the end of the round and thus rack up more points. The final round consists of 20-point toss-ups.

In the "Questions" section, we have just included the questions themselves. Turn to the "Answers" section for the correct answers, actual answers given by the contestants, and a running point tally.

1. What New Orleans-born author of *The Little Foxes* has crafted her dramatic work so as to speak out strongly for social justice? _____

2. There have been many attempts on the lives of U.S. presidents, but only four have been fatal. Name the four assassinated U.S. presidents.
   (1)_____
   (2)_____
   (3)_____
   (4)_____

3. Physical stress and stressful verbal interaction are key elements of a widely used method of personality alteration created in 1971 by Werner Erhard. What is its acronym name? _____

4. Some computer terms are acronyms, such as RAM for random access memory. In fact, some computer languages are acronyms themselves. For what do the computer acronyms BASIC and FORTRAN stand? _____
   _____
   _____

5. B. F. Skinner, the noted psychologist, could also be called the father of behaviorism. Identify these works by Skinner:
   (A) This 1948 utopian vision emphasizes operant behavior and instrumental conditioning _____
   (B) This 1971 work broadly applies the vision elaborated in (A) to the whole of culture _____

6. The U.S. has almost ⅓ of the world's known accessible coal reserves. Which nation currently produces the most coal annually? _____

7. Large airports are very busy places, serving thousands of passengers every day. Identify the cities near which the following airports are found:
   (A) Orly _____
   (B) Heathrow _____

8. She debuted as a director with the 1980 film *Fatso*. Her success as an actress can be measured by her Tony for *Two for the Seesaw* and her Tony-Oscar combination in stage and screen versions of *The Miracle Worker*. Name her. _____

9. It prohibited slavery north of latitude 36 degrees 30 minutes and admitted Maine as a free state. Name it. _____
   _____

10. The name of this sport is a curious condensation of the word "association." The game consists of two 45-minute halves of almost constant action between teams of 11 players each. Name the sport. _____

11. They were officially annexed by Israel on December 14, 1981. What two-word name is given to this territory captured in 1967 from Syria? _____

12. It has two heads but no arms. We, however, have one in each of our arms and it allows us to turn a doorknob. What is this important flexor muscle, whose name means "two-headed"? _____

13. *The Diary of Anne Frank* is one of the most touching and inspiring documents to come out of World War II. In what country did Frank live? _____

14. In Europe in 1870, at the outbreak of the Franco-Prussian War, she volunteered to

work at the front for the International Red Cross. It took her 11 years, but she finally received presidential authorization to establish the American National Red Cross. Who was this "angel of the battle-fields"? _____

15. They called her box-office poison in 1938 because of her stiff manner, but already she had won the Academy Award for her performance in *Morning Glory*. She went on to win three more Oscars, most recent-ly for Best Actress in "*On Golden Pond*." What is the name of this actress?

_____

16. Its weekly circulation is over five million. Founded in 1926, it has reached the top of its class by emphasizing sensational and off-beat stories. Identify this national tabloid newspaper. _____

_____

17. In 1903, this Russian physiologist won the Nobel Prize for his investigation of condi-tioned reflexes. What was the name of this famous scientist? _____

18. When the Yankee Clipper retired from baseball, the Yankees retired his number. Who was this legendary player?

_____

19. After 1965, he became an increasingly vocal critic of the Vietnam War and was the 1972 presidential nominee of the Peo-ple's Party. His name? _____

_____

20. Patient Randle Patrick McMurphy fights a guerilla campaign against Nurse Ratched in this 1962 novel by Ken Kesey. What is the title of the novel?_____

_____

21. Established as a singer, he showed himself a gifted comic actor in the "Road" film series with Bob Hope. His name?

_____

22. Believing that the key to most psychoses lies in the personal and collective con-sciousness, this psychologist broke from the theory of his teacher Sigmund Freud. Who was he? _____

23. The body constantly renews itself through two energy processes. Anabolism is the process of replacing old compounds and making new ones; catabolism is the pro-cess of breaking down compounds to free energy. Anabolism and catabolism are two subdivisions of what overall process?

_____

24. He was born on August 29, 1923 in Cam-bridge, England, the son of a historian. He made his first stage appearance in 1941 in O'Neill's *Ah! Wilderness,* and his film debut the next year in Noel Coward's *In Which We Serve*. As a director, among his first big successes was *A Bridge Too Far,* which shares its antiwar theme with his biggest success, *Gandhi*. Name him.

_____

25. In Shakespeare's *Julius Caesar*, Brutus addresses the crowd, "Romans, country-men, and lovers." How does Mark Anthony begin *his* address?_____

_____

26. On a musical score, it instructs the musi-cian to play the notes of a chord in rapid succession rather than simultaneously. Name this Italian word. _____

27. Many of the signers of the Declaration of
    Independence were in their 30s or 40s
    when they autographed that revolutionary
    document, but one signer was 70 years old.
    Who was he?

    _____

28. The growth process of common fungus
    forms enzymes, which makes it useful for
    making bread rise. What fungus are we
    talking about? _____

29. In 1984 in *The Adventures of Buckaroo
    Banzai Across the Eighth Dimension*, he
    played the evil Dr. Emilio Lazardo. His
    name? _____

30. Everything is bigger in Texas. In terms of
    population, what is the largest city in
    Texas? _____

31. Newark-born Joseph Levitch is well
    known for his charity work and for dozens
    of films including *Boeing-Boeing* and
    Three on a Couch. By what name is he
    usually known? _____

ANSWERS!

[Note: Jumps in the sequence and unaccounted-for points indicate visual, audio, or spelling questions we have left out.]

Ten-Point Toss-ups with 20-Point Bonus Opportunities

1. Lillian Hellman
   Answered correctly by teachers. Score: teachers 10, students 0

Teacher's Bonus:
2. Garfield, Kennedy, Lincoln, McKinley
   First three answered correctly by teachers. Score: teachers 25, students 0

3. EST
   Answered correctly by teachers. Score: teachers 35, students 0

Teacher's Bonus:
4. (A) Beginner's All-purpose Symbolic Instructional Code
   (B) Formula Translation
   (B) answered correctly by teachers. Score: teachers 45, students 0

Student's Bonus:
5. (A) *Walden Two*
   (B) *Beyond Freedom and Dignity*
   (A) answered correctly by students. Score: teachers 45, students 20.

Student's Bonus:
6. the Soviet Union
   Answered correctly by students. Score: students 50, teachers 45

Student's Bonus:
7. (A) Paris
   (B) London
   Answered correctly by students. Score: students 80, teachers 45.

8. Anne Bancroft
   Answered incorrectly by students ("Patty Duke Astin"). No score change.

Teacher's Challenge Round

9. the Missouri Compromise
   Answered incorrectly by teachers ("the Mason-Dixon Line"). No score change.

10. soccer
    Answered incorrectly by teachers ("football"). No score change.

11. the Golan Heights
    Answered incorrectly by teachers ("West Bank"). No score change.

12. bicep
    No answer by teachers. No score change.

13. the Netherlands
    Answered incorrectly by teachers ("France"). No score change.

14. Clara Barton
    Answered incorrectly by teachers ("Florence Nightingale"). No score change.

15. Katherine Hepburn
    Answered correctly by teachers. Score: students 80, teachers 65.

16. *The National Enquirer*
    Answered correctly by teachers. Score: students 80, teachers 75.

17. Ivan Pavlov
    Answered correctly by teachers. Score: teachers 85, students 80.

End of Teachers' Challenge Round.

Student's Challenge Round

18. Joe DiMaggio
    Answered incorrectly by students
    ("Rizzuto"). No score change.

19. Dr. Benjamin Spock
    Answered incorrectly by students
    ("George McGovern"), who buzzed
    before the host read the information that
    this candidate was from the People's
    Party. No score change.

20. *One Flew Over the Cuckoo's Nest*
    Answered correctly by students. Score:
    students 100, teachers 85.

21. Bing Crosby
    Answered correctly by students. Score:
    students 110, teachers 85.

22. Carl Jung
    Answered correctly by students. Score:
    students 120, teachers 85.

23. metabolism
    Answered correctly by students. Score:
    students 130, teachers 85.

24. Sir Richard Attenborough
    Answered incorrectly by students ("Ben
    Kingsley"). No score change.

25. "Friends, Romans, countrymen"
    Answered correctly by students. Score:
    students 140, teachers 85.

26. arpeggio
    Answered correctly by students. Score:
    students 150, teachers 85.

27. Benjamin Franklin
    Answered correctly by students. Score:
    students 160, teachers 85.

28. yeast
    Answered correctly by students. Score:
    students 170, teachers 85.

End of Students' Challenge Round.

20-Point Toss-ups

29. John Lithgow
    Answered correctly by students. Score:
    students 200, teachers 85.

30. Houston
    Answered correctly by teachers. Score:
    students 220, teachers 105.

31. Jerry Lewis
    No time for answer.

End of game.
Final score: students 220, teachers 105.

TEACHER CERTIFICATION

National Teacher Examination

*We lived on a small farm near Havre de Grace,
Maryland, during the Depression. A remarkable
man came to the back screen door one morning in
the early spring, asking for work in exchange for
meals and a place to sleep. Since our dad needed
help plowing and painting the barn, he set the man
to work. Those jobs were done, and well done, in
hardly any time at all. A small pile of apples left
from the prior autumn's harvest had begun to go
bad in the dirt cellar. The man stayed down there in
the cold all day, with only a candle for light, trying
to sort the bad ones from the good. At suppertime
when Dad asked him why it was taking him such a
long time to do such easy work when he'd handled
the big jobs so quickly, the hired man replied, "It
ain't the work, Mr. Bragdon, it's the decisions."*

While there still exists a bewildering variety of state-level teacher certification examinations, the National Teacher Exam, developed by Educational Testing Service (the same people who created the SAT) is becoming a mandatory part of the teacher certification process of an increasing number of state boards of education.

The NTE comprises two separate sets of tests: the so-called "Core Battery" tests and the subject-specific Specialty Area tests. The Core Battery tests are designed to measure the academic achievement and basic proficiency of college students entering, enrolled in, or completing teacher education programs. The battery consists of three separate two-hour tests: the Test of Communication Skills, the Test of General Knowledge, and the Test of Professional Knowledge. The General Knowledge and Professional Knowledge tests each include four 30-minute sections containing multiple-choice questions or problems. The test of Communication Skills consists of three 30-minute multiple-choice sections and a 30-minute essay, designed to assess the examinee's knowledge and skills in the areas of listening, reading, and writing. The Listening section consists of 40 questions testing the ability to retain and interpret spoken messages (examinees listen to statements, questions, or dialogues, and answer questions about them.) The Reading section consists of 30 multiple-choice questions that assess the examinee's ability to read for literal content and to analyze and evaluate prose selections. The multiple-choice Writing section consists of 40 multiple-choice questions that assess the examinee's ability to use standard written English correctly. For the essay component of the Writing section, examinees are asked to write for 30 minutes on an assigned topic. Scores are based on such things as the development of the central idea, consistency of point of view, rhetorical force, and correctness of mechanics and usage. (Each essay is read and rated on a six-point scale by two readers working independently. The score the essay receives is the sum of the two readers' ratings. If the two ratings differ by more than a point, the essay receives a third reading, and the two closest scores are the ones that count.)

The Test of General Knowledge assesses examinees' knowledge and understanding of various disciplines. The test consists of four separately timed 30-minute sections: Literature and Fine Arts, Mathematics, Science, and Social Studies.

The Test of Professional Knowledge (perhaps the most difficult Core Battery test for those of us lacking specialized teacher training or preparation) assesses examinees' understanding of the knowledge and skills that a beginning teacher uses in decision making, with emphasis on "context" and "process" teaching. Questions concerning the process of teaching assess knowledge of appropriate techniques or means of instructional planning, implementation, and evaluation, as well as knowledge of what constitutes acceptable professional behavior. Questions concerning the context of teaching assess examinees' ability to recognize constitutional rights of students and implications of state, federal, and judicial policy, and forces outside the classroom that influence teachers and students.

The Specialty Area tests assess knowledge in specific subjects, such as Biology, Chemistry, Foreign Languages, Social Studies, and Math, and are for the most part intended for those who plan to teach those subjects at the junior or senior high school level.

In the pages that follow, we have included questions representative of the Test of Communication Skills Reading and Writing sections; Test of General Knowledge Literature and Fine Arts, Mathematics, Science, and Social Studies sections; and the Test of Professional Knowledge. The sample represents about 10 percent of a complete exam, minus (for obvious reasons) the Listening section and the essay component of the Writing section.

Professional Knowledge

1. Ms. Jackson, the principal, announces over the intercom speaker that it is time to stand and salute the flag. Harry does not wish to participate. He has the right to

   I.   stand but remain silent
   II. stay seated at his desk
   III. chat with a friend, if he stands

   (A) I only
   (B) II only
   (C) III only
   (D) I and II only
   (E) none of the above

2. Mrs. Roberts is concerned that a few students in her class never seem to volunteer. Which of the following techniques would *not* be acceptable as a way to get these few students to participate in future lessons?
   (A) Call on them to make it clear that she expects every student to participate
   (B) Vary her questioning style so that students with different thinking styles are more likely to answer
   (C) Pull names out of a hat as a way of deciding who will answer questions
   (D) Try and ask some questions which she knows are related to these students' areas of interest
   (E) Alert these students to particular questions she may ask them during the next day's lesson

3. Mrs. Brownstein, a homeroom teacher for 10th-grade students, is asked by one of her 15-year-olds to see his records. She must
   (A) refer him to the guidance office
   (B) demand written permission from his parents
   (C) show them to him

   (D) explain that he cannot have access to them until he is 18
   (E) be polite, but firmly refuse

4. Two 3-year olds who are strangers to each other meet in a yard without other persons present. After they stare at each other, John hits Bob and stands back to watch while Bob cries. Bob stops crying. This sequence is repeated. What is the most likely motive for the hitting? John is
   (A) trying to establish social dominance
   (B) releasing hostility
   (C) exploring
   (D) probably unloved and punished too much at home
   (E) seeking attention

5. In which of the following situations may a teacher legally use force?

   I.   To discipline students
   II. To quell a disturbance
   III. In self-defense
   IV. To obtain a weapon a student has

   (A) II, III, and IV only
   (B) I only
   (C) III only
   (D) III and IV only
   (E) all four

6. In adolescence a conspicuous social-class difference is that
   (A) working-class girls have greater freedom than middle-class girls
   (B) working-class youths assume adult roles with less strain than middle-class youths
   (C) middle-class boys have greater sexual freedom than working-class boys
   (D) masturbation is more acceptable for working-class boys than for middle-

class boys
(E) working-class youths place greater value on education as a means of upward mobility

7. In the years since 1960, American education has been characterized by the increasing importance of
(A) centralization and lay control
(B) centralization and professional control
(C) decentralization and professional control
(D) decentralization and lay control
(E) none of the above

8. A curriculum committee recommends that children in the primary grades begin their social studies program with the consideration of relatively simple cultures, such as that of Eskimos. In later grades they would advance to the study of our own complex, industrial culture. Which one of the following statements most correctly evaluates this suggested program?
(A) The proposal is good, because it takes into consideration the relationship between interest and motivation
(B) The proposal is good, because it provides for intercultural education at the child's own level
(C) The proposal is poor, because the so-called simple cultures are foreign to the child in our society and actually present many complexities
(D) The proposal is poor, because most primary grade teachers have little background in anthropology and tend to overstress the odd or quaint factors in such studies
(E) The proposal is good, because children already know by experience the culture around them

9. A teacher notices that Linda, first violinist in the school orchestra, has quickly learned how to play the cello. This is an example of
(A) high motivation
(B) reinforcement
(C) learning by doing
(D) proactive inhibition
(E) positive transfer of training

10. The most basic recommendation concerning frustration and the school is to
(A) eliminate frustration whenever possible
(B) reduce irrelevant frustration to a minimum
(C) reduce frustration tolerance
(D) increase skipping to accommodate advanced students
(E) provide psychological services whenever children become frustrated

11. The teacher's greatest ally in the maintenance of classroom discipline is a
(A) clear understanding on the part of the students that nonsense will not be tolerated
(B) constructive program of classroom activities
(C) firm hand
(D) system of rewards for good behavior
(E) strong detention system

12. Joan cannot take the qualifying examination for the Music Award because of a religious holiday celebrated by her religion, but not by the school system. The result of this is that
(A) Joan loses her chance to compete
(B) Joan must be given another opportunity
(C) Joan should come to school just for the examination

(D) the music teacher must use other criteria to select a winner

(E) everyone must take the examination again, when Joan can take it

13. The nongraded school concept is significant chiefly because it provides for
(A) flexibility in the designation of grade levels
(B) implementation of the theory of continuous pupil progress
(C) longer periods of time for achieving certain learnings
(D) carefully developed subject-matter sequences
(E) an alternative to annual promotions

General Knowledge

Social Studies

1. Which one of the following is *incorrect* with regard to congressional organization and procedure?
(A) In each house, one-fifth of the members present are guaranteed the right to demand a record vote on any question
(B) The only congressional officers that are mentioned in the Constitution are the Speaker of the House of Representatives, the Vice-President, and the President Pro-Tempore of the Senate
(C) There is not a word in the Constitution about the committee structure of Congress
(D) The seniority system determines committee chairmanships
(E) Each house may punish its members for disorderly behavior or may, by a majority vote, expel a member

2. Of the following pairs, the one that *incorrectly* attributes a river system to a country is
(A) Yellow—China
(B) Vistula—Italy
(C) Murray Darling—Australia
(D) Loire—France
(E) Volga—Russia

3. Which statement best describes the reaction of many American colonists toward British colonial policy following the French and Indian War?
(A) They refused to accept the idea of Parliament's right to manage their internal affairs
(B) They petitioned the British Parliament for immediate independence
(C) They urged the colonial legislatures to enforce the taxation program of the British Parliament
(D) They opposed the withdrawal of British troops from the Ohio Territory
(E) They advocated higher taxes to cover the costs of war

4. Presidential electors in the United States must vote for their party's presidential candidate
(A) because of recent federal legislation
(B) as the result of a Supreme Court decision
(C) if legislation of their state so prescribes
(D) since the adoption of the 12th Amendment
(E) at all times

Literature and Fine Arts

Questions 1 and 2 refer to the following passage:

Behold him, Thebans; Oedipus, great and
  wise,
Who solved the famous riddle. This is he
    Whom all men gazed upon with envious
      eyes
Who now is struggling in a stormy sea,
    Crushed by the billows of his bitter woes.
Look to the end of mortal life. In vain
    We say a man is happy, till he goes
Beyond life's final border, free from pain.

1. The *sea* referred to is
    (A) life
    (B) the Aegean
    (C) a symbol for the city of Thebes
    (D) Oedipus' family
    (E) the rival to Greek city-states

2. The last three lines imply that life as we
    know it is
    (A) bound to get better if we are patient
    (B) bound to get worse, so we must pre-
        pare for it
    (C) unpredictable, so we must reserve
        judgment on others' fortunes
    (D) better for the great and wise, like
        Oedipus
    (E) worse for the old and poor, like the
        citizens of Thebes in general

3. Which of the following Shakespearean
    characters is *incorrectly* paired with the
    play in which he appears?
    (A) Prospero—*The Tempest*
    (B) Shylock—*The Merchant of Venice*
    (C) Christopher Sly—*The Taming of the
        Shrew*
    (D) Dogberry—*The Comedy of Errors*

(E) Francis Flute—*A Midsummer Night's
    Dream*

Question 4 is based on the following passage:

Now it is autumn/and the falling fruit
and the long journey towards oblivion.
The apples falling like great drops of dew
To bruise themselves an exit from themselves.
And it is time to go, to bid farewell
To one's own self, to find an exit
from the fallen self.

4. The poet uses the idea of falling to repre-
    sent
    (A) sleep
    (B) the end of the growth cycle
    (C) autumn, or fall
    (D) the frailty of human nature
    (E) the unity of man and his environment

Science

1. When small particles are added to a liq-
    uid, they can often be seen to be undergo-
    ing very rapid motion on the surface of
    the liquid. The explanation for this motion
    is best described as the
    (A) electrical interactions between the liq-
        uid and the suspended particles
    (B) molecular vibrations of the liquid
        causing collisions with the suspended
        particles
    (C) low density of the particles causing
        them to try to rise above the surface of
        the liquid
    (D) air currents above the liquid moving
        the particles
    (E) heat rising, causing the particles to
        move

2. Of the following, the only safe blood
    transfusion would be

(A) group A blood into a group O person
(B) group B blood into a group A person
(C) group O blood into a group AB person
(D) group AB blood into a group B person
(E) group B blood into a group A person

3. It is probable that a mammal smaller than a shrew could not exist because it would
    (A) not get sufficient oxygen
    (B) reproduce too rapidly
    (C) have to eat at too tremendous a rate
    (D) not be able to defend itself
    (E) be unable to bear live young

Communication Skills: Reading

1. Questions 1–4 refer to the following passage:

    If experimentation is defined as involving some new and untried element, or condition, then experimentation involves the evaluation of the effects of this condition or element. The condition or element being evaluated is referred to as the independent variable in the experiment, while the criteria by which it is to be evaluated are referred to as the dependent variables. Ideally, an experiment is so designed that there is a direct relationship between the independent and dependent variables— direct in the sense that it is reasonable to believe that whatever differences exist on the dependent variables after the experiment can be attributed to the independent variable. In most educational research this ideal design is not realizable, for other variables come between the independent and dependent variables. These other variables, referred to as intervening variables, can, in the simplest sense, be defined as all conditions which impede attributing all differences in dependent variables to the independent variable. Note that this definition does not require that the independent variables necessarily precede the intervening variables in time. A difference in intelligence between two groups being compared in a learning experiment would make intelligence an intervening variable, as it is defined here. Why? Because that initial difference in intelligence would impede attributing final differences on the dependent measures to the different learning processes studied.

1. In an experiment to determine if different class sizes will have an impact on reading scores, the variable *class size* is
    (A) the ideal design
    (B) the intervening variable
    (C) the dependent variable
    (D) the independent variable
    (E) not determinable from the information given

2. If, after an experiment, the researcher discovers that there are no differences on the dependent variable, he or she can conclude that
    (A) differences on the independent variable were not significant
    (B) the intervening variables were extremely powerful
    (C) differences in intelligence must have existed
    (D) the independent variables did not precede the dependent variables in time
    (E) the wrong criteria were chosen

3. With which of the following statements would this author probably agree?
    (A) Sound experimentation requires a clear identification of the possible intervening variables
    (B) Good educational experiments follow

the ideal design

(C) All groups must be equated for differences in intelligence

(D) Learning processes are the most important area for educational experimentation

(E) In sensible experiments there is a sequence in time of independent variables, intervening variables, and dependent variables

4. According to this author, when an experimenter uses the variable *intelligence* in an educational experiment, that variable

(A) is an intervening variable

(B) is too vague and ambiguous to be useful

(C) could be any of the three kinds of variable

(D) should be an independent variable in an ideal design

(E) will impede understanding the results

ANSWERS! ☛

Professional Knowledge

1. D
2. A
3. C
4. C
5. A
6. B
7. D
8. C
9. E
10. B
11. B
12. B
13. A

Explanations for Answers:

1. (D) This is a factual item and a series of legal decisions have indicated Harry's right not to participate provided he does not distract others.

2. (A) In the effort to increase volunteering, Mrs. Roberts could properly vary her style (B), make a game by pulling names out of a hat (C), and also try the techniques in options (D) and (E). (A) is the only behavior which would not be considered good questioning practice.

3. (C) This is a factual item. Legislation and court cases have made it clear that Mrs. Brownstein must show the student his records.

4. (C) At the age of 3 the most likely motivation for John's hitting is that he is exploring the nature of the relationship or the response pattern of Bob. He is too young to be establishing social dominance and without others around is not seeking attention. There is nothing in the situational description to suggest options (B) or (D).

5. (A) While there is some variation from state to state on teacher use of force, there is consensus both in certain legislation and legal decisions that a teacher may use force to stop a disturbance, in self-defense, and to obtain a weapon. There is general consensus as well that discipline should be achieved by means other than force.

6. (B) The literature on the sociology of education suggests and early and psychodynamically easier assumption of adult roles among working-class youth.

7. (D) One of the sharpest characteristics distinguishing American public education in the decades after 1960 is the ever-increasing importance of parental and public input and lay control. The decentralization of authority into smaller administrative units such as districts rather than citywide school boards has also happened. Option (D) includes both aspects of this movement.

8. (C) The proposal is poor because it is a simplification as well as an insulting comment reflecting little understanding of the complexities of Eskimo culture. While one could argue that in many school systems few teachers have any background in anthropology (D), the basic criticism of the proposal is its insensitivity to other cultures.

9. (E) Linda's ability to master the cello quickly suggests that her previous experience with a string instrument has expedited her learning of a second string instrument. This is the application of positive transfer training.

10. (B) The research on frustration is consistent in agreeing that irrelevant frustration is neither educationally nor personally productive. It also agrees that relevant frustration such as that encountered in coping with difficult but solvable problems is educationally productive. Thus (B) is the best response.

11. (B) While all of the responses listed would contribute to classroom discipline, the constructive program in option (B), by keeping students involved in positive activities, would be considered the greatest ally.

12. (B) Legal definitions of the schools' responsibilities to religious observers make clear that Joan must be given an opportunity to

take the qualifying examination.

13. (A) The primary significance of the non-graded school lies in the flexibility it provides teachers and administrators in designating grade levels. While it does provide extended time for study of certain areas (C) and is an alternative to annual promotion (E), neither of these is its primary function or unique to the nongraded concept.

General Knowledge
Social Studies
1. E
2. B
3. A
4. C

Literature and Fine Arts
1. A
2. C
3. D
4. D

Science
1. B
2. C
3. C

Communication Skills: Reading
1. D
2. A
3. A
4. C

Arithmetic—100 credits

1. A man at his death left his wife $2,500, which was one-half of five-sixths of his estate; she at her death left five-sevenths of her share to her daughter; what part of the father's estate did the daughter receive?

2. Bought a house for $2,500; two years and nine months after I sold it for $2,700. What rate did I make or lose upon my investment, money being worth 8 percent?

3. If a bin 8 ft long 41-5ft wide and 2½ ft deep holds 67½ bushels, how deep must another bin be made that is 18 ft long and 35-6 ft wide to hold 450 bu.?

4. A man paid $330 per week to 55 laborers consisting of men, women, and boys; to the men he paid $10 per week, to the woman $2 per week, and to the boys $1 per week. How many were there of each?

5. How many gallons will a tank hold, of cubical form, the area of whose faces is 3,750 sq. in.?

Grammar—100 credits

1. Correct grammatical errors in the following sentences, and give reasons for corrections:

   "Chess fascinates its votaries more perhaps than any game."

   "He must have certainly been detained."

   "I shall walk out in the afternoon unless it rains."

   "Please excuse my son's absence."

2. Diagram the following sentence:
   "Tell me not, in mournful numbers,
       Life is but an empty dream;
   For the soul is dead that slumbers
       And things are not what they seem."

Orthography—100 credits

Meerschaum	Chagrin
Traceable	Juiciness
Pneumonia	Panacea
Rarefy	Nucleus
Ecstacy	Modoc
Stanislans	Synecdoche
Banana	Embellish
Besiege	Dahlia
Pajaro	Ricochet
Chalybeate	Portemonnaie
Apteryx	Bordeaux
Satellite	Dove-cote
Weird	Guttural
Numskull	Carbuncle
Pleurisy	Sapphire
Argillaceous	Combustible
Belles Lettres	Nonsensical
Holocaust	Oscillate
Cozen	Chaparral
Tessellated	Souvenir
Saccharine	Sibyl
Embezzle	Phthisic
Yenisei	Copyist
Vaccinate	Irascible
Macerate	Harelip

Geography—50 credits

Designate and locate the following:
    Transvaal, Auckland, Yenisei, Auvergne,
    New Providence, Titicaca, Borgne, Mur-
    ray, Queenstown.

Word Analysis—25 credits

1. Give and define five Latin and five
   Greek prefixes.

2. What is the meaning of ars, techne, lit-
   tera, gramma, theos, deus?

Mental Arithmetic—25 credits

1. At 20 cents a quart, how many gallons of
   molasses will $4.80 buy?

2. If the difference in time of Boston and St.
   Louis is one hour and fifteen minutes,
   what is the difference of their longitude?

3. Two men hired a pasture for $36. One
   put in 2 horses for 3 weeks, the other 3
   horses for 4 weeks. What should each
   pay?

General Literature—25 credits

1. Name two authors contemporary with
   Shakespeare.

2. Who wrote the first five books of the
   bible?

U.S. History—50 credits

When was the national flag adopted? State
    the number at first of the stars and stripes
and their arrangement. State their number
and arrangement at present.

Music—25 credits

Write four different kinds of notes and their
    corresponding rests.

Entomology—25 credits

1. Into what divisions is the body of a true
   insect divided? How many legs has a true
   insect?

2. What insect sits upon its eggs until
   hatched and then broods its young as a
   hen does her chickens?

Physiology—50 credits

What is the distinctive function of the capil-
    laries? What veins do not lead toward the
heart?

Algebra

1. When the hour and minute hands of a
   clock are together between 8 and 9
   o'clock, what is the hour?

2. A man rode 24 miles, going at a certain
   rate; he then walked back at the rate of
   three miles an hour, and consumed
   twelve hours in making the trip. At what
   rate did he ride?

3. A man sold a horse for $24 and lost as
   much per cent as the horse cost. What
   did the horse cost?

TRAVEL AGENT

American College of Travel

"Fly the friendly but incomprehensible skies of PBA—uh—Bar Harbor Airways—un, unnh—Continental—er, ah—that will be $149 for 200 miles, LaGuardia to Hyannis, and $225 for 6000 miles, LaGuardia, San Francisco, LaGuardia. Sir. Please."

If you have an interest in the varied wonders of the world's cultural, political, and physical geography, you might have considered working as a travel agent, or maybe even dreamed of starting your own agency. In case you think that working in the travel business will satisfy your love of travel and adventure, however, you might want to pause and reflect that travel agents are paid to handle many of the mundane details that carefree vacationers would rather not worry about. That means keeping abreast of the latest fare schedules, memorizing regulations concerning carry-on luggage size restrictions on international flights, and spending long hours on the phone trying to get through to the airline operator. Indeed, the standard warning industry representatives issue to would-be travel agents is, as the American Society of Travel Agents puts it in its informational brochure, that "the travel agency industry is a highly specialized, intricate, and serious business—far from the occasional misconception of being a continuous round of carefree traveling."

Most agencies these days require a formal education in the more arcane aspects of reservation procedures, air travel regulations, the procurement of visas, booking package tours, writing tickets, and securing hotel, car rental company, tour operator, airline, cruise line, and railroad "appointments" from "suppliers" (a prerequisite to collecting sales commissions, the major source of revenue for a travel agency). American College of Travel, the contributor to this section, offers a basic, six-week training course covering the fundamental skills considered necessary for entry into the travel industry, a three-week course in airline computer systems, and a three-week advanced course featuring immersion in case-study situations.

The first set of questions in this section is from a test used by ACT to screen aspiring travel agents before they enter the training course; those who can correctly answer fewer than 75 percent might want to reconsider their choice of career. The remaining questions are from sections of the comprehensive Basic Training course, including Air Scheduling and Pre-Ticketing.

For more information about ACT's programs, write Michael Jago or Carol Steele at American College of Travel, 4020 Magnolia Blvd., #F, Burbank CA 91505, or call (818) 843-5347 or (213) 655-0997.

Multiple Choice

1. The Canary Islands are off the coast of
    (A) Spain
    (B) West Germany
    (C) Africa
    (D) Madagascar

2. Which is the most visited National Park in
    the U.S.A.?
    (A) Yosemite
    (B) Sequoia
    (C) Bryce Canyon
    (D) Yellowstone

3. Which of these is an American airline?
    (A) SAS
    (B) KLM
    (C) ANA
    (D) TWA

4. Which of the following is not popular with
    cruise ships?
    (A) Dead Sea
    (B) Aegean Sea
    (C) Mediterranean Sea
    (D) Caribbean Sea

5. Which of these attractions is not in
    Europe?
    (A) The terra-cotta army
    (B) The Parthenon
    (C) Big Ben
    (D) The Eiffel Tower

6. "Air tickets cost more money if you buy
    them from an agency rather than from an
    airline."
    (A) True
    (B) False

7. How many degrees does the world turn
    through each hour?

(A) 24
(B) 365
(C) 52
(D) 15

8. Which of these European cities is west of
    Frankfurt?
    (A) Vienna
    (B) Berlin
    (C) Prague
    (D) Paris

9. In which country is Macchu Picchu?
    (A) Romania
    (B) Peru
    (C) New Zealand
    (D) China

10. To obtain the least expensive round-trip air
    ticket you should
    (A) arrive at the airport two hours early
    (B) buy two one-way tickets
    (C) find three friends to travel with you
    (D) book well in advance

11. Most international travel requires a
    (A) voter's registration card
    (B) letter of credit from a bank
    (C) release form from your place of work
    (D) passport

12. Another name for Eire is
    (A) Iran
    (B) Ulster
    (C) British Virgin Islands
    (D) Ireland

13. Travel insurance protects against
    (A) trip cancellation
    (B) lost luggage
    (C) medical expenses while traveling
    (D) all of the above
    (E) none of the above

14. "Coach class" means
    (A) economy class on an airplane
    (B) steerage class on a ship
    (C) transportation by bus

15. "Airline computers are still an unnecessary luxury for travel agencies."
    (A) True
    (B) False

16. If you leave Santa Monica, California and drive east on Interstate 10, where do you run out of road?
    (A) Chicago
    (B) Jacksonville
    (C) Miami
    (D) Houston

17. "An agency that handles leisure travel cannot make your business travel reservations."
    (A) True
    (B) False

18. Travel agents travel free
    (A) sometimes
    (B) never
    (C) always

19. Which is the highest category of hotel?
    (A) first class
    (B) superior
    (C) tourist
    (D) deluxe

20. Zimbabwe used to be called
    (A) Upper Volta
    (B) British Honduras
    (C) Tanganyika
    (D) Rhodesia

21. "APEX" means
    (A) the highest point reached during a flight
    (B) advance purchase excursion
    (C) associated promotional expertise

22. Which of the following skills do you think is most important in the travel agency business?
    (A) Speaking four languages
    (B) The ability to fly a small plane
    (C) Interpersonal and sales skills

23. Europe and Asia meet at
    (A) Istanbul
    (B) Athens
    (C) Vienna
    (D) The Iron Curtain

24. Which of the following countries is governed by a constitutional monarchy?
    (A) Guam
    (B) Great Britain
    (C) Republic of China
    (D) Italy

25. Which of the following flights is the longest?
    (A) London to Istanbul
    (B) Beijing to Shanghai
    (C) Los Angeles to Honolulu

26. Which of the following cities is a ski destination?
    (A) Davos
    (B) Nice
    (C) Rome
    (D) Dublin

27. Abu Simbel is in
    (A) Israel
    (B) Egypt
    (C) Syria
    (D) Jordan

28. Which is the largest of these airplanes?
    (A) 707
    (B) 727
    (C) 737
    (D) 747
    (E) 767

29. If you cross the International Dateline traveling west, the time is
    (A) unchanged
    (B) the same time one day later
    (C) the same time one day earlier
    (D) none of the above

30. What are the Tropics?
    (A) A hot-blooded tribe in New Guinea
    (B) Daily travel news bulletins
    (C) Belts of the earth on each side of the equator

31. A stateroom is
    (A) an airport waiting room for VIPs
    (B) a cabin on a cruise ship
    (C) a governor's office

32. Which canal was nearly the scene of war in 1956?
    (A) The Suez Canal
    (B) The Isthmus of Corinth
    (C) The Panama Canal
    (D) The Kiel Canal

33. "It is illegal to fly on an airline ticket for which you have not paid."
    (A) True
    (B) False

34. If you cannot use an airline ticket you can
    (A) sell it to any other person
    (B) sell it to a member of your family with the same last name
    (C) either of the above
    (D) neither of the above

35. Which of the following cannot be imported to the U.S.A.?
    (A) Russian caviar
    (B) German World War II memorabilia
    (C) Havana cigars.
    (D) French dairy products

36. Berlin is best described as
    (A) a divided city
    (B) a free city
    (C) an open port
    (D) a border town

37. Which language is spoken in Brazil?
    (A) Spanish
    (B) Portuguese
    (C) Colombian
    (D) German

38. How many languages are officially spoken in Switzerland?
    (A) One
    (B) Two
    (C) Three
    (D) Four
    (E) Five

39. Which of these languages is not spoken in Switzerland?
    (A) Romansch
    (B) Hungarian
    (C) Italian

40. Thomas Cook was
    (A) the first man to make English food edible
    (B) the inventor of travelers' checks
    (C) the first group tour operator

41. The Renaissance began in
    (A) Heidelberg
    (B) Siena
    (C) Detroit
    (D) Shanghai

42. Where does the Bullet Train run?
    (A) Japan
    (B) Between old Wild West towns
    (C) From New York City to Washington
    (D) On the same route as the Orient Express

43. The Pedernales are a
    (A) South American tribe
    (B) school of Spanish painters
    (C) range of hills in Texas

44. Which country produces the most wine?
    (A) Norway
    (B) Italy
    (C) Saudi Arabia
    (D) Austria

45. "Perpendicular Gothic" signifies
    (A) a romantic novel in hardback
    (B) the family tree of the princes of Gotha
    (C) an architectural style

46. The Michelin guides are helpful for
    (A) choosing hotels and restaurants
    (B) ascertaining current tire prices
    (C) treasure hunting in the Caribbean

47. Where do the Ohio and Mississippi rivers meet?
    (A) Cairo, IL
    (B) St. Louis, MO
    (C) Kansas City, MO
    (D) Cincinnati, OH
    (E) Memphis, TN

48. The Lyndon B. Johnson library is at
    (A) Hyde Park, NY
    (B) Abilene, KS
    (C) Austin, TX
    (D) Dallas, TX

49. Which is the largest of the Great Lakes?
    (A) Lake Michigan
    (B) Lake Baikal
    (C) Lake Windermere
    (D) Lake Superior

50. An autobahn is a
    (A) shuttle between airport parking and terminals
    (B) freeway in Germany
    (C) self-service restaurant in New York

51. The southern tip of South America is called
    (A) The Falklands
    (B) Land's End
    (C) The Cape of Good Hope
    (D) Cape Horn

52. Which Russian city is closest to the U.S.A.?
    (A) Samarkand
    (B) Kiev
    (C) Minsk
    (D) Vladivostok

53. In which region of the U.S.A. is Santa Fe, NM?
    (A) Central
    (B) Southern
    (C) Far East
    (D) Southwest

54. Who were the Medicis?
    (A) A noble Florentine family
    (B) Greek colonial adventurers of the 5th century
    (C) Leaders of the Spanish Inquisition
    (D) Roman proconsuls

55. Travel agents generally earn money from
    (A) service charges paid by clients

(B) commission paid by hotels,
airlines, etc.
(C) profits from currency exchange

56. Which is the largest of these islands?
(A) Greenland
(B) Sicily
(C) Iceland
(D) New Guinea

57. Which of these cities is 8 hours "ahead" of
Los Angeles?
(A) Moscow
(B) London
(C) Cairo
(D) Tokyo

58. Which city is furthest south?
(A) Tehran
(B) Calcutta
(C) Irkutsk

Matching

1. Match each of the following with its
appropriate city
(A) United Nations   (1) Brussels
(B) NATO   (2) Leningrad
(C) Mardi Gras   (3) New York
(D) The Hermitage   (4) New Orleans

2. Match the island with its country
(A) Galapagos   (1) Great Britain
    Islands   (2) Spain
(B) Shetland Islands (3) Ecuador
(C) Canary Islands

3. Match these bridges with the towns where
they stand:
(A) Golden Gate   (1) Lake Havasu
    Bridge   (2) Venice
(B) Tower Bridge   (3) San Francisco
(C) London Bridge   (4) London
(D) Bridge of Sighs

4. Match these countries and currencies:
(A) Mark   (1) Mexico
(B) Guilder   (2) Poland
(C) Baht   (3) Netherlands
(D) Zloty   (4) Germany
(E) Peso   (5) Thailand

5. Match these cities and attractions
(A) Zona Rosa   (1) Cairns
(B) La Scala   (2) Freiburg
(C) Black Forest   (3) Beijing
(D) Forbidden City   (4) Mexico City
(E) Great Barrier   (5) Milan
    Reef

6. Match these cities and their English-
language equivalents
(A) Koln   (1) Canton
(B) Wien   (2) Venice
(C) Livorno   (3) Cologne
(D) Venezia   (4) Vienna
(E) Guangzhou   (5) Leghorn

Short Answer

1. What is the normal rate of commission for
(A) domestic airline tickets
(B) international airline tickets

2. What is a "multiline rep"?

3. What is an "outside sales" agent?

4. What are the new names for the following
places?
(A) Upper Volta
(B) Tanganyika
(C) Cyrenaica
(D) St. Petersburg
(E) Palestine
(F) S. Rhodesia

5. What is an "override" commission?

6. Where is
   (A) The Caspian Sea
   (B) The Dead Sea
   (C) The Sea of Marmara
   (D) The Aral Sea
   (E) The Black Sea
   (F) The Arabian Sea

7. Where are the following attractions?
   (A) The Blue Mosque
   (B) Amboseli National Park
   (C) The Shrine of the Book
   (D) The Stone Forest
   (E) The Wild Goose Pagoda
   (F) The Hermitage
   (G) The Aswan Dam
   (H) Angkor Wat

8. Which country surrounds Gambia?

9. How many time zones separate 150 degrees west of Greenwich from 105 degrees east of Greenwich?

10. Which mountains are the "backbone" of Italy?

11. What is the capital of Scotland?

12. What languages are spoken in the following countries
    (A) Corsica
    (B) Wales
    (C) Crete
    (D) Malta
    (E) GDR
    (F) Shetland Islands

13. How many countries border on France?

14. What is American AAdvantage?

15. Which airline(s) would you think of for an itinerary ATL/STL/BUR?

ANSWERS! ☛

Multiple Choice

1. C
2. D
3. D
4. A
5. A
6. B
7. D
8. D
9. B
10. D
11. D
12. D
13. D
14. A
15. B
16. B
17. B
18. A
19. D
20. D
21. B
22. C
23. A
24. B
25. C
26. A
27. B
28. D
29. B
30. C
31. B
32. A
33. B
34. D
35. C
36. A
37. B
38. D
39. B
40. C
41. B
42. A
43. C
44. B
45. C
46. A
47. A
48. C
49. B
50. D
51. B
52. D
53. D
54. A
55. B
56. A
57. B
58. B

Matching

1. A: 3
   B: 1
   C: 4
   D: 2

2. A: 3
   B: 1
   C: 2

3. A: 3
   B: 4
   C: 1
   D: 2

4. A: 4
   B: 3
   C: 5
   D: 2
   E: 1

5. A: 4
   B: 5
   C: 2

D: 3
E: 1

6. A: 3
    B: 4
    C: 5
    D: 2
    E: 1

Short Answer

1. (A) 10%
    (B) 8%
2. A representative of different travel products
3. An agent who sells travel outside an agency
4. (A) Burkina Faso
    (B) Tanzania
    (C) Libya
    (D) Leningrad
    (E) Israel
    (F) Zimbabwe
5. Additional commission
6. (A) Iran
    (B) Israel
    (C) Turkey
    (D) USSR
    (E) Turkey/USSR
    (F) Between the Mideast and Africa
7. (A) Istanbul
    (B) Kenya
    (C) Jerusalem
    (D) Kunming
    (E) Xian
    (F) Leningrad
    (G) Egypt
    (H) Cambodia
8. Senegal
9. eight
10. Apennines
11. Edinburgh
12. (A) Italian
    (B) Welsh/English
    (C) Greek
    (D) Italian/Maltese/English
    (E) German
    (F) English
13. eight
14. American Airlines' frequent flyer program
15. TWA

Credits

ASTROLOGY/ Milo Kovar Astro-Psychology Institute
Reproduced by permission of Milo Kovar Astro-Psychology Institute, 2640 Greenwich #403, San Francisco CA 94123, tel. (415) 921-1192.

AUTO MECHANICS
Questions 19–34 reprinted by permission of National Institute for Automotive Service Excellence, 1920 Association Drive, Reston VA 22091-1502 from *ASE Preparation Guides to Heavy-Duty Truck Testing and Automobile Technician Testing*.
Questions 1–18 and Matching question reprinted by permission of Denver Automotive and Diesel College, 460 South Lipan, Denver CO 80223, tel. (303) 722-5724.

BARBER/ Moler Barber College
Reproduced by permission of Moler Barber College, 517 NW 4th, Portland OR 97204, tel. (503) 223-9818.

BARTENDING/ Boston Bartenders School
Reproduced by permission of Boston Bartenders School, 719 Boylston Street, Boston MA 02116, tel. (617) 536-7272.

BROADCASTING/ Columbia School of Broadcasting
Reprinted by permission of Columbia School of Broadcasting, 5858 Hollywood Boulevard, Hollywood CA 90028-5619, tel. (213) 469-8321.

BUILDING CONTRACTOR/ American Schools
Reprinted by permission of American Schools, P. O. Box 2948, Torrance CA 90509, tel. 1-800-63-STUDY.

COSMETOLOGY
Reprinted by permission of the publisher, Keystone Publications, 1657 Broadway, New York NY 10019, from the book *State Board Review Examinations in Cosmetology* by Anthony B. Colletti, © 1983.

CPA/ American Institute of Certified Public Accountants
Material from *Uniform CPA Examination Questions and Unofficial Answers,* © 1987 by American Institute of Certified Public Accountants, Inc., is reprinted with permission.

EXECUTIVE SECRETARY/ Katharine Gibbs School
Reproduced by permission of Katharine Gibbs School, 866 Third Ave, New York NY 10022
School addresses:
　　Boston: 86 Beacon Street, Boston MA 02108, tel. (617) 262-7190
　　Huntington, Long Island: 535 Broad Hollow Road, Town of Huntington, Melville NY 11747, tel. (516) 293-2460
　　Montclair: 33 Plymouth Street, Montclair NJ 07042, tel. (201) 744-6967
　　New York: Pan Am Building, 200 Park Avenue, New York NY 10166, tel. (212) 867-9307
　　Norwalk: 142 East Avenue, Norwalk CT 06851, tel. (203) 838-4173
　　Philadelphia: Land Title Building, 10th Floor, 100 South Broad Street, Philadelphia PA 19110, tel. (215) 564-5035
　　Piscataway: 80 Kingsbridge Road, Piscataway NJ 08854, tel. (201) 885-1580
　　Providence: 178 Butler Avenue, Providence RI 02906, tel. (401) 861-1420.

FASHION DESIGN/ Progressive Fashion School
Reproduced by permissoin of Jean Salata, Progressive Fashion School, 2012 West 25, Suite 612, Cleveland OH 44113, tel. (216) 781-4595.

FLORAL DESIGN/ Rittners School of Floral Design
Reproduced by permission of Rittners School of Floral Design, 345 Marlborough Street, Boston MA 02115, tel. (617) 267-3824.

GEOGRAPHY
National Council for Geographic Education questions reprinted by permission of National Council for Geographic Education, 16A Leonard Hall, Indiana University of Pennsylvania, Indiana PA 15705.
CBS Affiliates questions reprinted by permission of WNEV-TV, Channel 7, Boston MA (A CBS affiliate station).
North Carolina University System questions reprinted by permission of Dr. Richard J. Kopec, Department of Geography, 323 Saunders Hall, University of North Carolina, Chapel Hill NC 27514.

GEOLOGY/ California State Board of Registration
Courtesy of California State Board of Registration for Geologists and Geophysicists.

GRAPHOLOGY
Material abridged from *Handwriting Analysis: A Guide to Personality* , © 1984 by David Battan, including the illustrations used as examples. Published by International Resources, P. O. Box 3113, Pismo Beach CA 93449.

MASSAGE/ Atlanta School of Massage
Reproduced by permission of Atlanta School of Massage, 2300 Peachford Road, Suite 3200, Atlanta GA 30338, tel. (404) 454-7167.

MATH/ National Assessment of Educational Progres
Courtesty of National Assessment of Educational Progress/The Nation's Report Card, P.O. Box 6710, Princeton NJ 08541-6710.

NOTARY PUBLIC/ State of California
Courtesy of State of California, Notary Public Division.

POSTAL SERVICE
Reprinted by permission of the publisher, Prentice Hall Press, New York NY, from the book *Civil Service Test Tutor Post Office Clerk-Carrier* by E. P. Steinberg, © 1987.

RESTAURATEUR, HOTELIER/ American College of Hotel and Restaurant Management
Reproduced by permission of American College of Hotel and Restaurant Management, 555 Universal Terrace Parkway, Suite 467, Universal City CA 91608, tel. (818) 505-9800.

SECURITIES/ Securities Training Corporation
Reproduced by permission of Securities Training Corporation, 17 Battery Place, New York NY 10004, tel. (800) 782-1223.

STUDENT vs. TEACHER CHALLENGE/ Rutgers New Jersey Bowl
Reproduced by permission of Office of TV and Radio, Rutgers State University of New Jersey, New Brunswick NJ 08903.

TEACHING/ National Teacher Examination
Questions 125–349 reprinted by permission of the publisher, Arco Publishing Inc., New York NY, from the book *NTE National Teacher Examinations* by David J. Fox, Ph.D., © 1988, 1984.

TRAVEL/ American College of Travel
Reproduced by permission of American College of Travel, 4020 West Magnolia Boulevard, #F, Burbank CA 91505, tel. (213) 655-0997.